THE SUEZ CRISIS OF 1956

DISCARD

THE
SUEZ CRISIS
OF 1956

BY ANTHONY EDEN

Consisting of Book One, Chapter 10 ("The Nile,
October 1951 – October 1954"), and all of Book
Three ("Suez") from *The Memoirs of
Anthony Eden, Full Circle*

BEACON PRESS   BOSTON

ACKNOWLEDGMENTS
TO
The Memoirs of Anthony Eden, Full Circle

I WISH to express my thanks to Mr. Alan Hodge for his help in the preparation of Books Two and Three of this volume, and to Mr. Bryan Cartledge for his help in respect of Book One. I would also like to thank Lord Furneaux and Mrs. B. W. Scott for their assistance on a number of chapters in the same Book. I am grateful to Mr. Robert Blake for both general and detailed advice at many stages of the work. Miss Edwards, my secretary, has typed the volume and facilitated its production.

The official documents printed in this volume are Crown Copyright, which is legally vested in the Controller of Her Majesty's Stationery Office, and I am obliged for permission to reproduce them.

FOREWORD
TO
The Memoirs of Anthony Eden, Full Circle

I BEGAN to think of writing a book about my years in office after my operation in the spring of 1957. My first intention was to proceed with it in the accepted order of time, from the early nineteen-thirties until the present day.

This method had the advantage that the lessons of the thirties and their application to the fifties, which are the themes of my memoirs, could be more easily displayed. It imposed a limitation, however, which I considered decisive. At least four years would have to elapse before my account of the more recent period could be presented. I thought that I should not wait so long. This book will expose wounds; by doing so it could help to heal them.

I was first connected with the foreign policy of my country in a modest capacity in 1926, when I became Parliamentary Private Secretary to Sir Austen Chamberlain. During the next nine years I held mostly junior offices, though towards the end of the period I was charged with missions which involved me in meetings and discussions with Hitler, Mussolini and Stalin, as well as with Ministers of the Western European democracies.

The years during which I held higher responsibility for the conduct of my country's foreign policy fall into two periods. The first was from 1935 until 1945, with a break of eighteen months from February 1938 until the early autumn of the following year, due to my resignation from Mr. Chamberlain's government. I resigned because of differences about policy towards the dictators. I returned to Cabinet office, in company with Mr. Churchill, on the outbreak of war on September 3 and became Foreign Secretary again towards the end of 1940.

The second period dates from the autumn of 1951 until January 1957, during the whole of which time I was either Foreign Secretary or Prime Minister. It is with this latter period that this volume deals, but the policies which I upheld and pursued during that time were based on my earlier experiences. In giving effect to them I found myself, from time to time, in disagreement with other opinions held in my own country and in allied countries. This has been a cause of regret to me.

So much of my life has been spent in the conduct or execution of foreign policy that I feel I should set down these events as they presented themselves to me. The reflections and decisions I record in this volume are those which I formed at the time. I hope that this account and my reasoning, as well as the experiences I lived through, may be of service to others.

My material has consisted of personal minutes which I wrote, often to Sir Winston Churchill as Prime Minister when I was Foreign Secretary, or to other colleagues when I was Prime Minister myself. Another source used has been the notes dictated to form the messages sent home when I was engaged upon a mission abroad, or sent abroad either to our embassies or to the statesmen of other lands. Yet another source has been the occasional notes jotted down at the moment and intended to be the basis for a fuller record when opportunity offered. But it is all the thought of the time on the action of the time set down at the time. I considered that such an account could be useful because, though the pattern of world politics may be modified and its contours appear smoother or more menacing, nothing can change man's need to take counsel with all who have pursued the endless adventure.

ANTHONY EDEN

September 1959
Fyfield Manor
Pewsey, Wiltshire

PREFACE: How To Settle the Middle East Crisis[1]

DURING THIS SUMMER we have witnessed one of the most astonishing feats of arms of our century, the brief Israeli-Arab war.

If we are to get anywhere in the Middle East imbroglio, we have to understand what are the essential issues. There is plenty to argue about, but much of it, though important, is relatively subsidiary and complexities can easily obscure realities.

There ought to be no dispute that it was the closing of the Gulf of Aqaba and the Straits of Tiran which started the inevitable chain reaction ending in the dramatic Israeli victory. It was well known that the United States, as well as Great Britain and France and other maritime nations, had committed themselves to keep those Straits open to commerce for all nations.

ACT OF AGGRESSION

It was no less evident that the purpose of the Egyptian action was to suffocate Israel's life, as the mobilization of Egyptian forces in the Sinai peninsula and the language of the Cairo radio — which was a call to butcher a whole people, a clamor for genocide — showed only too clearly.

The definition of an aggressor has frequently been the subject of debate, but my recollection is that as long ago as 1952 the Soviet Government, in a declaration before the United Nations, listed the establishment of a blockade as an act of aggression. Under that definition there can be no doubt who was the aggressor in this instance.

[1]Reprinted from "Topics" on the editorial page of *The New York Times*, September 2, 1967. © 1967 by The New York Times Company. Reprinted by permission.

FREEDOM OF ACCESS

Now, in the aftermath of the fighting, there is another opportunity for a Middle Eastern settlement. The objective this time must surely be to bring about a lasting peace throughout the area. That means the end of the period of belligerency, freedom of access and transit for shipping, a willingness to live and let live, an agreement over boundaries, and a comprehensive effort to further a solution of the refugee problem.

All this will take time but it is by no means impossible. It must be remembered that Israel's military action was taken solely to protect its right to live. Israel does not seek the destruction of any neighboring Arab state, but it does ask for the end of belligerence and there can be no lasting settlement in the Middle East without the acceptance of this condition. If this were guaranteed by the great powers and above all the super powers, it might be accompanied by a limitation of armaments which had some meaning.

Europe has had its frequent warring periods so that it does not perhaps lie with us to lecture others. Yet it remains true that if once toleration, let alone cooperation, could prevail for even a few years between Israel and her Arab neighbors, the economic opportunities would have a chance to be spelled out.

The World Bank could then really get to work. Water schemes, communications, joint exploitation of resources, these could transform the area, raise human standards, and create openings to resolve its refugee problem with scope for work rather than charity. But for all this and much more to be possible, there is one absolute condition: belligerency must come to an end.

NO POLITICAL SHUTTLECOCK

This is necessary for technical as well as for political reasons. The refugee problem is an outstanding example, for this humanitarian question has been sadly plagued by politics for years. Even with goodwill it will take some time to resolve, but as long as it remains a political shuttlecock no real progress is possible. On the other hand, given an end to the condition and threat of war, practical schemes and financial aid could soon be applied effectively.

International and individual enterprise could then play their parts in settlement schemes with a real hope of success, and they would bring with them advantageous results for the refugees and their neighbors. Equally, beneficial water schemes, some of which have been in existence for years, could make an early contribution to the economy of the whole area, if once there was a real assurance that settled conditions would give economic development a fair chance to thrive.

TIME FOR STATESMANSHIP

The same limiting conditions at present apply to communications. A glance at the map will show how much a cooperative approach to these problems could benefit Arab lands, even more than Israel. There is no insuperable obstacle to the development of such plans except confidence, which has no hope of breathing in the choked atmosphere of constantly proclaimed belligerency.

For twenty years now the continuing state of war has bedeviled every attempt to put joint effort before rancor and progress before prejudice. To be rid of it is surely something to work for and our generation must show enough statesmanship to make this possible.

CONTENTS

*Anthony Eden was Foreign Secretary during the period covered
in Chapter 1 and Prime Minister during the period covered in
Chapters 2 – 10.*

THE SUEZ CRISIS OF 1956

THE
MIDDLE EAST

Countries of the Baghdad Pact shown thus:

1

THE NILE
October 1951–October 1954

The Wafd — Nahas Pasha — Anglo-Egyptian Treaty denounced — Egypt and the Sudan — Riots in Cairo — Fall of Nahas — American views on Sudan — Military revolt and General Neguib — King Farouk abdicates — Changes in Middle East strategy — Sudanese self-government — Anglo-American discussions — Arms to Egypt — Nasser gains power — Anglo-Egyptian Treaty

EGYPT IN THE THIRTIES and forties has been described as a three-legged stool, the King, the Wafd and the British. The three legs might be uneven in length, the stool might rock and tilt, but somehow it contrived to stay up. Mussolini's ambitions in the Mediterranean had encouraged acceptance of the British by the Egyptians. Better the devil you know.

In 1936 an Anglo-Egyptian Treaty was arduously negotiated in Cairo by our High Commissioner and later Ambassador, Sir Miles Lampson, and signed by me in London with representatives of all Egyptian political parties, a total of thirteen. This multitude of signatures was an unusual but necessary precaution, though criticized at the time by the Opposition at home as being undemocratic. The procedure shared responsibility and made it difficult for any Egyptian party to evade the agreement later. The occasion of the signing of this treaty was the only time that I appeared on a set of postage stamps, and they were Egyptian.

A considerable party came to London for the event, including the wives of several of the representatives. Some of these had never left Cairo before and I arranged a special luncheon party for them. Thinking I might add to their entertainment by giving them unusual fare, I arranged for grouse to be sent down from Yorkshire for the meal, it being then mid-August. Afterwards I asked how the luncheon had gone off and received the reply, "I am sorry, but it was not a success; the ladies complained of being given old crows to eat."

The 1936 treaty gave the Egyptian Government increased authority and served us well in the war years. For some time afterwards the three-legged system continued to function. Even in the opening months of 1951, the casual observer felt no concern. The Wafd had recently been re-elected with a large majority. Its Prime Minister, Nahas Pasha, who had signed the 1936 treaty, had many years of leadership to sustain him. But the decay was there. The economic situation was deteriorating and the Government's inefficiency was blatant. Corruption was frequently practised and more frequently rumoured, with Madame Nahas and the Minister of the Interior as commonly canvassed offenders. The Prime Minister was senile and there was no effective Opposition. Even by Egyptian standards, this was a dismal and discreditable state of the nation.

It would be a mistake to regard the Wafd as commanding national support in the same sense as a political party in Britain or the United States can do. The elections were a caricature, with only a little more real freedom of expression than exists in a Communist state. In the elections in January 1950, the Wafd was at the height of its power. Even so, only fifteen per cent of the electorate in Cairo cast their votes. It was a rich party and a party of rich men, many of whom had grown fat at the expense of the state.

The King might have been able to halt the deterioration, but his reputation and authority were at a low ebb. His second marriage brought him no popularity, and his absence for three and a half months, on what was judged to be an unedifying holiday by the Mediterranean, led to personal attacks upon him in the press in terms unbelievable a year before.

Increasingly plagued by its internal troubles, the Wafd chose the remedy of history: it sought out foreign quarrels. Even so, it might have ridden the storm, had it remained in control of the forces it let loose. The Wafd made hardly any attempt to do so. For months past, Egyptian Ministers had been privately assuring the Labour Government, which was then in power in Britain, that they were sincere in wishing to negotiate a new Anglo-Egyptian agreement. When that Government produced its proposals for the revision of the treaty, the Wafd rejected them out of hand.

The evacuation of the British management and staff from Abadan and the loss of the refinery had its immediate consequence. The press in Egypt did not hesitate to draw a lesson from Musaddiq's "firm stand," as it was proclaimed. This proved to their satisfaction that the British would yield to a campaign of threats and violence.

In October, Nahas Pasha, to deafening plaudits, denounced the Anglo-Egyptian Treaty, which had still five years to run. Even before this, terrorist activity had been growing, especially in the Suez Canal zone. It now multiplied, encouraged by a violently extremist press, which on this scale was a new phenomenon in Egyptian life.

The position I had to face in Egypt was more forbidding than anything which was happening in Persia. I was convinced that there the situation had been made worse by some unimaginative mishandling, which I believed could be remedied. In Egypt the outlook was much darker; almost everything seemed rotten in the state. Food prices were rising sharply and income tax had been increased upon all but those best able to pay. "Liberation squads" were occupied extorting subscriptions, but thousands who had left work with the British forces found none elsewhere. Many of these had given up their employment with regret, intimidation was rife. Contact between communities in the canal zone had virtually ceased. The Labour Government had just ordered reinforcements to the canal zone, where the military commitment was already a heavy one.

On taking over, I caused a note to be delivered by our Ambassador in Cairo informing the Egyptian Government that we intended to uphold our treaty rights. The text of this note should be recalled, for its first paragraph was consistently applied by us to later events. Failure by the world to heed this truth is, in my judgment, the chief cause of the deterioration in international relations. Bad practices have been indulged and they have grown and multiplied:

The Anglo-Egyptian Treaty of friendship and alliance of 1936 contains no provision for unilateral denunciation at any time. If the principle were accepted that one party to such a treaty were entitled to denounce that treaty unilaterally, no reliance could be placed on any international agreement, and the whole basis and structure of international relations would cease to exist.

The action of the Egyptian Government in repudiating this treaty is therefore illegal and without validity, and entirely contrary to the principles of the Charter of the United Nations, paragraph 3 of the preamble to which expressly states that one of the main purposes of the organization is "to establish conditions under which justice and respect for the obligations arising from treaties and other sources of international law can be maintained."

His Majesty's Government are willing, as were their predecessors, to enter into negotiation at any time for a revision of the treaty of 1936, under the procedure set forth in Articles 8 and 16 of that treaty. Meanwhile they regard the treaty and the condominium agreements of 1899 as remaining in force, and intend fully to maintain their rights under those instruments.

In addition they hold the Egyptian Government responsible for any breach of the peace and any damage to life or property that may result from their purported abrogation of those instruments.

The United Nations were due to hold their annual General Assembly within a few days of my return to the Foreign Office. The meeting was in Paris and I decided to use this occasion to display Western unity in Middle Eastern affairs. I intended to anticipate criticism from Arab states against the Middle Eastern defence plan of our predecessors and I prepared a text accordingly. After discussion with our allies, I abandoned my draft and agreed to work upon an American text.

This became a document of some importance. It set out our intentions, and the advantages in equipment and unity which went with them. In a four-power statement agreed by the United States,

France, Turkey and ourselves, we explained that the Middle East command would be an integrated allied command. All states which joined would be individual and equal. Any facilities which they granted to the command would be the subject of specific agreement. "A continuing objective of the Middle East command," we said, "is to reduce such deficiencies as exist at present in organization and capacity for defence in a vitally important area." As a result, the part played by countries in the area would increase in peacetime. Equally important to them, the part played by countries not in the area would decrease proportionately. These were reasonable explanations, but they did not suffice.

Patiently as the four Governments had worked for this proposal, it never really had a chance. The Syrian reaction was characteristic. The Prime Minister, Khaled el Azm, who had shown courage in supporting the Middle East command, had fallen. The Syrian President was backing him and he might have returned, but his Cabinet was against him. The Syrian representative at U.N., to whom I commended the defence proposals, replied in terms expressive of much Arab opinion, then and since. "The people of Syria," he said, "are by no means opposed to the Anglo-Saxon countries, nor do they have strong anti-Soviet feelings; they have, in fact, very little feeling at all about the Soviet Union. The threat of aggression to them is not from Russia, but from Israel." When Syria learns that this is a mistaken view, it is unlikely that she will be in a position to use her knowledge. The Egyptian Government having recalled Amr Pasha, their friendly and experienced Ambassador in London, I used the occasion of this Assembly meeting for a direct talk with the Egyptian Foreign Minister, Salah ed-Din.

I complained of the attacks on Egyptian members of our Embassy in Cairo and on British forces in the canal zone. In both cases the Egyptian authorities had shown themselves to be openly hostile. I deplored the present state of Anglo-Egyptian relations. If they were to improve these incidents must cease. When this had been brought about, I recommended the four-power proposals as a fair basis for a settlement. My report continued:

The Minister agreed that the incidents were regrettable. He then spoke on familiar terms about the impossibility of

Egypt accepting British or any other foreign "occupation" and said that the Egyptian Government had rejected the four-power proposals after close study had shown them to differ little from the earlier and equally rejected proposals of April.

I said I could not accept the Minister's view of the four-power proposals, which had been worked out most carefully with the object of meeting as far as possible Egyptian requirements. I then enumerated the specific advantages which the proposals offered to Egypt. I was confident that the points of difference could be ironed out if only the proposals could be discussed. I made it quite plain that we could not meet the Egyptian demand for evacuation and that it was no good the Egyptian Minister expecting it.

After further discussion the Minister said he would report our conversation to his Government, putting to them the suggestion that efforts should now be made to bring incidents to an end (as regards which I said we had already done our part by excluding our forces from Port Said, Suez and Ismailia), and that thereafter both sides should consider the four-power proposals without commitment. I said I was ready to contemplate talks either in London or Cairo. The Minister said he was proposing to return to Cairo in a month. No mention was made of the Sudan. I cannot tell whether anything will come out of this talk. I gave nothing away and the Minister seemed in a more reasonable mood than I had anticipated. We agreed that the press should be told simply that we had had a general exchange of views on Anglo-Egyptian relations.

Although I had not discussed the Sudan with the Egyptian Foreign Minister, I was aware of Egyptian activities in that country and of their purpose, the unity of the two countries under the Egyptian crown. If this was what the Sudanese wanted, which I doubted, there was no cause for us to stand in the way, but I was definitely not prepared to allow the Egyptians to bounce the Sudanese into a union which was not to their liking. We had done well by the Sudan. The country was admirably administered by a small Civil Service of the highest quality. We intended that the Sudan should have early self-government, but it must be free to make its own decisions about its future.

I thought it desirable to state this plainly, publicly and soon.
On my return from Paris, I made an announcement to the House
of Commons, having first secured its approval by my colleagues.
In the course of this I said:

> In view of the uncertainty caused in the Sudan and elsewhere
> by the Egyptian Government's unilateral action in purporting
> to abrogate the 1936 treaty of alliance and the two condo-
> minium agreements of 1899, His Majesty's Government find
> it necessary to reaffirm that they regard the Governor-Gen-
> eral and the present Sudan Government as fully responsible
> for continuing the administration of the Sudan.
>
> His Majesty's Government are glad to note that the Sudan
> has for some time been, and is now, moving rapidly in the
> direction of self-government. In their view this progress can
> and should continue on the lines already laid down. . . . His
> Majesty's Government are glad to know that a constitution
> providing for self-government may be completed and in opera-
> tion by the end of 1952.
>
> Having attained self-government, it will be for the Sudanese
> people to choose their own future status and relationship
> with the United Kingdom and with Egypt.

The Governor-General reported that this statement was welcomed all over the Sudan and went far to counter the sentiment
that, Egypt having revoked the condominium agreement, the Sudan
should automatically be released from foreign tutelage of any sort.
Many Sudanese were shrewd enough to observe that Egypt's
clamour for the Sudan's freedom was not disinterested. There was
an Egyptian price.

The United States Government were, however, uneasy about
the Sudan and the effect of Egyptian propaganda moves, as my
record of December 5 shows:

> When the United States Ambassador came to see me this
> morning he said he had been instructed to speak to me about
> the Sudan.
>
> The State Department had been rather troubled by the

Egyptian Foreign Minister's challenge about a plebiscite in the Sudan. They thought that perhaps we should make some reply, or at least make plain our reasons for not acceding to this request. I replied that I had considered the matter carefully, and my own strong present view was that Salah ed-Din's proposal should be left alone. It did not cause any great stir in the world. I should prefer to let it die. It was, of course, quite impracticable, and was a mere propaganda move. Discussion about it would really be playing the Egyptian game. The Ambassador, who seemed already aware of our point of view, said he understood that we would therefore prefer the Americans not to talk about it either. I said "Yes" and he appeared to accept this conclusion.

Despite Mr. Gifford's understanding, we continued to be urged by the United States Government to recognize King Farouk as King of the Sudan. A few days later the American Ambassador came to see me again to renew this suggestion, which was to be part of a "package deal." I repeated that we could not yield on the Sudan.

This Egyptian move advocating the acceptance of King Farouk as King of the Sudan, subject to ratification by the Sudanese, was astute. Endorsement by us of such a title, even provisionally, would be taken by many in the Sudan to mean that we were no longer interested in the matter, and that we acknowledged the King of Egypt as the future ruler of the country. They would conclude that it was of no use for them to resist this decision and they would vote for the King of Egypt. This would not be a true expression of Sudanese opinion. The Pakistani High Commissioner also drew my attention to this danger.

It was unfortunate that the British and American points of view about the Sudan at this time were known to be out of line. In an interview after his return, the Egyptian Ambassador warned me that the American Ambassador in Cairo, Mr. Jefferson Caffery, "was not wholly behind us over the question of the Sudan." This hardly surprised me, but I was determined that there should be no misunderstanding of where the United Kingdom Government stood. Accordingly I concluded a despatch, in which I later instructed Sir Ralph Stevenson, our Ambassador in Cairo, to open discussions with a new Egyptian Government, with these words:

> It must be quite clear that sincerely as Her Majesty's Government wish for agreement with Egypt on the future of the Sudan, they neither can nor will make a bargain with Egypt over the heads of the Sudanese, in return for strategic concessions in the canal zone.

In the last week of January 1952, the Prime Minister was sailing the Atlantic on a return journey from the United States and I was in charge in his absence. There had been a bloody affray in the canal zone on January 25, between our forces and two Egyptian police posts, with heavy casualties to the Egyptians. The next day demonstrations took place in Cairo, in the dust and confusion of which small gangs of men appeared suddenly in a number of places in the centre of the city and began systematically firing buildings. All eye-witness accounts agreed that these gangs were very well organized; they worked on a carefully prepared plan and carried with them lists of their targets. They had battering rams, rags soaked in kerosene and all the paraphernalia of arson. A number of British-owned buildings were set on fire, as well as cinemas, restaurants, cafés and department stores. Some of these were owned by British subjects, but not all. Nevertheless, the violence was in the main anti-British. The most tragic occurrence was at the Turf Club, where the Canadian Trade Commissioner and nine British subjects were killed, most of them murdered by the mob.

It is impossible to determine how far the Government were implicated in all this. The Minister of the Interior, Serag ed-Din, probably knew what was intended. Outside the Turf Club, forty police were usually stationed because of repeated threats. That morning they had been reduced to four.

The material damage in central Cairo was later estimated to amount to three or four million pounds to British interests alone. The fire brigades had been prevented from working and much of their equipment had been destroyed. Had there been any wind that day, most of Cairo east of the Nile would have burnt out. The army was called in and arrived at the centre of the city in the late afternoon, whereupon the gangs melted away, leaving only the mob, which was easily dealt with.

The destructive work of the day was caused by two different elements, the organized gangs which destroyed specific objectives, and the mob which followed in their wake like jackals after the larger beasts of prey. The gangs showed extraordinary efficiency and discipline. Several organizations are thought to have played a part. The Peace Movement, a semi-Communist body, was one of these. The Socialist Party, led by Ahmed Hussein, was also under suspicion, and some members of the Muslim Brotherhood may have had a hand. I think it probable that an expert Communist organizer, perhaps a member of the Peace Movement, controlled the business, which had a definite revolutionary flavour.

While Cairo blazed, messages began to come through from the Embassy to the Foreign Office and on the teleprinter from our military headquarters in the canal zone to the War Office. A plan had been worked out under which our forces would intervene in Cairo and Alexandria to protect the lives and property of British subjects, including Maltese. However, during this Saturday, a message arrived from the British command in Egypt expressing concern at the resistance shown in the recent fighting at the police post. Serious doubts were expressed as to whether the forces available from the canal zone would be enough for the tasks allotted them under the plan. Most of my senior Cabinet colleagues were away from London that Saturday. The Lord Chancellor, Lord Simonds, was at hand and I asked him to come round to my flat in Carlton Gardens. I told him of the position and showed him a message I was sending to our Commander, saying that if instructed to intervene he must do so, whatever the risks. The Lord Chancellor firmly agreed.

The belief that we had the forces and the conviction that we were prepared to use them were powerful arguments in prodding the Egyptian army to quell the riots. Whether at the order of King or Government, this military action saved Cairo. The fear that our forces were arriving also exerted an influence the next day, when, after prolonged discussions at the Palace, the King dismissed Nahas Pasha and called upon Ali Maher to form a

Government. Though so recently all-conquering, the Wafd never returned to power. It had been the fleshy body of Egyptian politics since 1920. The Wafd had destroyed itself by its excesses and almost destroyed Egypt by its example.

The country was teetering on the edge of anarchy. Ali Maher was old, skilled and cunning, but he had an almost impossible task. Much of Cairo was still smouldering, so was the Wafd, with its agents among the King's company. Ali Maher only lasted five weeks. His success was that he restored order, stopped the radio excesses, called off the "liberation squads" and reduced the cost of living. His was the first Government for years to do anything for the poor of Egypt — no mean record. He promised to arraign the Wafd for their corruption, but he put it off from day to day. His brother had been assassinated and he did not want to share his fate.

Ali Maher served his country well, yet the King was wise to make a change. With Hilali Pasha, who was vigorous and sincere, at its head and Ali Maher's two strongest Ministers to help him at the Treasury and the Interior, the new Government had a fair chance to survive, particularly if our negotiations for a treaty could make progress. Here we were back in the public-opinion dilemma created by the Wafd. We could not make the concessions which the Wafd had demanded, because some were at the expense of another country. It was difficult for Hilali to take less. We had, therefore, to find a new approach and sufficient cover to satisfy opinion while we went to work.

At the end of March, the United States Government pressed us to hasten our discussions with Egypt. "Our information," they told us, "leads us to believe that as each day passes without definite progress towards resolving outstanding issues, the eventual survival of the present Government is placed increasingly in jeopardy." An immediate start on the withdrawal of our forces from Egypt was urged upon us. The United States Ambassador in London was understanding, as usual, and admitted that there was perhaps something of the cloister about the study which he presented on behalf of his Government.

I was concerned at the implication of this American proposal for the Sudan. It included British recognition of the title "King of the Sudan" for the Egyptian King. As I had explained several times before, any such recognition, except by agreement with the Sudanese, which was not likely to be forthcoming, would be regarded in the Sudan as a betrayal. I expressed to the Ambassador the hope that Mr. Caffery would not continue to think it impossible to reach an agreement with the Egyptians without recognition by us of the title.

In my written reply to this United States document, I also explained the problem of the redeployment of our forces in the Middle East. Gaza had been examined and rejected as a possible alternative station. Other areas had other limitations. "All this," I wrote, "does not make it easier for us to agree to a large and immediate withdrawal of troops from the canal zone, while continuing to prepare for the defence of the Middle East against outside aggression." While I set out our difficulties to the United States Government, who were naturally impatient, I was trying to find a solution of Egyptian-Sudanese relations which would not be a breach of our engagement to the Sudan. I called home the Governor-General, Sir Robert Howe, and our Ambassador in Cairo, Sir Ralph Stevenson, and held a number of meetings with them and my Foreign Office advisers. As a result of these consultations we evolved the following formula, which the Governor-General was authorized to put to the Executive Council in Khartoum, while our Ambassador in Cairo approached the Egyptian Government:

The Egyptian Government having declared that His Majesty King Farouk holds the title of King of Egypt and the Sudan, Her Majesty's Government reaffirm that they would accept either the unity of Egypt and the Sudan under the Egyptian Crown or any other status for the Sudan, provided that it resulted from the exercise of the right of the Sudanese people freely to decide their future status, which right is recognized and accepted by both Governments. Her Majesty's Government realize that there are differences of opinion between the two Governments as to the question of the King's title during the interim period before self-determination. They therefore also declare that they are ready to enter into immediate consultation with the Sudanese in regard to this matter, in order to ascertain whether any solution is possible, agreeable to the Sudanese and consistent with the pledges given by Her Majesty's Government to them.

I had some hopes that our statement would bring about joint discussions between the Egyptians and the Sudanese. I was ready to encourage these, especially with Hilali's Government, but I was not prepared to dragoon the Sudanese against their better judgment.

The Governor-General reported that the immediate reaction of the Sudanese members of his Council was one of caution and suspicion. They felt that there must be a catch somewhere, and the psychological effect of the reference to King Farouk's title of "King of the Sudan" in the opening sentence was evident. Some of them raised the question which the Governor-General had anticipated. Would Her Majesty's Government, after consultation, insist on recognition of the title, even if the Sudanese were opposed to it? Clearly we could not do this.

The Egyptian Ambassador in London, Amr Pasha, continued to work for agreement, and was able to report some progress at the Cairo end of the line. I told him that if relations continued to improve, we could make a start with some deliveries of military equipment, at least for training purposes.

Direct discussions between Egypt and the Sudan made little progress. Throughout May and June, at meetings and in despatches, American pressure was heavy upon us to put pressure on the Sudanese. At one of these discussions I had to say bluntly that we could not keep the Egyptian Government alive by feeding the Sudanese to them.

Early in June, Mr. Henry Byroade visited London after a tour of the Middle East, made on behalf of the American State Department. He suggested that some really authoritative figure might visit the Sudan, and so explain matters to the Sudanese that they would be prepared to acquiesce in the title.

The business could not, however, be settled so simply. The Sudanese desire for independence was deep and real; so was their suspicion of the Egyptians. By the end of the month it was clear that the Sudanese were not prepared to accept King Farouk's claim to be their King. While the visit of the Sudanese delegation to Cairo had, for the first time, injected some realism into relations between Egypt and the Sudan, no Egyptian Government dared to reach an agreement with us without some satisfaction on the Sudan, which the Sudanese were not prepared to give. When the Wafd Government had denounced their treaty with us, they had also abrogated the condominium agreement by which our two countries held joint responsibility in the Sudan. That was not the fault of the present Egyptian Government, who wanted to regain the position the Wafd had thrown away. We were ready to help them as far as we could do so, without being false to our own engagement to the Sudan.

The position was usefully discussed at meetings with Mr. Acheson at the Foreign Office at the end of June, which both the Governor-General of the Sudan and our Ambassador in Cairo attended. The United States Ambassador in London and Mr. Acheson's Middle Eastern advisers came with him. We explained the deadlock in our negotiations with Egypt over the question of the recognition of King Farouk's title. Sir Sayed Abdul Rahman el Mahdi was not prepared to accept that claim. As one of the two principal leaders in the Sudan, and chief of the largest political party, the Sayed's representative had been in Cairo and failed to agree with his hosts. On the other hand we wished to help the present Egyptian Government. It was my hope that we might be able to handle together the programme of constitutional development for the Sudan. Accordingly, I proposed to invite the Egyptians to discuss with us a draft statute submitted by the Governor-General for the self-government of the country.

I explained that while the Sudanese were against the King's title, they did recognize the need for close relations with Egypt. I thought that my method would take account of these realities, and enable Egypt and ourselves to help the Sudan's political development. The first Sudanese Parliament would be elected in the autumn. It could pronounce on the King's title, and, though it might not be anxious to do so, we were ready to give encouragement. By promoting direct talks between the Egyptians and Sudanese, we thought we had opened a back door which might help us to get round the question of the King's title. I was proposing to open another door by enabling the Egyptians to associate themselves with the last stages of constitutional development in the Sudan.

Our American guests accepted these plans as useful, but they continued to hover round the title, and thought we should talk to the Sudanese and impress upon them the importance of agreement with Egypt.

We had scarcely dispersed, when bad news came out of Egypt. Hilali's Government was firm and honest. I thought it the best the country had known for years. It was making ready to arraign those who had waxed on previous systems of graft. The Wafd leaders were to be indicted. It was also reported that the Finance Minister intended to press the Government's claims against Abboud Pasha, for unpaid taxes amounting to several millions of pounds. Abboud was a man of immense riches, the source of some of whose fortune was known to the Wafd. Into this morass Hilali resolved to move. I admired his courage, but in a state rotted by bribery and sodden with favouritism, the path of the reformer is slippery and full of peril.

Threatened with these unpleasant exposures, Abboud took action at the Palace, paying large sums of money in Swiss francs to two of its less creditable but influential hangers-on, Elias Andraos Pasha and Kerim Tabet Pasha. These two worthies were to engineer Hilali's downfall. The Prime Minister soon found himself entangled in a financial and political mesh, characteristic of Egypt. The combination of Abboud Pasha, who feared he might have to pay taxes, and ex-Wafdist Ministers, who saw themselves being indicted for corruption, overthrew Hilali Pasha.

This palace intrigue was damaging to the country and to the King. Hafiz Afifi Pasha, his senior adviser, had tried to save King Farouk from the consequences of his own acts. Seeing clearly the dangers, this loyal servant did everything he could to persuade Hilali to carry on. He failed, and the Prime Minister's resignation marked the beginning of the end of royal rule in Egypt.

A confused and decaying interlude followed, in which small men had their way. Sirry Pasha was sent for by the King to form a Government. He was an unimpressive personality with little following, and there was no rush to serve. The faithful Hafiz Afifi was at work meanwhile attempting to secure the appointment of a

Prime Minister of repute and some integrity. He was still trying to save the reputation of the King. On his pleading, Bahi ed-Din Barakat Pasha was sent for to form a Government. He could have met the needs of the hour but King Farouk's evil star was now guiding him. Barakat Pasha had been at work only a few hours, when the King changed his mind and summoned Sirry Pasha once again, in the middle of the night of July 1–2. This time he formed a Government of underlings and the unknown, the inclusion of Kerim Tabet Pasha being a sinister warning. There were to be no more attempts to root out corruption. Egypt was back in its dirty financial groove.

I thought that these events heralded the return of the Wafd, and so it seemed to many in Egypt. Pictures were shown of the former Prime Minister, Nahas Pasha, in his silk dressing-gown welcoming back his most discreditable colleague, Serag ed-Din, who had been under restraint for corruption and his alleged part in the Cairo riots.

The affairs of Egypt were now sharply set upon a downward course. The intriguers were triumphant, and honest men hid their heads. They would be lucky if they did not find themselves in prison. The King knew well enough that the British Government deplored and resented the fall of Hilali, but this did not trouble him. He felt no need to take account of us. He thought that he could always prevent Britain from taking strong action in Egypt by appealing to the United States and working on their Ambassador's fears of a revolution. He also thought that if a revolution occurred, British forces would in the last resort come to his rescue. In this he was mistaken. Although we had a plan for intervention, should a crisis threaten British lives, we had decided that it could only be brought into action by a Ministerial decision. It would be wrong to place heavy political responsibility on the Commander-in-Chief.

Our Chargé d'Affaires in Cairo commented, in a despatch, that it was necessary to make an end to Egypt's practice of playing on American fears and on the vanity of the United States Ambassador in Cairo. The King must be urged to restore to power men of proven character and resolute in action. As a result of this message, I instructed a senior member of the Foreign Office to see the United States Ambassador and put the position clearly before him. He gave Mr. Gifford our information and told him that we knew that the United States Ambassador in Cairo, Mr. Caffery, had had talks with Abboud Pasha and Kerim Tabet before the recent change of Government in Egypt. We did not suppose that Mr. Caffery had told these men that the United States would favour a change of Government leading to the return of the Wafd, but the fact that he had talked to them had been widely misinterpreted in Egypt.

As usual, Mr. Gifford was most helpful and did everything he could to bring our policies into line. Unfortunately he was only partly successful. He could only agree that Egyptian opinion knew of the divergencies between our two Governments. In particular, Egypt was aware of Mr. Caffery's insistence on the importance of the King's dual title, Egypt and the Sudan. The Foreign Office representative commented to the Ambassador: "It was unfortunate that the United States Government found such difficulty generally in the Middle East in giving Her Majesty's Government support in the only way in which the Oriental understood the word." Egyptians, and King Farouk in particular, he said, must be made to realize that they could not rely on driving a wedge between us and the Americans.

These differences were also known in the Sudan, where in an interview Sir Sayed Abdul Rahman expressed a hope that constitutional progress in the Sudan would not be held up, despite American pressure on Her Majesty's Government to yield to Egyptian demands.

The rottenness and inefficiency of the new administration in Egypt were soon apparent. Sirry Pasha's Government lasted barely three weeks, the monarchy a few days more. The new Prime Minister took over the portfolios of War and Marine, as well as a number of other offices. The King appointed one of his favourites, General Hussein Sirry Amer, to the committee of the Officers' Club, the epitome of the military life of Egypt. The General was most unpopular and suspected of murdering a fellow officer. When the King's appointment was rejected, he retaliated by dismissing the committee. The Prime Minister was troubled that discipline might collapse, and said as much in a letter to our Embassy asking for the release of British war material. On July 20 it became known that the Prime Minister had submitted his resignation as a result of a difference with the King over the appointment of a new Minister of War.

The Prime Minister had proposed to appoint General Neguib, thinking that his popularity with junior officers would help. The King would not agree and once again proposed General Hussein Sirry Amer for yet another appointment. It is likely that the decision to attempt the military revolution was taken during this Cabinet crisis. Meanwhile, the King had become frightened by the growing unpopularity of his actions and, stimulated by his fears, he called upon Hilali Pasha to form a second Government. This time Hilali rightly laid down certain conditions before accepting. These were that the purge of corrupters should continue; that the electoral laws should be amended; that elections should be held when he himself thought it advisable; that martial law should continue, but only against those accused of taking part in the burning of Cairo; most important of all, that there should be no interference by "irresponsibles," the Palace hangers-on.

King Farouk had been scared by the disapproval of the Sirry Pasha Government all over Egypt, as well as abroad, and by unrest in the army, which was symptomatic of the general discontent. Year by year, after 1948, the army brooded over its ignominious defeats by the Israelis. Without much difficulty the young officers persuaded themselves that the fault was not theirs. A scapegoat must be found. They had been let down by the Palace and its minions and by corruption in high places. This was the motive power which led to the King's downfall and the establishment of military rule.

King Farouk sent for Hilali Pasha too late, the army was already on the move. The King and the diplomatic corps were at this time in Alexandria. During the night of July 22–23 a group of dissident officers took over control in Cairo. The police obeyed their orders.

In the early hours of the morning the conspirators moved on Abbassia barracks, and by 7 A.M. it was clear that all army units in the capital supported General Neguib. The revolt had been entirely successful. This tactical victory was no doubt facilitated by the absence of the King and Ministers from Cairo, as was the custom during the summer months.

From 8 A.M. onwards, the King was frequently on the telephone to the United States Ambassador. He repeated, each time more clearly, that only foreign intervention could save him and his dynasty. He did not ask explicitly for British military action, but the implication was obvious. I had frequently indicated to our Embassy that British forces would not intervene to keep King Farouk on his throne. Our Chargé d'Affaires had this in mind and gave no encouraging reply to Mr. Caffery's messages.

I thought it necessary that we should at once make our position clear to General Neguib, and I instructed our Embassy in Cairo to send Mr. John Hamilton* to see Neguib at once and to tell him that, while we had no wish to intervene in internal affairs in Egypt, we should not hesitate to do so if we thought it necessary to protect British lives. For this reason we had issued instructions to our forces which would bring them to a state of readiness. We had noted General Neguib's statement that the Egyptian army would be responsible for the protection of foreign lives and property, and we sincerely hoped that no intervention by British forces would therefore be necessary. The military preparations which we were making were in no way directed against Egyptian armed forces and every effort would be made by us to avoid the possibility of any incident.

A reply came back promptly:

> Action duly taken 2300 hours to-day. General thanked Assistant Military Attaché and myself for delivery of message and repeated his assurance regarding protection foreign lives. In so far as possible to gauge in short time, headquarters seemed both calm and confident.

General Neguib had good reasons for his confidence. Meanwhile, in Alexandria, Hilali's Government despatched Maraghi Pasha, a man of firmness and resolution, to Cairo to talk matters over with the General. Before the Government's emissary could arrive, General Neguib demanded the appointment of Ali Maher Pasha as Prime Minister and the King yielded. He also insisted on the dismissal of a number of the King's favourites, including Kerim

---

* Counsellor at Her Majesty's Embassy in Cairo and a man of much experience in Egyptian affairs.

Tabet and Elias Andraos, the two men who bore the chief responsibility for the fall of Hilali's first Government; the second had only lasted a few hours. Ali Maher's Government was not impressive, but he himself retained most of the important offices. I did not consider that this could be more than an interim arrangement.

Alexandria was entered by General Neguib on July 25. He was accompanied by a force of troops, tanks and artillery. There was little enthusiasm, and uncertainty brooded on the scene. A number of senior officers from the army and the police were arrested by Neguib in Cairo and, on the following day, in Alexandria.

Early the next morning, aircraft flew low over the royal palaces, and armoured units and tanks broke into their gardens. There was very little firing.

The King had continued in close contact throughout these days with the United States Ambassador and made a last appeal to him for help. No help was forthcoming, and the King accepted General Neguib's demands that he should abdicate before noon and leave the country that evening. At the appointed hour of six o'clock, a little group composed of the Prime Minister, the American Ambassador, some officers of the Palace guard and and domestic servants, saw the King and his family leave Egyptian soil. Neguib and his followers arrived too late for any parting, a mishap which appeared to annoy the General. All reports agreed that there was little excitement and that the Royal departure did not stir the nation.

It was a misfortune for King Farouk that he succeeded to the throne so young. He had been entered as a cadet at Woolwich just before his father died and a toughening training might have added strength to his intelligence and character to his nimble wits. Back in Cairo as a King, with one or two sage advisers amid a flock of toadies and panders, he found it too easy to drift with the tide. The outcome was unhappy for him and disastrous for his country. With a discredited monarchy and despised political parties, all was made ready for a military dictatorship, which was later to fall under aggressive leadership with baleful consequences.

At this stage, General Neguib's revolt was accepted rather than acclaimed. The revolution had one immediate and unfortunate consequence for the relations between our two countries. The Egyptian Ambassador, Amr Pasha, a patriot and a man of courage who was prepared to take risks in the real interests of our two countries, was succeeded by Mahmoud Fawzi.

Once the General was installed, numerous arrests followed of public men, deserving and undeserving. Loyal servants of Egypt were imprisoned, including the former Prime Minister Hilali, Maraghi and Hafiz Afifi. A number of prominent Wafdists shared their fate and better deserved it.

A new wind began to blow in Egypt and I had now to decide on our attitude to the revolutionary leaders. General Neguib posed many problems. I knew that he was partly Sudanese and had been educated at Gordon College in Khartoum. Men spoke well of him, his honesty and his intentions. He had fought bravely in the Israeli war and been wounded. His powers of leadership were more doubtful and I was disturbed to notice that in his earlier meetings with our Ambassador or our Chargé d'Affaires he was never alone and did not appear to lead his side. There were risks in any course. General Neguib was at least a better bet than either King or Wafd. He must be given his chance to cleanse the Egyptian stable. As the King had embarked on his launch to leave his country, he observed tartly to Ali Maher that his Premiership would not last long. The prophecy was soon fulfilled, and within six weeks Neguib had taken over in fact as well as in name.

Her Majesty's Government had first to test the new Egyptian Government in negotiation, beginning, as usual, with the vexing question of the Sudan. The abdication of the King had at least removed the significance of one of the most troublesome Egyptian demands, that of his dual title. I would normally have given the new Government time to settle down before making any approaches, but I had to act promptly because of our joint responsibilities in the Sudan. A draft statute, which was to be its constitution, had been prepared for that country. By November 8, when the new Sudanese Parliament was due to meet, it had to be determined.

I had to make plain our own attitude at least a month before, and preferred to do so in harmony with General Neguib, if I could. Accordingly, I addressed a comprehensive despatch to our Ambassador in Cairo in which I set out our plan. I explained that I wanted agreement with Egypt, but that I could not on this account delay the elections in the Sudan indefinitely, nor hold up the constitution. The new Egyptian Government must be aware of the feelings of the Sudanese. Sayed Abdul Rahman's representative had been in discussion in Cairo. The Sayed had intended to follow this up with a personal visit, but he cancelled it on learning of the military revolt in Egypt. After the Sudanese constitution had been brought into force there would be an interim period, under the arrangements we had agreed, before the Sudanese determined their future. I wanted the Egyptian Government to be associated with us during that time. I asked our Ambassador to put all this to Neguib.

Meanwhile, Sir Sayed Abdul Rahman el Mahdi came to see me in London and I had some memorable discussions with this remarkable man, whose father had led a religious movement which had swept the Sudan and driven out Egyptians and British. We had returned by force, but the administration which followed had cared for the welfare of the Sudanese, and the people knew that. I was not surprised when the Mahdi, criticizing condominium rule as anomalous, added that trouble had only been avoided by the wisdom of British officials in the Sudan. We discussed the inevitable difficulties which beset the first steps in democratic government in the Sudan, when the elections ought to be held and how long they should take. The Sayed was concerned that his country should, from the outset, be guided by a responsible Parliament from which the Sudanese Cabinet could be drawn. He wanted more direct elections and a time limit for self-determination, not later than the end of 1953. I said that the date was a matter for the new Sudanese Parliament. If they decided as he proposed, I would have no objection, provided that they were ready for it. I enjoyed his visit and respected his personality and the directness of his approach.

The "National Front" also came to see me. They did not want elections or self-government followed by self-determination. They wanted a plebiscite at once to decide the future of the Sudan. I could not agree with them, but they were told that if all parties in the new Sudanese Parliament wanted a plebiscite, they could hold one. In the event, as I expected, they did no such thing. On October 22 I announced in Parliament that Her Majesty's Government had given their consent to action by the Governor-General to bring the self-government statute into force.

★ ★ ★ ★ ★

The autumn brought an important and welcome change. Greece and Turkey became allies in N.A.T.O., with strategic consequences which affected our Middle Eastern deployment. I was particularly delighted at this new relationship with Turkey. I had always deplored the hostilities with that country in the first world war and their legacy. One of my first speeches in Parliament was in 1924 in support of the Treaty of Lausanne, which made peace between us. I admired the peasant toughness of the Turk and knew him for a loyal friend.

At this time I sent a despatch to our Ambassador in Cairo which included the following observations on the situation as I saw it then:

> While I do not expect the new Egyptian Government to show any marked friendliness towards us, they do seem to be approaching Anglo-Egyptian problems in a more practical way and this is at last beginning to show results.
>
> The new regime in Egypt is not, however, the only change influencing our attitude to Egypt on defence problems. Other major factors are:
>
> (a) the entry of Turkey into the Middle Eastern picture as a firm ally;
>
> (b) the possibility that financial considerations may make necessary the reduction of the forces which we are able to maintain in the Middle East in peacetime; and that the forces deployed in the Middle East in the first six months of war may be smaller than previously envisaged;
>
> (c) the steps taken towards the setting up of a Middle East defence organization: this is now designed in the first instance as a planning organization and references in my despatch No. 65 to a supreme allied commander and a Middle East command are therefore no longer appropriate.

If, however, further progress is to be made with setting up an organization on these lines, the solution of Anglo-Egyptian problems should fit in with the form of the organization.

These considerations, and particularly the first two, have made it necessary to review in detail our whole strategy in the Middle East. This review is now proceeding, and it may well emerge that a base in Egypt, although desirable, is no longer absolutely essential to our interests. Hitherto the basis of our policy towards Egypt has been the advice which we have received that is essential to maintain in peacetime the Egypt base if the Middle East is to be successfully defended in war. If this advice is to be modified — and I must emphasize that it has not yet been modified — we may find it easier to come to terms with Egypt.

Early in December Her Majesty's Government decided in principle to transfer the joint headquarters in the Middle East to Cyprus. They authorized the expenditure of up to half a million pounds on preparatory work. This predictive decision was welcomed by Turkey. Cyprus as an air base was within range of the Persian Gulf, but the island unfortunately had no natural harbour. The cost of building one would have been very high. We did not do so and were to pay dearly for that omission.

On the last day of the year I had a talk with the Turkish Ambassador, who was urging me to conclude an agreement with the present Egyptian Government. I explained that I was having a great deal of difficulty. General Neguib was by no means easy to negotiate with and his speeches were a constant irritant to us. If he really wanted to work with us he must stop threatening. The Ambassador replied that I should understand General Neguib's internal difficulties. I said I thought I did, and hoped our Turkish friends would continue to impress upon him that he must go some way to meet us.

As I reflected at the end of the year upon our responsibilities in this part of the world, I thought that there had been some improvement in politics, but the economic situation in Egypt was bad and growing worse. This had already dimmed much of the popularity of the new military rulers. It could have more serious consequences in the New Year.

★ ★ ★ ★ ★

Sudanese affairs underwent a sea change in the autumn of 1952. The Egyptian Government could no longer make the claim that the King of Egypt was King of Sudan; by an act of statesmanship General Neguib dropped the claim to the unity of Egypt and the Sudan. This was, of course, extremely welcome to the Sudanese, whose political parties made a number of agreements with the Government of Egypt in the next few weeks.

Britain also negotiated with the Egyptian Government in these new conditions. The agreement which we reached expressly recognized the right of the Sudanese people to self-determination and to its effective exercise at the right time with the necessary safeguards. The problem of the South, and of the replacement of British officials in the Sudan service by Sudanese, presented considerable difficulties, but on the whole the arrangements made were acceptable. Two commissions were to be set up, one to assist the Governor-General in the exercise of certain of his powers. This would consist of a Pakistani as chairman and two Sudanese, proposed by ourselves and the Egyptian Government in agreement, and approved by the Sudanese Parliament. The second was an electoral commission which would supervise the preparations and conduct the elections. This would have seven members, three Sudanese, appointed by the Governor-General, one British, one Egyptian, one American and one Indian, who was to be chairman. In the event, both these commissions did their work quite well.

I was anxious that Her Majesty's Government should endorse this agreement without delay. The Sudanese had been led to expect self-government by the end of 1952. It would be much easier to defend the agreement we had now negotiated with the Egyptians, which included reasonable provision for replacing British officials and for safeguarding the southern provinces, than to accept the much less satisfactory agreements which the Egyptians had negotiated with the Sudanese political parties behind our backs. The Sudanese elections ought to be held before the rainy season began, and this would be impossible unless the preliminary arrangements were completed by the end of February.

The Government discussed the agreement, but some felt that there was misunderstanding and uncertainty about it in the House of Commons. I therefore undertook to explain the agreement to a meeting of Government supporters that evening. My colleagues accepted that if I were satisfied that I could command enough support they would then authorize the conclusion of the agreement. At my request, the final decision was to be taken that night after I had addressed the meeting.

I had no doubt which was our right course. If we delayed, made difficulties and refused to conclude the agreement, the Sudanese would put the chief blame upon us for the inevitable postponement of the elections and any other political difficulties which might result. The Egyptians would no doubt try to mount an anti-British campaign, but that campaign was less likely to be successful with the Sudanese if we maintained a consistent attitude. In the autumn of 1951, I had publicly pledged the Government, without dissent in Parliament, to self-government for the Sudan. To go back or hestitate now would be to play into the hands of the Egyptians and to cause dismay and despair among our friends in the Sudan. Admittedly the choice was between difficulties, as too often happens in foreign affairs, but the wise course, to go ahead with the agreements, was also the one that we were in duty bound to follow. I felt sure that if we held steadily to our decision, the violence of the Egyptian campaign to induce the Sudanese to align their future with Egypt would, in time, produce its own reaction. Egypt and the Sudan had many reasons for living on friendly terms and we had no wish that they should not do so. But if the Egyptians were going to bribe or bully the Sudanese into unity they would soon, I believed, be taught a sharp lesson. However events worked out, it must be to our advantage to pursue a consistent course. I explained the position to the Conservative Members of Parliament and was thought to have dispelled many of their doubts and anxieties. The Government endorsed my proposal late that evening and I made a statement in Parliament the next day. I should have had to resign if I had not got my way.

This was one of the rare occasions when I differed from Sir

Winston Churchill on a matter of foreign policy. As he remarked
on another occasion, you could put each of us in a separate room,
put any questions of foreign policy to us and nine times out of
ten we would give the same answer. This was certainly true and I
think that Sir Winston was influenced on this occasion by his own
memories of the Sudan many years before. Also, he probably
felt, as I did, that the agreement could have been greatly improved upon.

The aftermath proved the Government's decision to have been
correct. While the pro-Egyptian parties gained a narrow victory
at the polls, they did not remain united for long. Dissensions
broke out among them and exasperation at Egyptian interference
increased steadily, with the result that within a year or two the
Sudan was firmly set upon its independent course. Whether or
not the Sudan and Egypt come closer together in the future, the
Sudan has been given every opportunity to evolve its national
life as it wills. We could not ensure more than this.

Eighteen months later I commented to the House of Commons:

> We want to have friendship ourselves both with Egypt and
> the Sudan, but we trust that all concerned will give to the
> Sudan a real opportunity to decide its own national life
> and future. All the reports we have had for the last few
> months show that there is an increasing determination in the
> Sudan to do just that. Beyond that, we have no claim which
> it would be within our rights to make.

Early in the New Year of 1953, I gave much time to setting
out in the clearest terms our requirements in Egypt, the offer we
proposed to make to the Egyptian Government and the part which
we hoped that the United States Government would play. After
a number of discussions with my colleagues, I set down the ideas
which I thought a general settlement should include:

1. A phased withdrawal of British troops from Egypt.
2. Maintenance of a military base in the canal zone in
peace under conditions which would enable us and our allies
to have immediate use of it in war.

3. An Anglo-Egyptian organization for the air defence of Egypt.

4. Egypt's participation in a Middle East defence organization.

5. A programme of military and economic assistance to Egypt by the United Kingdom and the United States.

All these proposals I considered to be interdependent and I wrote:

> We must be sure that the base will be readily available in a future war. Middle East defence organization must be more than a paper plan and Egypt must prove that she intends to back it. If France and other maritime nations are to be satisfied that free passage of the canal will continue, we must show that some satisfactory alternative for protection by British troops has been provided. The United States must be closely associated with Middle East defence organization.

Here was an early indication of the canal problem which would vex us so much in the future.

In January the Prime Minister paid a visit to the United States and saw the President-elect. During his discussions with Mr. Eisenhower, he emphasized the importance we attached to full sympathy and support from the United States during our negotiations with Egypt. We were not asking them, we explained, to give us any military help in Egypt at present. We had ample forces of our own there.

The Government considered my proposals in the light of the Prime Minister's discussions in the United States and of the negotiations I had been holding with the State Department. I had already had a number of exchanges through diplomatic channels with the United States Government, which encouraged me to think that they would agree with us. Two days later, they did so. All seemed to be going well. A week after this, however, the Prime Minister told me that while the President accepted our proposals, he wanted to discuss with me, when I came to Washington, the question of sending a United States military representative. This arose from a suggestion by the Prime Minister that in negotiations of this character, which were so largely military, the Ambassadors should be double-banked by military representation. I welcomed this, for Neguib was also a soldier. Field-Marshal Sir William Slim was to be our representative.

Throughout my stay I kept in the closest touch with the Prime Minister. When negotiating for my country abroad I have often found it useful to receive a current commentary from those at home as I went along, and I have tried to provide it for others who are in the same position. In discussion with a foreign power one is sometimes drawn almost insensibly towards their point of view. Even on minor points this can add up to a considerable shift of emphasis. While, therefore, a negotiator is entitled to a fair latitude, it can help him to be reminded of his point of departure. It may be irritating to have one's elbow jogged too much; it is much worse to feel that what one is trying to do is not understood. In all the years that Sir Winston Churchill and I worked together, it was this comprehension at the end of the wire that was most remarkable. I suppose that it was in part the result of our lifetimes' experience of world affairs.

On the day of my arrival in Washington I had a conversation with the President at which Mr. Dulles and our Ambassador were present. The following is the text of my personal message to the Prime Minister that night, retailing the part of our conversation which dealt with Egypt:

The President agreed with me that it was essential to maintain the base in Egypt and that if we were to evacuate the canal zone before making a Middle Eastern defence arrangement we should be exposing ourselves to Egyptian blackmail. In contrast to Dulles, he was clear and firm on this point. I put it to him strongly that Egypt was the key to Middle East defence but that if we were to secure a satisfactory agreement, we must act together. I pressed him repeatedly to send a military adviser to Cairo to work with Slim. He seemed finally to agree with this. His difficulty was to find a suitable officer. But he said that he would consider

the possibility of sending General Hull (the Deputy Chief
of Staff and an entirely suitable man) accompanied by a
personal message to Neguib stressing the importance which
he attached to the setting up of an effective defence organization in the Middle East and the securing of a base on the
canal.

Towards the end of the conversation I expressed my anxiety
to try to reach an agreed policy with him on the Middle East
during this visit. The President thought that this would be
possible and asked me to go over the ground with Mr. Dulles,
preparatory to a further talk with him on Friday, March 6.
I shall do this, and shall hope to make progress. The prospects
in regard to Egypt seem fairly hopeful but I foresee the greatest
difficulty in regard to Persia.

The President could not have been more friendly and said
that he wanted to have more than one further talk with me
while I was here.

On March 6 I had a long discussion with Mr. Dulles and his
advisers under six different headings, one of which was Egypt.
In the course of this exchange we reached agreement on a formula
to cover our negotiations, which I would refer to the Government at home and he to the President.

We followed this up in a conversation with the President later
the same day. At this meeting, the President said he was prepared
to make General John Hull available to assist the United States
Ambassador in Cairo for a period of about six weeks, provided
the terms of reference were agreed. General Hull would be available from March 9. But there was a preliminary point: he was
not willing to gate-crash the negotiation, and the Egyptians
would have to invite the Americans to participate. They had at
present no basis for intervention. I observed that the Egyptian
army would have to be equipped largely from American resources
and that the Egyptians had already asked to be supplied with
arms. There was a direct relationship between the arming of the
Egyptians and defence arrangements in the Middle East. The
President admitted this, but maintained his view that the Egyptians
must assent to United States participation in the talks. Subject

to this he would accept the terms of reference which Mr. Dulles and I had proposed. I undertook to report the position we had reached to my colleagues.

Our original proposal contained a number of choices known as Case A, Case B and Case C. In all three schemes the canal zone would be handed over to Egypt. In Case A, up to seven thousand British servicemen would run the existing depots and installations; in Case B, this would be done by the Egyptians under our supervision; in Case C, our role would be restricted to one of periodical inspection. It was estimated that A would enable us to put the base on a war footing immediately, but that under B and C delays of sixty and ninety days would be inevitable. Case A contained the terms of settlement which we all wished to see. The Government in London had not agreed to go beyond this, though the United States Government had been fully informed of the other courses.

Overnight a telegram arrived from the Foreign Office stressing the importance of preserving, in any text agreed with the Americans, a suitable reference to the package proposal and suggesting that an additional paragraph should be included in the agreement to the following effect:

The United States and the United Kingdom Governments will propose to the Egyptian Government a general settlement comprising:

(a) the maintenance of the canal zone base in peace with a view to its immediate reactivation in the event of war;

(b) an arrangement for the air defence of Egypt;

(c) a phased withdrawal of British armed forces from Egyptian territory;

(d) the participation of Egypt in a Middle East defence organization; and

(e) a programme of military and economic assistance to Egypt.

The representatives will indicate that if British forces are to be withdrawn from the canal zone, it is imperative that alternative arrangements be made at the same time for the

defence of the Middle East as a whole. It is for this reason
that all the terms comprising the proposed general settlement
should be treated as interdependent.

On March 9 I again saw the President and reported to the Prime
Minister on the outcome:

I had a good talk with the President on Egypt. He spoke
very fully about the necessity of having a workable base in
Egypt. He wants to get a base which is workable in peacetime
(Case A) and will strive for this. If we cannot get it, then we
must have a base which can be reactivated as soon as possible
after the outbreak of war and in no event in more than two
months. In the second case he spoke firmly of the necessity
of keeping certain installations and depots under British
technical supervision and control. But our two soldiers in
his opinion should be allowed to judge the technical conditions which are necessary to achieve this objective, and he
thinks that they should have latitude to make modifications
in the optimum plan which they both agree.

I read to the President the "package" proposals, and he
thought they were good, but in paragraph (a) he would
speak of the "earliest possible" rather than the "immediate"
reactivation of the base on the understanding recorded in
the preceding paragraph of this telegram.

I can assure you that both the President and Bedell Smith
are perfectly clear about the issues involved and on what is
required for an operational base in Egypt.

The President said he would send a personal message to
Neguib by General Hull, who has already begun work setting
out his position and interest in these defence negotiations.

I concluded my visit with a further message to the Prime Minister:

My telegram [just quoted] was read out by Her Majesty's
Ambassador to Mr. Bedell Smith on the conclusion of our
meetings this morning. He agreed that this accurately set
out the position we had reached. If, as I devoutly hope,
these arrangements are acceptable, the next step is the joint

approach by the two Ambassadors to the Egyptian Government of which Caffery has already been warned.

I am leaving for New York in an hour and you will no doubt send the necessary instructions to Her Majesty's Ambassador, Cairo, repeating to Washington, so that this joint step can be taken as soon as possible.

Hull is ready to start and, the moment the Ambassadors give the all clear, will fly direct to Cairo by special aircraft.

Americans at one time suggested that conversations should start without waiting for Hull's arrival. I deprecated this because of my mistrust of Caffery, which they understand, and, while acutely conscious of the time factor, they have agreed to wait for Hull.

Our communiqué said little, as is usual with such documents. On the flight to New York, where I was to speak to the Foreign Policy Association that night, I thought with satisfaction on the outcome.

When I got home, I was able to tell my colleagues that as a result of my discussions in Washington full agreement had been reached on Egyptian negotiations. Unfortunately, an unexpected hitch was to derail these carefully prepared plans. The Egyptians rejected the idea that the Americans should participate, and the President had made Egyptian acceptance a condition for taking part. The Egyptian argument for their refusal was that an agreement must first be reached on evacuating British troops from Egypt. Middle East defence as a whole could be considered afterwards. We were not prepared to discuss our exodus in isolation. There was, in consequence, no basis on which to begin the negotiation.

I have given a detailed account of these exchanges because of their importance and because they were characteristic of so much diplomacy then and later. If we had been able to bring about joint Anglo-American negotiations with Egypt at this stage, as the Prime Minister and I both wished to do, the future position in the Middle East would have worked out differently. It was unfortunate that the United States Government and, in particular, their Ambassador in Cairo, were not prepared to put any pressure upon the Egyptians to bring this about. In view of the help, financial and other, which the United States had given and was proposing to give to Egypt, it would, in my judgment, have been possible for them to make a firm request to attend without being accused of gate-crashing. However, it was impossible to persuade the Americans to make any further effort to attend the meeting. The Egyptians were left to act as they wished and they preferred to divide both the discussions and the allies.

On my return to Britain, my attention was soon drawn to a pending delivery of arms from the United States to Egypt. I asked the United States Ambassador to come to see me and told him that I wanted to be quite clear where we were in respect of United States delivery of arms for Egypt. As I understood it, although the Americans had made a general offer of arms to the Egyptian Government, they did not contemplate the delivery of any lethal weapons while the political situation in Egypt and relations with us remained disturbed. The Ambassador said that this was also his understanding of the position, though he had heard nothing on the subject lately. He had always taken the view, and expressed it, that the Americans could not supply weapons to Egypt which might be used to kill British troops. I thanked the Ambassador and said that he would remember that this was a topic on which I had made strong representations to Mr. Dulles. In view of the difficulties which we were now encountering in opening our negotiations, I would send him a brief memorandum of our views. I said that I would be grateful if he would transmit this to the State Department and make sure that there was no doubt on the subject.

Meanwhile, Mr. Selwyn Lloyd, the Minister of State at the Foreign Office, on his way back from the Sudan, had some conversations in Cairo with both General Neguib and Colonel Nasser, who was becoming a rival leader on the Revolutionary Council. To the former he said that, in the present situation, the delivery of more jet aircraft was impossible. The present attacks on the British administration in the Sudan and upon Her Majesty's Government were such as to make it exceedingly difficult to carry out the agreement. Towards the end of this discussion, General Neguib repeated that he did not want any Egyptians to interfere with the course of the Sudanese elections and that he promised to stop them going. The Minister of State asked General Neguib whether he could quote him on this point. The General replied that he could and Mr. Lloyd wrote on a piece of paper these words, with Egyptian agreement: "General Neguib affirmed that it was not the desire of the Egyptian Government to interfere with the complete freedom of the elections in the Sudan." I have no doubt that Neguib intended these words to be observed. His personal position in the Sudan was strong and he may have known that extraneous Egyptian activities would not help him there. Others in Egypt thought and acted differently.

* * * * *

Illness laid me aside from any further participation in Egyptian discussions during the next six months, during which time sinister portents began to appear. General Neguib was not in good health and his authority weakened. His policies had been restrained and civilized, but they did not always prevail against the will of Colonel Nasser and other officers of the C.R.C., the Council for the Revolutionary Command. Outside opposition was being progressively smothered. The Wafd counted for less, which was no bad thing, and Gestapo methods for more, which was ominous. The Council declared a republic and seized the royal family's property without compensation, contrary, it was rumoured, to the wishes of both General Neguib and Colonel Nasser. Neguib's own period of restraint was not far off.

At this time, negotiations between the British and Egyptian Governments were being held intermittently and both sides moved nearer agreement. Cairo admitted that the canal base need not be only Egyptian, while London suggested reducing the numbers of British technicians to be stationed there. We made no better progress on my return in October, "availability" and the status of our technicians held up agreement. The first was the more important issue. The Egyptians accepted our use of the base if an Arab country were attacked, while we held that we must be able to return to it if Iran or Turkey were involved. By the end of October this deadlock had made further negotiations useless.

On the other hand there were signs that the Egyptians wanted a settlement and that their rejection of our proposals was only a tactical move. The Egyptian press was abusive over the Sudan elections, but silent about the defence negotiations; the raids on the Suez Canal zone were rarer and weaker than in the past. The Egyptian Government could afford to wait for the results of the Sudan elections, which were to be held in November. Their candidates would be handicapped if Egypt were simultaneously running an anti-British campaign in the Sudan, and negotiating for friendly Anglo-Egyptian relations in Cairo. If they won the elections they would be in a stronger position.

At the end of November, the Sudanese National Unionist Party, supported by the Egyptians and aided by their opponents' divisions, gained a small over-all majority. Although the N.U.P. included extremist groups like the Ashigga, I doubted if the majority of the party would work for union with Egypt. I thought it more likely that the victory would encourage the Egyptian Government to take some hostile action against us. They could renew their attacks on our forces, victimize British subjects, or even make a pact with Russia. Many of our own supporters in the Commons held strong views on the future of the base: they wanted the Government to break off negotiations completely.

I was not impressed by their arguments and still hoped for an agreement with the Egyptian Government. If we failed, we should be confronted with the choice of several undoubted evils: first, to stay on indefinitely in the canal zone, despite Egyptian hostility and attempts to remove us by international action; second, to announce that we should liquidate the base, evacuate the canal zone and deploy elsewhere in the Middle East the forces which we considered necessary, making it clear that we would do so in our own time, but aiming to complete the operation by December 1956; third, to state that we were prepared to revise the 1936 treaty, and as agreement with the Egyptians upon revision was impossible, we were prepared to go to arbitration upon it in accordance with the treaty.

The first course, advocated by a minority of the Conservative Party, had many disadvantages, political, military and economic. It would ensure complete hostility from Egypt and a deterioration of our relations with other Arab powers. Friendly states like Iraq and Pakistan were at that time anxious that we should come to terms with Egypt. Ambitious plans for a militant dictatorship and for an Egyptian hegemony were then unknown. General Neguib did not harbour them. If Egypt invoked international authority, the verdict was likely to be against us. The attacks on our base would be intensified; we would be unable to find any Egyptian labour; our water supply, by the Sweet Water Canal, might be cut off, or the filter plants sabotaged. Without these plants the water was undrinkable. So many troops would be tied down in the canal zone that we should be unable to meet any crisis elsewhere.

If we chose the second course, we would abandon our position in Egypt without securing any alternative base. The effect upon our authority throughout the Middle East would be damaging.

If the Egyptians refused arbitration, the choice of the third course would improve our position in any quarrel. It would be defensible to our friends and allies, and it would allow us to redeploy our forces in our own time. It was clear that this plan was the lesser evil, but it was equally plain that a successful treaty was our best chance. My colleagues shared this view. If we were forced to redeploy our troops, a base in Turkey would allow us to cover Egypt and the northern frontier of Iraq. Gaza was ruled out by the absence of a harbour and of fresh-water supplies.

Anglo-American differences about Egyptian policy persisted. In a report home on the year our Ambassador in Cairo commented that American policy in general seemed to be conditioned by a belief that Egypt was still the victim of British "colonialism," and as such deserving of American sympathy. It also appeared to be influenced by a desire to reach a quick solution almost at any cost and by a pathetic belief that, once agreement was reached, all would be well. These considerations, combined with a horror of unpopularity and fear of losing their influence with the new regime, particularly on the part of the United States Embassy in Cairo, and also an apparent disinclination by the United States Government to take second place even in an area where primary responsibility was not theirs, resulted in the Americans, at least locally, withholding the wholehearted support which their partner in N.A.T.O. had the right to expect and which would have been of great, if not decisive, influence on our negotiations. Inevitably the Egyptians exploited the equivocal American attitude.

The instability of the Egyptian Government showed itself in the first months of 1954. On January 12, the Revolutionary Council dissolved the Muslim Brotherhood after a clash between their respective supporters at Cairo University. The Brotherhood had been a religious, political and social organization, with a private army of over 10,000 men. Although it had taken no part in the original revolt, which put the officers in power, it had, at times, played an important role in keeping them in that position. The Brotherhood's demands for a law based on the Qurân and for a purifying of the country's morality reached far further than the Revolutionary Council's tentative plans for reform. Their political ambition, their claim for treatment as an equal force with the C.R.C., and their request for a veto over legislation, led to frequent quarrels and intrigues on both sides. From our point of view the outcome was satisfactory. Although El Hodeibi, the Supreme Guide of the Brotherhood, had been anxious for friendly relations with us, the majority of his followers were set against any settlement acceptable to us until after evacuation and many of the worst terrorists and rioters were members.

At the end of February, a more serious clash threatened to split the army junta, which had ruled Egypt for the last eighteen months. Throughout this period General Neguib's position had been anomalous. President, Prime Minister and Chairman of the C.R.C., his popularity in the Sudan was immense. The local boy who had made good was Egypt's best chance of union. But as the leader of a successful revolution in his own country his position was remarkably weak. In spite of his imposing titles, his actual power was scarcely greater than that of any other member of the junta.

The formal inauguration of the Sudan Parliament, to which he was invited, gave General Neguib an opportunity to increase his authority at home. During his attempts to do so, he made a tactical resignation, which he must have thought safe at a time when his presence in Khartoum would soon be essential to Egyptian interests. He had miscalculated. His resignation was unanimously accepted and Colonel Nasser was appointed Premier and Chairman of the C.R.C. Reaction in Egypt was immediate and violent. Although the civilian population was puzzled, passive and, at the most, disapproving, the cavalry immediately came out in support of General Neguib. Colonel Nasser and General Amer, the Commander-in-Chief, were forced to choose between conciliation and civil war, with the certain loss of the Sudan. They yielded and invited Neguib to return on February 27, only two days after his resignation.

The effect of these events on Sudanese opinion was to leave the General as the only member of the Egyptian Government with any following in the Sudan. Major Salem was pointedly ignored when he arrived on March 1 for the reopening of Parliament. More serious, he and the General were greeted in Khartoum by anti-Egyptian riots organized by the Ansar. These developed into a violent battle with the police, who mostly belonged to the rival Khatmiya sect. Over thirty people were killed, including the British Commandant of the Khartoum police, and several hundred injured.

In Egypt, the return of General Neguib to Cairo had left every issue undecided. Any prospect of an understanding between him and Colonel Nasser was soon dispelled. Neguib was anxious to check the army extremists, but he had failed to build up his own power. The General had never contemplated dictatorship, and on March 8, on his initiative, the abolition of press censorship was announced and a constituent assembly promised for July. On March 25 the C.R.C. voted its own dissolution to take place in July and allowed the immediate re-establishment of political parties.

The press revelled in their new freedom, General Neguib and the junta being attacked in terms which the newspapers would not have dared to use a few weeks before. The students in Cairo University demonstrated in favour of a return to constitutional life. But their efforts were dwarfed by an impressive strike organized by the C.R.C. in protest against its own dissolution, a truly Egyptian twist to events, which succeeded. Under this

self-imposed pressure the C.R.C. was able, on March 29, to postpone its liberal measures. This decision was followed on April 5
by the announcement of the need to purge the press, restore
discipline among the students, eliminate the politically corrupt
from public life and "safeguard the Revolution" by law.

Although General Neguib lost none of his positions during
these intrigues, Colonel Nasser emerged from them with the full
support of the army. The reversal of General Neguib's reforms
was followed by the systematic destruction of opposition to the
C.R.C. All Ministers who had held office under the royal government since 1942 were deprived of their political rights for ten
years. This trend was intensified when illness forced General
Neguib to ask Colonel Nasser to form a Cabinet. Arrests of
cavalry officers and civilians followed, on charges of plotting to
restore parliamentary government. Two leading newspaper owners
were imprisoned for ten and fifteen years, their papers placed
under Government control.

In October a member of the Muslim Brotherhood attempted to
assassinate Colonel Nasser during the latter's speech at Alexandria.
His shot missed and his failure gave Nasser the opportunity to
attack El Hodeibi and General Neguib, the two most serious
obstacles in his path. At the trial of the assassin, the General
was accused of allowing his jealousy of Nasser to make him
a tool in the hands of the Brotherhood. The Supreme Guide and
four hundred followers were arrested. Shortly afterwards Neguib
was deposed, but he was never brought to trial. He is still under
restraint.* Uncompromising laws against subversive activity
and harsh sentences on El Hodeibi and his followers left the
C.R.C. supreme in power.

★   ★   ★   ★   ★

During this turmoil our negotiations followed a troubled course.
In the summer of 1953, the Egyptians had said that they would not
let us use the base if Turkey or Iran were threatened with attack.
In the autumn they had rejected a formula which would have made
the United Nations an arbiter in the decision. Six months later they

* As of August 1959.

modified this position and said that they would be willing to let us re-enter the base, if Turkey were threatened with aggression. I thought this an important concession because of Turkey's geographical position and because she was our ally in N.A.T.O. Noting this sign of grace, Her Majesty's Government decided to persist in negotiation.

Meanwhile relations were growing closer between Turkey and Pakistan. I encouraged this development and helped it all I could. Noting this tendency in the northern tier, I thought it seemed worth while to make another effort to bring about military talks with the United States on the whole Middle East. When Mr. Henry Byroade, Assistant Secretary of State, passed through London on his way home from a conference of American Heads of Missions at Istanbul, I was glad to learn that he favoured such exchanges. Hitherto the Americans had held out against involving themselves in anything of the kind. I was all the more anxious to bring about discussions, because the State Department was once again canvassing economic aid to Egypt, as a sweetener, pending the conclusion of our negotiations.

An opportunity shortly presented itself for an Anglo-American meeting. The Prime Minister and I paid a visit to Washington late in June 1954, when Egyptian negotiations were again a principal topic. The Americans agreed to use their economic help as an incentive to induce the Egyptians to make and keep an agreement on acceptable terms. This was to be understood by all concerned, but not blatantly expressed. The United States Government also undertook at this meeting to support in public the principle of freedom of transit through the Suez Canal, which we and the Egyptians were to reaffirm. We plunged back into the cauldron of negotiation.

Many influences were at work on Anglo-Egyptian relations that summer; the most powerful was self-interest. Time and modern needs were bringing changes. The Suez Canal remained of supreme importance, the base was yearly less so. The tangled mass of workshops and railways in an area the size of Wales was cumbersome and dependent upon Egyptian labour. It did not seem likely that in this nuclear age we should ever need a base on the past scale. Smaller bases, redeployment and dispersal would serve our purpose better. The Minister of Defence, Lord Alexander, favoured agreement, so did the Secretary of State for War, Mr. Antony Head, and most military opinion. A treaty seemed to them a method of resolving an outdated commitment. Service in the canal zone was also a poor recruiting agent.

Politically there were hazards either way. Apart from pressure from the United States, our friends in the Arab world were eager for agreement. The new administration in Egypt was admittedly a question mark and General Neguib's fall had inked it in. It seemed, however, free of some of the vices of the Wafd and showed no signs as yet of those wider ambitions of empire which Colonel Nasser was later to proclaim and pursue. On balance the agreement seemed to our advantage and worth a trial.

The Government having taken this decision, Mr. Head was chosen to lead our delegation in Cairo and did so admirably. In a few days he established heads of agreement which covered the future of the base. This included its organization and services in peace and the facilities needed to place it on a war footing, including the use of Egyptian ports. There were also over-flying and landing facilities for the R.A.F. Her Majesty's forces would be completely withdrawn from Egyptian territory within a period of twenty months from the signature of the agreement. Both parties would uphold the 1888 Convention guaranteeing freedom of navigation of the canal.

Later discussions in Cairo elaborated these arrangements, Mr. Anthony Nutting representing Her Majesty's Government. Signatures were affixed on October 19, 1954.

This agreement was a declaration of convenience for Britain and Egypt. Neither country wanted the existing state of affairs to continue. The agreement's most serious weakness was not recognized by many at the time. Egypt still proclaimed herself at war with Israel and there was nothing in the clauses to limit or restrain future Egyptian ambitions, except a reaffirmation of the freedom of the Suez Canal. Nor were there any evident reasons for insisting on this. The hope was rather that Anglo-American co-operation, strengthened by the agreements, could work more effectively for improved relations between Israel and the Arab states. During the next twelve months our two Governments plodded steadily after schemes to that end. I did not then foresee the extent of Egyptian expansionist aims over other Arab states, nor the growing menace which Egyptian words and acts, such as the *fedayeen* raids, would later bring upon Israel. It is probable that the absence of British forces from the canal zone, however circumscribed they had been, facilitated aggressive Egyptian activities, both overt and covert, against her neighbours. Even so, the 1936 treaty did not give us a right to a base in Egypt, nor to the large forces we maintained there. Under that treaty, no British troops could have been on the canal in the autumn of 1956, for by then it would have expired

2

THEFT
July 19–August 2, 1956

The Aswan Dam — Nasser seeks a loan — Egyptian-Soviet intrigues — Anglo-American misgivings — Mr. Dulles calls off the loan — Visit of the King of Iraq — The canal is seized — Implications of Nasser's action — Meeting with M. Pineau — The Government's decision — My telegram informing President Eisenhower — Financial and economic measures — Reflections on dictators — Proposal for a conference of maritime powers — Talks with M. Pineau and Mr. Murphy — Mr. Dulles' declared sympathy with our aims — Canal dues — General agreement in the House of Commons

WHEN THE JULY DAYS came our thoughts turned to holiday plans. The year before they had not worked out, but this time my wife and I had firm hopes of three weeks' rest in August. We both longed above all things for hot sunshine and seas in which to bathe. The Governor of Malta, Sir Robert Laycock, had most kindly found for us one of the loveliest villas in the island, by the sea. We began to count the days.

All through the summer Middle Eastern problems had continued to plague us. In particular, the conduct of Egypt over the project for building the Aswan Dam made things increasingly difficult. In 1955 the Egyptian Government came forward with an ambitious scheme to improve the irrigation of the Nile Valley and develop hydro-electricity. To do this they planned to build a new high dam, three miles long, across the river a few miles south of the existing dam at Aswan. Her Majesty's Government were prepared to help. We knew of Egypt's needs, her growing population and falling standard of living. But this scheme raised many problems, among them the division of the Nile waters between the Sudan and

Egypt, upon which the two countries were not agreed. It also raised intricate questions of finance. The total cost over a period of sixteen years was estimated at $300 million. Large sums in foreign exchange were involved, which Egypt could certainly not meet out of her own resources. Her balance of payments was precarious.

British, French and German firms were involved in a consortium for carrying out the project. The Governments of all three countries were willing to back their contractors with financial aid. To help meet the considerable risks, we enlisted the aid of the United States Government and of the World Bank. A plan was devised, involving the participation of us all, which was expensive but workable. The initial Anglo-American grant towards the cost was to be $70 million, of which our share was to be $14 million, and the World Bank agreed to lend $200 million.

The Soviet Government then made tempting overtures for the contract. They offered to build the High Dam on terms which were uneconomic and all the more attractive for being so. I did not want to see Soviet influence expand in Africa, and in November 1955 we discussed the threat of this with the United States Government and determined to persist.

In the new year of 1956, agreement had nearly been reached with the Egyptians. Then they began to raise more and more difficulties over the terms suggested by the World Bank for the issue of a loan. Every effort was made by Her Majesty's Government and our allies to make these terms acceptable to Egypt, and the World Bank did its share. However, head in air as a result of Soviet promises, Egypt declared in January that the guarantees required for such a large outlay of international money amounted to a demand for "the control of the Egyptian economy." These guarantees were not drastic; a promise that the Egyptians would give the dam priority over other projects, that contracts would be awarded on a competitive basis and that aid from Communist sources would be refused.

As the months passed a growing proportion of Egyptian revenues was directed to meeting payments for arms from behind the Iron Curtain. We were disturbed at this mortgaging of the country's economy. Appeals and remonstrances to Colonel Nasser on this account were met by evasions or counter-complaints against Israel. The Egyptian financial position deteriorated and it became more and more doubtful whether the Egyptian Government would be able to cover their part of the inevitable expenditure for the dam project.

The more uncertain the Egyptian contribution, the greater our liability loomed. There was a point beyond which we could not go in financing this venture. There was not only a limit to what we could afford, we had also to take account of the position of our allies, notably Iraq, who had their own needs. Already at the beginning of the year the Iraqi Government were complaining that the Egyptians had done better out of the West by bullying than they had by co-operating. The Iraqis had got £3 million and a few tanks; the Egyptians seemed about to get the Aswan Dam. If there was to be charity, then friendly Arab countries had the right to apply. They could hardly be expected to view with enthusiasm the advance of large sums for an Egyptian project, while that country was becoming ever more closely linked with Soviet Russia and while Egyptian propaganda was viciously attacking both them and us.

Throughout that summer we had increasing evidence, from secret sources and otherwise, of the activity of Egyptian agents in all Middle Eastern lands. In Libya, the Egyptian Military Attaché had been busy trying to undermine the authority of the King and substitute an administration more subservient to Nasser. He was sent home. There were similar activities in the Lebanon, where President Chamoun's refusal to display anti-Western fanaticism won him Nasser's unrelenting hostility. In Jordan, there were plots against the King, the extent of which the Jordan Government revealed many months later. In Iraq, there were intrigues and attempted assassinations; again a military attaché had to be sent back to Egypt. In the Sudan, subversion was active, aided by the inflated staff of the Soviet mission. Throughout the Middle East the "Voice of the Arabs" from Cairo was blaring out hostility to the West and to the lackeys of imperialism, as our friends were called. In the same breath, more money was being demanded for the scheme to build the dam.

The Foreign Secretary, Mr. Selwyn Lloyd, set to work to exchange views on this state of affairs with the United States Government, and found that the State Department shared both our doubts for the present and our apprehension for the future of the scheme. Consultation continued between a number of my colleagues, in which the Chancellor of the Exchequer, the Foreign Secretary and I took a leading part. In mid-July, after the most careful canvassing of all the arguments, the Government came to the conclusion that they could not go on with a project likely to become increasingly onerous in finance and unsatisfactory in practice.

I would have preferred to play this long and not to have forced the issue. There was no need to hurry. Unhappily things did not work out that way. The Egyptian Government no doubt sensed Western reluctance to promise ever larger sums for the scheme, when they were themselves jeopardizing their own contribution. They tried to clinch the business on their own terms. The Egyptian Finance Minister, Dr. Kaissouny, arrived in Washington and had a series of interviews with the World Bank and with the State Department. On July 19, for reasons connected with the Senate's attitude to foreign aid and the critical climate towards neutralism then prevalent in Washington, Mr. Dulles felt obliged to tell the Egyptian Ambassador that the deal was off. We were informed but not consulted and so had no prior opportunity for criticism or comment. As a result of this decision the loan from the World Bank was also cancelled, for the two transactions were interdependent.

We were sorry that the matter was carried through so abruptly, because it gave our two countries no chance to concert either timing or methods, though these were quite as important as the substance. At this moment Colonel Nasser was in Brioni at a meeting with Marshal Tito and Mr. Nehru, and the news was wounding to his pride.

★   ★   ★   ★   ★

In July the King of Iraq, with his uncle, who had recently been Prince Regent, and Nuri es-Said, the veteran Prime Minister who had been a personal friend of mine for thirty years, were paying a state visit to London. Nasser was then campaigning vehemently against Iraq. During the ceremonies and discussions the King impressed everyone with his sincerity and natural charm. He was familiar with the development plans upon which his Government had embarked and was eager to speed them. He seemed to be the best type of young ruler, caring for his people, modest in his living and direct in his approach. As I listened to his speech at the dinner given in his honour at Buckingham Palace, my mind went back to my first meeting with his grandfather, founder of Iraq and of his dynasty, who had ridden with Lawrence and been our ally in the first world war. Faisal I would have been proud of his grandson that evening.

I had a conversation with Nuri es-Said after dinner at Buckingham Palace. I found him deafer, but as resolute as ever and without illusions. We spoke of the past and of our first meeting in Baghdad in 1925 and of the personalities, British and Iraqi, in his country at that time; of General Jafar and the King, of Sir Francis Humphreys and Miss Gertrude Bell. Then of the present; Nuri es-Said was coldly aware of the menace to him and to the work he was doing for his country, of Nasser and his virulent brand of demagogy. He knew that Iraq's development board and all its works were a race against time. Once the people saw the results of these projects and benefited from them, they would understand and they would not let them go. But this would take time, and whether they had time enough would depend upon the support we and the Americans gave Iraq. He spoke warmly of the work of our Ambassador, Sir Michael Wright. As I listened I felt, as so often before, admiration for this man who was such a tough and resilient fighter in politics and in war, and my heart warmed to him. I knew how active and unscrupulous were Nasser's agents and that the Iraqi was an obstacle to the Egyptian's schemes of empire. There had been at least one recent plot against Nuri es-Said's life, but I knew, too, the young King's popularity, especially among the tribes. I little thought that this was the last intimate talk we were to hold together.

Two years later King Faisal was massacred in Baghdad with his uncle and relations, men, women and children, Ministers and friends, in conditions of exceptional barbarity even by modern standards. The nearest parallel in my lifetime was the murder in

1903 of King Alexander and Queen Draga in Belgrade, who were flung from the windows of their palace to the street below. When they tried to hold on to the window's edge, their hands were hacked away. Then, a thrill of horror ran through Europe. The Baghdad massacre was more degrading and more widespread. The naked bodies of the former Regent and of Nuri es-Said were dragged through the streets of Baghdad amid scenes of unmentionable beastliness. A British officer was shot within the Embassy. Three Americans were torn to pieces by the mob, with faint protest by their Government. Within a few days the free nations of the West recognized the Government which had endorsed, if it had not sanctioned, the gruesome deeds. In London, only the initiative of friends, who included Ministers, working against ecclesiastical difficulties, organized a small service in memory of these national figures whose friendship proved faithful unto death. This did not seem enough to mark our country's respect and gratitude.

★   ★   ★   ★   ★

On the night of July 26, the King and other Iraqi leaders were dining with me at Downing Street. While we were at dinner, one of my private secretaries came in with the news that Nasser had seized the Suez Canal and forcibly taken over all the properties of the company which had administered it under international agreement. In a speech at Alexandria he had declared that Egypt herself would find the funds with which to build the Aswan Dam. The means lay ready to hand. He would seize the canal and draw upon its revenues for the capital he needed.

I told my guests. They saw clearly that here was an event which changed all perspectives, and understood at once how much would depend upon the resolution with which the act of defiance was met. Our party broke up early, its social purpose now out of joint. Mr. Selwyn Lloyd, Lord Salisbury and Lord Home were dining with me, and we adjourned to the Cabinet room to discuss our course of action. The Lord Chancellor and the Chiefs of Staff also joined us. I had no doubt how Nasser's deed would be read, from Agadir to Karachi. This was a seizure of Western property in reply to the action of the United States Government. On its outcome would depend whose authority would prevail.

We decided to invite the French Ambassador, M. Chauvel, and the United States Chargé d'Affaires, Mr. Foster, to take part in our consultation. When they arrived I told them what we knew. In our judgment the economic life of Western Europe was threatened with disruption by the Egyptian seizure of the canal. Here was an issue of the first importance, in which an international agreement was at stake. We ought immediately to concert steps between our three Governments. The French and American representatives were given the terms of a statement I proposed to make in the House of Commons next morning. They undertook to ask their Governments to take similar action. Telegrams were despatched in the early hours of the morning to our Embassies in Paris and Washington informing them of this step.

On the morning of July 27, in the House of Commons, I answered a Private Notice question put by the Leader of the Opposition. I said:

> The unilateral decision of the Egyptian Government to expropriate the Suez Canal Company, without notice and in breach of the Concession agreements, affects the rights and interests of many nations. Her Majesty's Government are consulting other Governments immediately concerned with regard to the serious situation thus created. The consultations will cover both the effect of this arbitrary action upon the operation of the Suez Canal and also the wider questions which it raises.

Mr. Gaitskell declared that: "On this side of the House we deeply deplore this high-handed and totally unjustifiable step by the Egyptian Government." At that moment, as the House understood, I could say no more about the exchanges we had initiated less than twelve hours earlier.

I then discussed the situation with my colleagues and with the Chiefs of Staff. We had seen the text of Colonel Nasser's speech, which was a vehement nationalistic manifesto and a catalogue of supposed grievances:

> This, O citizens, is the battle in which we are now involved. It is a battle against imperialism and the methods and tactics of imperialism, and a battle against Israel, the vanguard of

imperialism . . . As I told you, Arab nationalism has been set
on fire from the Atlantic Ocean to the Persian Gulf. Arab
nationalism feels its existence, its structure and strength.

This was the context in which Nasser chose to set his action.
Egypt, he claimed, had forced Britain to evacuate the canal zone
base. She had applied to Britain for arms for use against Israel
and been refused. Russia, on the other hand, had supplied her
needs without attaching conditions. When Egypt had appealed
for financial aid with which to build the Aswan Dam, the World
Bank had sought to impose conditions which would have subjected
the Egyptian economy to Western tutelage. The American offer of
funds had been withdrawn for the political reason that Egypt was
opposed to the Baghdad Pact. The canal would therefore now be
nationalized in retaliation, and also because the Canal Company
had usurped the rights of the Egyptian people.

As we debated the action we should take, we were aware of
Nasser's intentions to milk the revenues of the canal and divert
them to the finance of his High Dam. He was, in fact, taking
over the money of an international company and intending to
use it for his own internal purposes. He soon gave an earnest of
his methods. The branch of the Ottoman Bank in Cairo was ordered
to hand over the balance of the Suez Canal Company's account
which it held. Five million Egyptian pounds thus passed into
Colonel Nasser's hands. As I wrote in one of my telegrams despatched that day, a man with Colonel Nasser's record could not
be allowed "to have his thumb on our windpipe."

The Government considered the situation fully that Friday
morning and decided that they could not allow Nasser to seize
control of the canal in defiance of international agreements. The
canal was an international asset and had been recognized as such
ever since the Convention of 1888. In recent years its importance had been greatly increased by the development of the Middle
Eastern oilfields and by the dependence of Western Europe on
them for a large part of its oil supplies. In 1955, 14,666 ships
had passed through the canal. Three-quarters of them belonged
to N.A.T.O. countries and nearly one-third were British. The
Government determined that our essential interests in this area

must be safeguarded, if necessary by military action, and that the needful preparations must be made. Failure to keep the canal international would inevitably lead to the loss one by one of all our interests and assets in the Middle East, and even if Her Majesty's Government had to act alone they could not stop short of using force to protect their position. This was our recorded opinion, which I still hold.

The Government had at this stage to consider both matters of principle and immediate practical steps. We took a number of decisions which were to guide our course through the next three months. We resolved that, in the first instance, President Eisenhower should be invited to send a representative to London to discuss the situation and align a joint policy with the Foreign Secretary and the French Foreign Minister. M. Pineau was, by a previous arrangement, due to arrive in England on the following Sunday, July 29.

The Government foresaw that some friends, especially in the Commonwealth, might urge us to refer the problem of Suez at once to the Security Council of the United Nations. Though we favoured using every method of conciliation, we were not convinced that it was wise to begin by a reference to the Security Council. The precedents were discouraging. During the past four years Egypt had flagrantly disregarded the Security Council's resolution that Israeli ships should have freedom of passage through the canal. The Russians, who were the armers and backers of Colonel Nasser, had the power of veto in the Council, and would not hesitate to use it. They could nullify any resolution taken by a majority of the Security Council. When discussions opened between the three powers, the Americans and French agreed with us that reference to the Security Council at this stage would be a mistake.

The next question the Government faced was the crucial one. Should we be prepared in the last resort to use force to dislodge Colonel Nasser from the canal? It was our intention first to bring the maximum political pressure to bear upon him. The means would be worked out in the tripartite talks of the next few days. Economic weapons were also at our disposal and the Chancellor of the Exchequer had prepared financial measures which were to come into operaton at midnight that night. But economic and political pressures alone might not succeed in checking Nasser and re-establishing international control over the canal. From the start we had to prepare to back our remonstrances with military action. The Chiefs of Staff were instructed to get ready a plan and a time-table for an operation designed to occupy and secure the canal, should other methods fail. We hoped to count upon the participa-tion of the French in any expedition which was mounted. We expected that the United States would at least be neutral. But if assistance were not forthcoming from our friends, we had to be in a position to take action alone. I informed the President of this decision in the telegram I sent him on the evening of July 27. The Commonwealth Prime Ministers were also informed through their High Commissioners in London. In my telegram to Mr. Eisenhower I said:

> This morning I have reviewed the whole position with my Cabinet colleagues and Chiefs of Staff. We are all agreed that we cannot afford to allow Nasser to seize control of the canal in this way, in defiance of international agreements. If we take a firm stand over this now we shall have the support of all the maritime powers. If we do not, our influence and yours throughout the Middle East will, we are all convinced, be finally destroyed.
>
> The immediate threat is to the oil supplies to Western Europe, a great part of which flows through the canal. . . . If the canal were closed we should have to ask you to help us by reducing the amount which you draw from the pipeline terminals in the eastern Mediterranean and possibly by send-ing us supplementary supplies for a time from your side of the world.
>
> It is, however, the outlook for the longer term which is more threatening. The canal is an international asset and facility, which is vital to the free world. The maritime powers cannot afford to allow Egypt to expropriate it and to exploit it by using the revenues for her own internal purposes irre-spective of the interests of the canal and of the canal users. . . .
>
> We should not allow ourselves to become involved in legal

quibbles about the rights of the Egyptian Government to nationalize what is technically an Egyptian company, or in financial arguments about their capacity to pay the compensation which they have offered. I feel sure that we should take issue with Nasser on the broader international grounds.

As we see it we are unlikely to attain our objectives by economic pressures alone. I gather that Egypt is not due to receive any further aid from you. No large payments from her sterling balances here are due before January. We ought in the first instance to bring the maximum political pressure to bear on Egypt. For this, apart from our own action, we should invoke the support of all the interested powers. My colleagues and I are convinced that we must be ready, in the last resort, to use force to bring Nasser to his senses. For our part we are prepared to do so. I have this morning instructed our Chiefs of Staff to prepare a military plan accordingly.

However, the first step must be for you and us and France to exchange views, align our policies and concert together how we can best bring the maximum pressure to bear on the Egyptian Government.

The recent behaviour of the Egyptian Government did not give us confidence that in the long term they would manage the canal with a full sense of international obligations. If they won sole control, further pressure must be expected in time, on Israel and others. We were convinced that the answer to Nasser must take account of the modern trend towards internationalism and away from nationalism. Our object must be to undo his action and to place the management of the canal firmly in international custody. The Suez Canal Company doubted the technical capacity of the Egyptians to widen and deepen the canal and accommodate the larger oil tankers and heavy traffic of the future. The Commonwealth Governments were informed of these reflections.

★   ★   ★   ★   ★

During our deliberations on that Friday, a number of decisions were taken and put into effect. The Bank of England and the commercial banks were given authority to block the current Egyptian sterling balances held in London. The funds and assets of the Suez Canal Company in London were protected against Egyptian expropriation. The export of arms and military materials to Egypt was banned. Four Egyptian destroyers, at that time in the harbours of the United Kingdom and Malta, were to have their sailings delayed by every means short of physical interference. Our own shipping position was to be examined, with a view to any requisitioning which might be necessary for a military operation. The Foreign Office was to warn British subjects resident in Egypt of likely developments.

A formal note of protest against the seizure of the canal was delivered to the Egyptian Government. Later that night the Egyptians sent back our note with an unsigned slip attached, which read: "Returned to British Embassy."

We estimated that the United Kingdom had reserves of oil which would last for six weeks, and that the other countries of Western Europe owned comparatively smaller stocks. The continuing supply of fuel, which was a vital source of power to the economy of Britain, was now subject to Colonel Nasser's whim. The oilfields of the Middle East were then producing about 145 million tons a year. Nearly 70 million tons of oil had passed through the Suez Canal in 1955, almost all of it destined for Western Europe. Another 40 million tons of oil reached the ports of the Levant by pipelines running through the territories of Egypt's then allies, Syria and Saudi Arabia.

More than half of Britain's annual imports of oil came through the canal. At any time the Egyptians might decide to interfere with its passage. They might also prompt their allies to cut the pipelines. We had to gauge the implications of bringing oil from the Persian Gulf by the long haul around the Cape of Good Hope.

A criticism was subsequently made that we and the French, as the powers principally concerned, should have reacted at once and forcibly reoccupied the canal. The argument runs, especially in the United States, that if we had done so there could have been little complaint. There are two answers to this.

The first answer is political. As signatories of the Charter of the United Nations, we were bound first to seek redress by peaceful means. Though we were conscious of the Soviet veto and of the weakness of the United Nations as an executive body, we knew that we must at some time take the issue to the Security Council. We might even be able to prod them into action. To accept this did not mean abandoning the use of force as a last resort. This was always the position of Her Majesty's Government and of the French Government at all stages of the dispute. We made it clear repeatedly, in public and in private, from the first day to the last.

The second is military. Unless the action could have been carried through exclusively by airborne troops, there was no alternative to an expedition from Malta. Unless we could fly all the forces needed, they had to swim. The nearest place from which to swim was Malta, a thousand miles away. Cyprus has no sufficient harbour for landing craft or transports. There is no escape from these logistics. We had nothing like enough airborne troops for an operation of this kind. The French had more, but together we could not have mustered a full division with artillery support. The follow-up would have taken several weeks to organize, even with the most brilliant improvisation.

The invasion of Sicily from North Africa took six weeks to prepare in the midst of the second world war. True, action against Egyptians is not militarily comparable with action against Germans, as I was constantly urging. On the other hand, our resources in the Mediterranean at this time were not comparable with those of the British and United States forces at the height of their power.

Earlier that summer my family and I had been watching Trooping the Colour on Horse Guards' Parade. As we walked back across Downing Street garden, I asked my son what he thought of it. He replied, "I should be happier if they were paratroopers." It may be a fair criticism that after the Berlin airlift and the threat to the West which had to be met there, our military plans had been too closely concentrated on the defence of free Europe by land, sea and air against Soviet attack. Between 1947 and 1956, preparations for airborne action on an important scale had not been made. I was not satisfied, and earlier in July the Government had taken the decision to create a reserve in England which would be mobile by air. There had not been time to give effect to this. Neither the aeroplanes

nor the men could be conjured up overnight. They could only
have been made ready over the years.

★ ★ ★ ★ ★

Modern dictatorships are not all of a type. The example that
comes most readily to mind is also the most dangerous, the dictator
who has a streak of paranoia. He sees himself as a conqueror on
behalf of his people, dominating a large part of the world. He feeds
the mob with demagogy, the mob feeds him with power; it is a
mutual indulgence. His megalomania need not exclude a quick,
subtle or scheming mind, nor a personality which gulls interviewers.
He may attract the devotion of large numbers of his countrymen
and echo their patriotic aspirations in his frantic oratory. He may
even command brilliant gifts of statesmanship. Evil lies in the use
he makes of them.

All dictatorships are repressive governments, intolerant of opposition, but in degrees that vary widely. There is the redemptive
type of dictator, whose rule is comparatively mild and beneficial.
A nation, through war or other calamity, meets disaster. The call
is for a man who by his qualities and experience can lead the
people and redeem their fortunes within their own land. Mustapha
Kemal in Turkey was one of these, during and after the Graeco-
Turkish war of 1920–22. Dr. Salazar in Portugal is another example,
restoring his country's economy after recurrent crises in the early
twenties.

Communist states fall into another category; they are totalitarian
in the sense that they have neither the spirit nor the machinery of
democracy. They are one-party states, but those who rule in Communist countries, though they may have seized power, only wield
it for a spell. The Communist dictators are working for a cause,
world domination by communism, not necessarily to be realized in
their lifetime. Communist rulers are the primitive and ruthless
priests of a modern religion, more skilful and more cautious than
the megalomaniacal dictator, who is compelled to achieve power and
fulfil his ambitions before he dies.

It is important to reduce the stature of the megalomaniacal
dictator at an early stage. A check to Hitler when he moved to

reoccupy the Rhineland would not have destroyed him, but it would have made him pause. The world would then have had time to assess the truth, and the Germans occasion to question themselves. This process would have been altogether salutary. "Though your enemy be an ant," runs the Turkish proverb, "imagine that he is an elephant." Nowadays it is considered immoral to recognize an enemy. Some say that Nasser is no Hitler or Mussolini. Allowing for a difference in scale, I am not so sure. He has followed Hitler's pattern, even to concentration camps and the propagation of *Mein Kampf* among his officers.* He has understood and used the Goebbels pattern of propaganda in all its lying ruthlessness. Egypt's strategic position increases the threat to others from any aggressive militant dictatorship there.

If any dictatorial government has it in mind to pursue an aggressive policy, it will do well to label itself "Socialist" from the start. Hitler was the first to understand the value of this camouflage. Despite the world's experience of German National Socialism, there is still a tendency to regard even a Government like Nasser's as Socialist and therefore as having a left-wing colouring. I have observed with amazement how national leaders in other countries, who hold left-wing views, have thought that they had more affinity with, for example, Colonel Nasser in Egypt than with Nuri es-Said in Iraq. The administration of Iraq under Nuri was infinitely more progressive and mindful of its people's welfare than the Egyptian. Three-quarters of Iraq's revenues from oil were devoted to public works, irrigation, electrification and improved living conditions. Only Kuwait, in a much smaller area, has attempted anything comparable. The poverty of the Egyptians further deepened when Colonel Nasser forced out General Neguib: arms before bread.

★   ★   ★   ★   ★

On Saturday morning, July 28, there was a meeting of the ministerial group which had been set up on the previous day to

---

* A number of Arabic translations of Hitler's *Mein Kampf* were found by the Israeli army in the possession of Egyptian officers after the Sinai campaign. These were not a standard issue, but the quantity of copies showed that the book had a highly popular appeal.

keep in contact with the situation on behalf of the Cabinet. They had to work out plans day by day to put our policy into effect. Six of my colleagues, in addition to myself, were permanent members of this group and other Ministers frequently joined in our deliberations. The Chiefs of Staff were in attendance when required. In the months ahead we held many meetings and the Cabinet were kept in touch with our work. That morning I told my colleagues of a message I had received from President Eisenhower, who was anxious that the largest possible number of maritime nations affected by the seizure of the canal should be brought quickly into consultation. He was sending Mr. Murphy of the State Department to represent the United States in talks with M. Pineau and the Foreign Secretary. Mr. Dulles at that moment was touring South America. He was in Peru.

At the beginning of the crisis the Americans appeared to wish to isolate Egypt among the nations of the world, and to bring the moral pressure of combined opinion to bear upon Colonel Nasser. This was an acceptable intention, but it took no account of the probability that Nasser would show himself impervious to moral pressure. In practice it was to mean conferences and resolutions, but no action. The result was words. Some suspicion of this difference in our approach was already beginning to appear in reports we were receiving of initial reactions in Washington. It became more pronounced during the consultations of the following week, though we had hopes of bridging it. For the time being we assumed that the American attitude, in the absence of the Secretary of State, was one of prudence rather than divergence.

Her Majesty's Government agreed to summon a conference of maritime powers. Its composition and its timing were the problems now to be considered. We favoured restricting representation to the six or ten powers who were the principal users of the canal in terms of tonnage and trade. It would be a matter for discussion with M. Pineau and Mr. Murphy whether an Anglo-French note should be immediately presented to Egypt. A tripartite note was greatly to be preferred, but American participation in such a step was doubtful. The alternative would be to delay diplomatic action until after the conference had met, and then to make a move on behalf of as many of the maritime powers as would associate themselves with us. In that event, if we got no satisfactory reply from Egypt, we must be ready for the possibility of having to back our joint requirements by military action.

That Saturday afternoon my wife and I motored to Broad Chalke. The cottage there was a haven. My wife had bought it several years before we married. It lies in the fields at the lane's end; its western windows overlook Gainsborough scenery in the Ebble Valley, its eastern gives on to downland. The garden is small, but cleverly laid out and large enough for us to plan and battle in. It is a frost pocket and the soil is chalk and stony and not too amenable. None of this mattered, for scenery, setting and friends outdid all. Forty-eight hours at the cottage were worth a week's holiday to me.

Throughout Sunday in Wiltshire I was in frequent touch with the Foreign Secretary, who was opening his conversations with M. Pineau and Mr. Murphy in London. In the evening I returned to London, for I had a statement to make in the House of Commons next day. After Questions on Monday, July 30, I told the House of the financial measures we had put into effect to freeze the Egyptian sterling balances and safeguard the assets of the Canal Company. I announced that conversations had begun with M. Pineau and Mr. Murphy, and that we were in close touch with the Governments of the Commonwealth countries. Within the next few days, and before the House rose for the summer recess, I hoped to make a further statement. Should the House wish to debate the subject, I was agreeable, but we would need to consider the world-wide repercussions of anything that was said. Our position was clear and I defined it in these words:

> No arrangements for the future of this great international waterway could be acceptable to Her Majesty's Government which would leave it in the unfettered control of a single power which could, as recent events have shown, exploit it purely for purposes of national policy.

This often quoted statement of our aims was acclaimed, no one in the House dissented. Our aims were not fulfilled.

★   ★   ★   ★   ★

Meanwhile, talks were continuing in London between the Foreign Secretary, M. Pineau and Mr. Murphy. They made slow progress. All agreed that the operation of the canal must be placed under international authority, but there were differences as to the best means to adopt. Our Ambassador in Washington had already reported to us that he had found the State Department cool and hesitant about taking urgent action. The Department gave the impression of wishing to stand aloof from the dispute with Egypt. Its officials were much concerned about the effects of any possible action on American public opinion, especially if there was an interruption in the passage of oil tankers through the canal. No doubt the impending American election also cast its shadow.

Mr. Murphy, on his arrival in London, soon made plain that his approach was a legal one. He wished to invoke the Convention of Constantinople, signed in 1888. This document guaranteed for all time the international character of the canal, irrespective of any particular concession from the rulers of Egypt to the Suez Canal Company. The Convention was an important element in our case, but it was by no means the whole story. Moreover, the Russians had signed it, but the United States had not. This was likely to land us in vexing problems if we were to base our action on the Convention alone. The Americans were not in favour of referring the problem to the United Nations at this stage, but they thought that a special agency of the United Nations should be entrusted with the control of the canal. We agreed that any canal authority which might be set up should work in association with the United Nations.

On August 1 Mr. Dulles arrived in London. He advanced much the same view as his assistants and advisers, but with new arguments. He showed that he and his department had other grounds for their insistence upon taking action under the Constantinople Convention. If military measures became unavoidable, the President would need the authority of Congress for any American commitment. In the eyes of Dulles and Murphy it was therefore essential that the legal basis of our joint proceedings should be unimpeachable. I found it encouraging that the United States Government should be thinking in the context of military action at all.

There was another preoccupation in American minds which was gradually revealed as the talks progressed. It was a very proper one. The Americans were nervous about the Panama Canal. They were anxious to emphasize that the problem of Suez was of a totally different order from any dispute that might arise in connection with Panama. Suez was an international matter, as the Constantinople Convention went to prove. The Panama Canal, on the contrary, was a private affair, regulated by a treaty between the Governments of the United States and the Panamanian Republic only. According to this agreement, the zone through which the Panama Canal ran was leased in perpetuity to the United States. It was thus an American and not an international waterway. The United States Government were determined to keep it so. They wished to distinguish forthrightly between their privileged position on the Isthmus of Panama and the international complexities of Suez.

No such hesitations disturbed the French. M. Pineau was a man of independent mind who could argue clearly, even vehemently, for his cause. He had had considerable ministerial experience and was apt to be impatient of diplomatic detail, which was no bad thing. We always found him a vigorous but loyal colleague, unwilling to dupe himself or others and stalwart in critical hours.

Pineau now declared that his Government were unanimous in desiring urgent and decisive action. The Suez Canal had been built by the French. Moreover, the repercussions of Nasser's action touched France closely in another and vital sphere. From the first, Pineau emphasized the effects that it would have in Algeria and upon the entire French position in North Africa. If Egypt were allowed to succeed in grabbing the canal, the Algerian nationalists would take fresh heart. They would also look to Egypt for backing, which they would certainly receive, both in arms and clamour. France could not permit this threat to develop. We agreed with M. Pineau's forecast and supported his views. He proved himself a true prophet. The Americans were less receptive, in part because their inveterate distrust of "colonialism" left them basically out of sympathy with French problems in North Africa.

M. Pineau had another grievance. Nasser had described his action as retaliation for the refusal to finance the Aswan Dam. The

United States had a responsibility for this decision and should not, Pineau felt, disinterest itself from the consequences. Murphy and Dulles both maintained that Nasser's action was not retaliatory and had long been in his mind. They did not convince Pineau.

The French attitude to the crisis was far nearer to ours than the American, though French interests in Asia and Africa differed in kind and in degree from ours. The French had a war on their hands in North Africa which was being inflamed, and to some extent supplied, by Cairo. They had opposed the Baghdad Pact, though M. Mollet had loyally refrained from criticizing it since his visit to me at Chequers earlier in the year, when we had done good work in aligning our policies.

While the United Kingdom had far-reaching treaty engagements with Jordan, France's relations with Israel were very close. There was national sympathy in France for a small country seeking to maintain itself in the face of a trade boycott and the hostility of larger neighbours. Our divergencies could be reconciled by diplomacy and events, but at this time they had not been.

At an early stage in their discussions, the three Foreign Secretaries agreed that the Arab-Israeli dispute should be treated as a separate matter from the future of the canal. Israel had suffered for five years from the Egyptian refusal to obey the United Nations resolution to give free passage through the canal. Her shipping had been unjustly barred from using it. The Security Council resolution of September 1, 1951, was specific. It found that the Egyptian action was "inconsistent with the objectives of a peaceful settlement between the parties and the establishment of a permanent peace in Palestine set forth in the armistice agreement." Israel was also the frequent victim of Egyptian armed raids. Though this was all too true, to associate Israel's problems with those arising from the nationalization of the canal would, at this time, have tangled them to Nasser's advantage. If we were to get action, we had to keep the issues crisp.

Mr. Dulles brought with him a message from the President, who was emphatic upon the importance of negotiation. The President did not rule out the use of force. He recognized the transcendent worth of the canal to the free world and the possibility that the eventual use of force might become necessary in order to protect international rights. But he felt that every possibility of peaceful settlement must be exhausted before this was done.

At his first meeting with the other Foreign Secretaries on August 1 Mr. Dulles summed up his views as follows:

> 1. It was intolerable that the canal should be under the domination of any single country without any international control;
>
> 2. We should use the 1888 Convention as a basis for discussion in order to avoid complications with the Panama Canal;
>
> 3. Force was the last method to be tried, but the United States did not exclude the use of force if all other methods failed;
>
> 4. We should mobilize world opinion in favour of international operation of the canal;
>
> 5. We should attempt to get our tripartite views accepted by at least a two-thirds majority of the conference that was to be called.

In further discussion at this meeting on the 1st, Mr. Dulles said:

> A way had to be found to make Nasser disgorge what he was attempting to swallow. . . . We must make a genuine effort to bring world opinion to favour the international operation of the canal. . . . It should be possible to create a world opinion so adverse to Nasser that he would be isolated. Then if a military operation had to be undertaken it would be more apt to succeed and have less grave repercussions than if it had been undertaken precipitately.

Dulles had several conversations with the Foreign Secretary, and one at Downing Street with both of us, in addition to the three-power meetings. We were encouraged by his statements. He agreed emphatically that the seizure of a great international waterway was intolerable. This was still more so when the single nation that set out to dominate the canal was Egypt. Nasser must be made, as Mr. Dulles put it to me, "to disgorge." These were forthright words. They rang in my ears for months.

I did not wish to conceal anything from Mr. Dulles and I told him that the United States Naval Attaché had been asking for information about our military preparations. I said that we were quite ready to give this, but that I wanted first to make sure that the United States Government really wished to have it. Mr. Dulles replied that the United States Government perfectly well understood the purpose of our preparations and he thought that they had had a good effect. It was preferable that the United States Government should not seek detailed information.

I felt a great sense of relief that evening. Every allowance had to be made for a different approach between us and the Americans, and for a differing sense of urgency. But if Nasser had in the end "to disgorge," the result would be plain for all to see. Theft would not have paid off, a breach of agreement would not have been endured, a wholesome lesson would have been taught in respect for the sanctity of agreements. The United States, we were told by Mr. Dulles, did not exclude the use of force if all other methods failed, but there must be genuine efforts first to reach a settlement by negotiation. Mr. Eisenhower believed that our countries could marshal world opinion in support of a conciliatory but firm position, and that an international conference of canal users would have, at the least, a profound educational effect throughout the world. Such was also my hope. But I did not wish to lose momentum, or to allow discussions to drag on from conference to conference.

The three Governments were now committed to summon an international conference. Britain and France would have preferred it to meet as soon as possible; Dulles favoured several weeks of preparation. In the end we compromised and August 16 was the date fixed. We also compromised on membership. We accepted the American request that invitations should be sent to the eight signatories of the Constantinople Convention, Russia included. The Americans agreed that invitations should likewise be sent to the sixteen principal users of the canal, selected in terms of tonnage and trade. These twenty-four countries were listed in the statement issued at the close of the consultations on the evening of August 2.

One further difficult question aroused much discussion at these three-power meetings. It concerned the payment of canal dues in the weeks ahead. Most British shipowners paid their dues into the account of the Suez Canal Company in London; the French paid in Paris. A number of other countries, including the United States, were in the habit of paying in Egypt. Normally 55 per cent of the dues was annually collected in London, 35 per cent in Egypt and 10 per cent in Paris. We wished British shipowners to continue to pay the legitimate Canal Company in London until such time as a new international authority was established. If the new Egyptian authority attempted to exact payments, we might have to instruct British shipowners to reroute their ships by the Cape. The French and ourselves intended that as little money as possible from ships passing through the canal should find its way into Egyptian hands. On this we found it hard to secure American co-operation. Mr. Dulles could not say how the United States shipowners would react to any advice given them. Moreover, the American Government had no power to give instructions to the numerous American-owned ships, registered in Panama, Liberia and elsewhere, and flying the flags of those countries. Our talks on this point were inconclusive and the problems of dues remained to perplex us for many a long day and night.

★   ★   ★   ★   ★

Some agreement was won at these London talks. A positive statement containing precise proposals was issued on behalf of the three powers. This first defined the deed:

> The present action involves far more than a simple act of nationalization. It involves the arbitrary and unilateral seizure by one nation of an international agency which has the responsibility to maintain and to operate the Suez Canal so that all the signatories to, and beneficiaries of, the treaty of 1888 can effectively enjoy the use of an international waterway upon which the economy, commerce, and security of much of the world depends.

The Convention of 1888 had guaranteed these benefits "for all the world . . . and for all time." The statement recalled that as recently as October 1954 Egypt had renewed her undertakings to uphold the

Convention. "The action taken by the Egyptian Government," the three powers declared, "threatens the freedom and security of the canal." This made it necessary that the signatories to the Convention, and all other nations entitled to enjoy its benefits, should take steps to safeguard their rights. In consequence, "operating arrangements under an international system" should be restored. Respect would be shown for legitimate Egyptian interests. Finally, the three powers formally convened a conference of the twenty-four nations principally concerned with the use of the canal.

In the event, all except Egypt and Greece accepted our invitations and attended. Three days later the proposals of the three powers on the purposes and functions of an international authority were despatched for the invited nations to consider.

Some hours before the statement of August 2 was issued I opened a debate on the Suez Canal in the House of Commons. I was not yet able to quote the three-power statement, which was still being drafted. But I emphasized once more that:

> . . . the freedom and security of transit through the canal can only be effectively secured by an international authority. It is upon this that we must insist. It is upon this we are working in negotiation at this moment with other powers deeply concerned.

I outlined the history of the Constantinople Convention, and also of the concessionary agreements between Egypt and the Suez Canal Company. The agreements had been last endorsed by Nasser's Government only six weeks before. "These undertakings," I said, "are now torn up, and one can have no confidence in the word of a man who does that." The Leader of the Opposition and the large majority of speakers in the debate on both sides of the House were at that time in general agreement. The House did not seem to be divided on party lines. Mr. Herbert Morrison, a former Foreign Secretary, wished us luck in solving this problem. He said: "I ask the Government not to be too nervous, because if they are too nervous we shall begin to evolve a situation in which countries can set themselves up against international practice, international morals and international interests, and, in that case, we are not helping the peace of the world." Other Opposition speakers echoed this theme with variations of their own. Mr. Gaitskell said of Nasser's attitude: "It is all very familiar. It is exactly the same that we encountered from Mussolini and Hitler in those years before the war." He added that, "I believe we were right to react sharply to this move."

To one Socialist peer who was listening, these comments seemed more warlike than mine. Lord Stansgate, who observed the events of that day from the Gallery of our House, reported on them as follows to his own House an hour or two later: "I went to another place this morning and I can correctly and sincerely say that I found much more reason, common sense and conviction in the Prime Minister's speech than there was in the rather heady wine which was produced by my own Front Bench."

During my speech I announced the precautionary measures we were taking to strengthen our position in the eastern Mediterranean. These included the movement from Britain of a number of navy, army and air force units, and the calling up of about twenty thousand army reservists. The concentration had its effect upon Colonel Nasser. He did not interfere with our ships, nor try to compel them to pay to his nationalized authority. He recognized what the consequences would be if he attempted to do so. The memory of the massacres in Cairo in 1952 was also fresh in my mind. Such a tragedy might recur, and there were some 13,000 British subjects still in Egypt. We had to be able to protect them.

At this period there was a general conviction throughout the country that Nasser must not be allowed to get away with his theft and that we would be fully justified in taking forcible steps to prevent him. *The Times* on August 1, the day before the Parliamentary debate just described, contained a leading article whose opening paragraphs deserve quotation:

> When the Commons take up Suez tomorrow there is one thing they can be sure of. It must be their guiding thought. If Nasser is allowed to get way with his *coup* all the British and other Western interests in the Middle East will crumble. The modern world has suffered many acts, like Hitler's march into the Rhineland or the Stalinist overthrow of freedom in Czech-

oslovakia, which were claimed to be assertions of domestic sovereignty. They were, in fact, hinges of history. Nasser's seizure of the Canal Company is another such turning point. Quibbling over whether or not he was "legally entitled" to make the grab will delight the finicky and comfort the faint-hearted, but entirely misses the real issues.

The first is quite simple. Freedom of passage through the Suez Canal, in peace or war, is a prime Western interest. That freedom can be assured only if the canal is in friendly and trustworthy hands. Nasser's grab and his accompanying speeches give final proof that he is both unfriendly and un-trustworthy. The second issue is no less obvious. The great oil works and fields of the Middle East are one of the main foundations of Britain's and Western Europe's industry and security. Anyone who thinks that a victory for Nasser would not encourage other extremist demands against the oilfields — and against strategic bases — should confine himself to tid-dleywinks or blind man's buff. The third issue is wider still. There can be no stability and confidence in the world so long as agreements can be scrapped with impunity.

3

EIGHTEEN POWERS

August 2–23

Nasser's abusive speech — Arab nationalism — The Russian
attitude to the Conference — Views of Mr. Nehru — Problem of
the reservists — National unity and the Left — Firmer attitude
in Washington — My broadcast — Mr. Menzies — The London
Conference meets — Decision in favour of international control
— Indian Government dissents — Mr. Menzies agrees to help

A FORTNIGHT WENT BY before the conference of twenty-two powers
opened in London. This period was filled with diplomatic activity
and with the mounting of our military precautions. Reactions at
home and abroad were generally favourable to the idea and purpose of the conference, except in one quarter. Egypt took up a
rigid position, after consultation with the Russians. The contacts
between the two countries were close. We learnt from Colonel
Nasser that Russia proposed to attend the London Conference,
some time before our Ambassador in Moscow was so informed.

The Egyptian Government called the London Conference im-
perialistic. International authority was the same thing as colonialism, they said. Such perversion of the ordinary terms of language
is common to dictatorships and in this, as in other matters, Nasser
was following the example of his European predecessors. At the
same time the Egyptians professed their belief in freedom and
mutual respect. What they meant by "mutual respect" we soon
found out. Their Foreign Minister informed the United States
Ambassador that if their plans and actions were not accepted by the
rest of the world, there would be "great disturbance" throughout
Africa and the Middle East.

A few days before the Conference was due to start, Nasser made
a speech of the abusive kind to which we were by now accustomed.

He accused the free world of "imperialism and the bloodsucking of peoples." The proposed internationalization of the canal he described as a "conspiracy." He went on once more to invoke the Arab world against the West: "One day after the nationalization of the Suez Canal, voices in the Arab world began to say: 'This is not called the Suez Canal, it is called the Arabs' Canal.' Arab nationalism began to appear in its full shape and in its best form. Support for Egypt began to pour in from kings and leaders of the Arabs." This was not fact, but wishful thinking. According to our information, the Governments of several Arab states were alarmed that Nasser might be allowed to get away with his pillage. If a sharp check were not administered to him now, his wishful thoughts might largely be fulfilled, at the expense of the independence of Middle Eastern and African peoples.

A Nigerian chief of the Muslim faith was at this time passing through Cairo, where an attempt was made to persuade him to sign a paper for publication endorsing Nasser's seizure of the canal. To the chief's credit, he not only refused, he tore the paper up. What would his attitude be if Nasser were allowed by the world to seize his spoil and keep it? The policy of plunder would have been seen to pay off.

In Moscow, meanwhile, Mr. Shepilov, the Foreign Minister, had some conversations with our Ambassador. I was fairly satisfied with these. The Soviet Government recognized our special interests in the Middle East. Marshal Bulganin and Mr. Khrushchev had evidently recalled our conversations at Downing Street earlier in the year. The Russians may also have remembered that not many years before, during negotiations over the passage from the Black Sea to the Aegean, they had demanded international control of Suez. They did not oppose the holding of a conference, but they raised some demur about its composition, its place and its timing. The Russians wanted to delay it until the end of August, they would prefer it to be held in Cairo and they wished us to invite some twenty further countries, many of them in the Soviet orbit and others under Nasser's influence. As I had expected, they did not fail to point out that the United States had not signed the Convention of 1888 and ought not to be one of the inviting powers. They expressed concern at our military precautions, though not in terms suggesting that they were unduly worried. Having registered all these points, they accepted our invitation.

It was clear to us that they would attend the Conference as watchdogs for Nasser, making use of any opportunity which might arise to widen divergences among the powers.

When Egypt first seized the canal, the Indian Government showed some embarrassment, no doubt accentuated by the fact that Mr. Nehru had been the guest of Colonel Nasser in Cairo only a few days before. With the passage of time the Indians embarked actively upon a policy which, they assured us, was an attempt to reach a compromise between two points of view. In effect, their policy really meant that Nasser must be appeased. Their representatives in Cairo, and the aviatory Mr. Krishna Menon, kept in constant touch with the Egyptian Government and freely offered advice to Her Majesty's Government. The Indians did not believe in setting up an international authority with more than advisory powers. This would have been entirely ineffective in giving any kind of guarantee to the users of the canal.

★ ★ ★ ★ ★

On August 8, I broadcast to the country:

> The alternatives are now clear to see. If we all join together to create an international system for the canal and spend its revenues as they should be spent, to develop it rapidly, that can bring growing prosperity to East and West alike, the countries that produce the oil and the countries which buy it. There will then be wealth for all to share, including Egypt. There is no question of denying her a fair deal, or a just return. But if anyone is going to snatch and grab and try to pocket what really belongs to the world, the result will be impoverishment for all, and a refusal by some countries at least to lead their life at such a hazard. Meanwhile, we have too much at risk not to take precautions. We have done so. That is the meaning of the movements by land, sea and air of which you have heard in the last few days.
>
> We do not seek a solution by force, but by the broadest pos-

sible international agreement. That is why we have called the conference. We shall do all we can to help its work, but this I must make plain. We cannot agree that an act of plunder which threatens the livelihood of many nations shall be allowed to succeed. And we must make sure that the life of the great trading nations of the world cannot, in the future, be strangled at any moment by some interruption to the free passage of the canal.

Meanwhile, public opinion in our own country held steadier than appeared from press reports. Left-wing and doubtful-minded journals saw in the possible use of force a handy stick with which to beat the Government. From early August onwards they did not hesitate to employ it. Left-wing Governments, if they are firm in the discharge of their responsibilities in international affairs, can always count on national support. Right-wing Governments cannot always do so. It was perhaps fortunate that it was a Labour Government which had to expose Soviet behaviour after the war and break the blockade of Berlin by the airlift.

One of our difficulties was the problem of the reservists. These men were indispensable if our forces were to be immediately ready for use. They were, most of them, taken from important work in civil life. The service which they had to be ready to give was often tedious and entailed much waiting about, as is always the lot of those who serve in the armed forces. Most of the reservists bore up cheerfully and without complaint. A few became restive and some newspapers made use of this to fan every incident and exaggerate every discontent.

On August 13 the Opposition Shadow Cabinet issued a statement. The retreat then began amid a clatter of excuses. The most contradictory of these maintained that forcible action was certainly justified if it had the sanction of the United Nations. From the first the Soviet Government made it plain that they would give diplomatic support to the Egyptians. This meant that Moscow would run no risks, but would take every political pot-shot from behind cover. The use of the veto in the Security Council was the easiest of these, for it was an exercise which never gave the Kremlin the slightest embarrassment. Apparently the Soviet veto was at Nasser's

disposal, as in fact it proved to be when the eighteen-power proposals came before the Security Council two months later. Nor
would any initiative in the General Assembly meet with success in
the face of Afro-Asian extremists supported by the Soviets. Therefore the condition of United Nations approval for the use of force
by Britain and France was equivalent to denying its use.

Not all those who advocated forcible action, subject to this limitation, understood what they were saying to Nasser, but some did.
Those who did would more fairly have expressed their attitude by
declaring "forcible action will not be possible, because it cannot be
employed without the sanction of the United Nations and in view
of the Soviet use of the veto that sanction cannot be expected."
This would have been an honest attitude, the implications of which
ought to be considered, for it inhibits action by the free nations
while permitting the use of force to the Communist powers, who
accept no limitations by the United Nations on their actions, as the
treatment of Hungary showed.

It is pardonable not to see the danger. It is excusable to see it and
declare it and do nothing effective about it on moral grounds. It is
unpardonable to see it and make a pretence of meeting it by
methods one knows in one's heart to be totally ineffective.

Despite all this, in August 1956 the nation understood the issues
at stake and the instability of opinion was very much less than it was
pictured to be. But there can be no question that what was
believed to be the deep division in the country created difficulties
for our diplomacy almost from the start. Doubt about British
national unity had its repercussions in the United States. It was
constantly quoted to us by American negotiators and helped to
weaken American resolution.

Following my usual custom, I maintained my hopes of American
support, and had written to Mr. Eisenhower on August 5 after the
three-power talks, expressing the belief that we could now "display
to Nasser and to the world a united front between our two countries
and the French." I added that "we must prepare to meet the
eventuality that Nasser would refuse to accept the outcome of the
conference." The President let me know that he had a great deal of
sympathy with our line of thought. Our Ambassador in Washington, Sir Roger Makins, assured us at this time that the Administra-

tion completely accepted the impossibility of leaving the control of the Suez Canal in the hands of a man like Nasser. Though they would strain every nerve to bring about a settlement by negotiation, they realized that in the last resort force might have to be used and they understood the necessity for the military precautions which we and the French were taking. The Ambassador thought that there would be a deep division of opinion in the United States on the use of force and that the political problems which it would raise in an election year would be appalling. Nasser could hardly have chosen a better time for his action in terms of American domestic politics. Even so, the Ambassador reported, the President and Mr. Dulles were showing firmness, and the attitude of the Administration was becoming more robust. There was talk in Washington of calling a special session of Congress in order to give the President emergency powers. The State Department was working out the details of a proposal for an international authority. Consultations were going forward on oil supplies, should passage through the canal be stopped.

Our relations with the French throughout this period were very good. The task of co-ordinating our policy and our precautions went forward steadily day by day. At the same time, we sought to reach agreement with them over a variety of problems in the Middle East, where there had been some sharp differences in our outlook since 1918.

★ ★ ★ ★ ★

In the days before the London Conference met, Mr. Menzies, the Prime Minister of Australia, joined us. When the Suez crisis began, he had been in the United States and was about to pay a visit to Japan and the Far East. The gravity of events was not lost upon him and he cancelled his tour. When he told me of his decision, I at once invited him to join us in London and take part in our councils. He generously consented to do so. We could not have had a wiser or more forthright colleague.

I had first met Bob Menzies in 1935 when he was Attorney-General and I came to know him well in the dark days of 1941, perhaps the worst period of the second world war. I had come back from the Middle East, where I had taken a prominent part in difficult decisions about the Greek campaign. Events have since proved that our decisions were right, but at the time they were much criticized. Since Australia made a generous contribution to the military operation, it was inevitable that some of the blame should fall, albeit unjustly, upon Mr. Menzies, who was the Commonwealth Prime Minister. He was himself in London during part of the time when the decisions were taken. I admired his courage then for endorsing what he believed to be right. He stood by it, even when he was involved in some obloquy at home, and lost a general election.

I remember that when I arrived back in London from Cairo and attended my first Cabinet, I found Menzies sitting next to me. He passed a note, "This is the strangest Cabinet I ever sat in. Since you have been away I have only heard one voice. Do none of them ever speak up?" I explained to him afterwards how the technique worked. The War Cabinet did not wish to be immersed in the details of military operations. Whatever the Prime Minister had to say on these topics, which sometimes filled the greater part of our discussions, was not usually commented upon then, because it was the Defence Committee which handled those affairs.

Later I had been Menzies' guest in Australia when he was Leader of the Opposition and I was also out of office. Our friendship had grown through the years and I felt a deep affection both for him and his charming family. Menzies shows his legal training in the lucidity of his mind and a penetrating intelligence. His statesmanship is something more. He has an instinct for great affairs and he cannot tolerate humbug.

When Menzies came to London at this critical time, I gained an immense reinforcement from his knowledge and experience. "It is lonely at the top," as Stanley Baldwin used to say. There are political colleagues with whom one has been through the toughest experiences. This was true of Lord Salisbury, and also of Oliver Lyttelton, who was a member of the War Cabinet and the Defence Committee for long periods during my service there. It was true more especially of my relations with Sir Winston Churchill. Now, at this sharp testing time for myself, it was good to be able to sit down and assess the problems with Mr. Menzies. We had been through this kind of thing together before.

At this period I had a strange interlude with the British Broadcasting Corporation. In conversation with Menzies, a day or two after his arrival, I asked him if he would comment publicly on the situation, preferably in a television broadcast. He replied that he would do anything he could to help. I said I had no doubt that this would be very welcome and passed on the information to the B.B.C. A little while later I learnt, almost by accident, that Mr. Menzies had not been asked to speak. I made inquiry why this was so. I was told that as I had already appeared and, I think, some other speaker who shared my point of view, it was felt that if Mr. Menzies were to be asked to speak, someone who clearly disagreed, Mr. Emrys Hughes was the name mentioned, should be put on the air to balance the presentation of views. I thought that this attitude was insulting to a Commonwealth Prime Minister, whatever his politics, and Mr. Menzies was invited to speak on television, which he did admirably.

During these weeks I took one night off, our wedding anniversary. On that evening my wife and I went to see *Romanoff and Juliet* and enjoyed its wit. When we returned to Downing Street, we found a group of students of varied nationalities vociferating in the wake of two Members of Parliament. Their boos drowned the cheers of supporters, and we ate our supper to a noise like a palace revolution. Strange wedding bells, but it seemed a fitting epilogue to our play.

★ ★ ★ ★ ★

A week before the London Conference was due to begin, most of the powers had accepted our invitations. I wanted two results from the Conference. First, that it should reach agreement by a large majority on the international control of the canal. Secondly, that it should decide upon the steps to take to effect this. I wished to secure a declaration from the Conference that, if Egypt rejected its recommendations for international control, the powers using the canal would refuse to pay their transit dues to the Egyptian company. A firm sanction would then be at our command. At present, Nasser was still getting about 35 per cent of the dues, most of this from American sources. I wanted the nations to proclaim their intention of paying their dues into a blocked account, to be held, perhaps by the World Bank, until an international authority was in operation.

We realized that some delegates at the Conference might press for the early reference of the issue to the United Nations. I could sympathize with this line of thought, but I knew that it was not well-founded, having taken a leading part myself in working out the terms of the United Nations Charter at San Francisco. This was a type of emergency which had been allowed for at the time. Article 33 of the Charter did not demand that every international dispute should be taken to the Security Council or the General Assembly. It stated:

> The parties to any dispute, the continuance of which is likely to endanger the maintenance of international peace and security, shall, first of all, seek a solution by negotiation, inquiry, mediation, conciliation, arbitration, judicial settlement, resort to regional agencies or arrangements, or other peaceful means of their own choice.

Setting up a regional agency was exactly the purpose of the Conference. A link between it and the United Nations could be worked out later.

★ ★ ★ ★ ★

The Conference held its first session on August 16 at Lancaster House, attracting considerable attention from the holiday crowds always in London during that month. After I had briefly opened the proceedings with a warning that all had a common interest in the sanctity of agreements, the Foreign Secretary took the chair. The Americans were at first doubtful whether he, or any representative of the three powers, should do so. They found the majority of delegates content that the host country should preside.

Mr. Selwyn Lloyd handled the proceedings of the London Conference with skill and despatch. He also had a number of private conversations with the Foreign Secretaries of all the powers and their advisers. In the course of these, we were quickly assured of the support of at least two-thirds of the members of the Conference,

Australia and New Zealand being wholly with us. The maritime powers of Europe, with some reserve on the part of Spain, were all in favour of reasserting international control over the canal The powers of the Baghdad Pact who were present, Iran, Pakistan and Turkey, thought the same. They held that we must bring Nasser to accept the rule of law. If we failed to do so, we should pile up fresh difficulties for the future. They thought it possible that, for political ends, Colonel Nasser would interfere with their trade and shipping.

There was general alarm at the Egyptian threat to freedom of navigation. Portugal, for instance, was perturbed about her communications with Goa. The Netherlands feared for their East Indian commerce. The Dutch were particularly indignant that only the Indonesians had been sent a special message by the United States, urging them to attend the Conference. Their leaders had recently received a public blessing from Mr. Dulles in Djakarta, yet only a while before, Indonesia had repudiated her debts to the Netherlands. The Dutch had forebodings that, encouraged by Nasser's action, Indonesia would next confiscate the assets of Dutch companies.

So it proved. A year later Indonesia made a brazen attempt to blackmail the Netherlands into abandoning its sovereignty over New Guinea. They seized shipping plying between the islands. They confiscated Dutch properties wholesale and compelled thousands of Netherlands citizens, who had never known any other home, to flee as refugees. No compensation of any kind was paid to these companies or to those who worked for them; no action was taken by the United Nations. After all, the Netherlands was only a colonial power. Cynically, the Indonesian Government remarked that compensation would only be paid when the Netherlands had abandoned western New Guinea. So the pattern of pillage spread.

At the Conference some of the powers, and particularly those of the Baghdad Pact, wished to emphasize Egyptian sovereignty over the canal, at the same time asserting the need for international control. They had national problems of their own in mind, which we understood. The question of sovereignty, we told them, was not a matter of absolutes. The British Government had sovereign rights in Uganda, at the headwaters of the Nile. We should not think our sovereignty infringed if, to reassure Egypt and the Sudan, we waived our right to divert the waters of the river. It was no inroad on Egyptian sovereignty to ask for international control of passage through the canal in exchange for a fair financial return. At the Conference we were able to meet the Pakistani, Iranian and Turkish point of view by accepting their amendments.

By August 22 the business of the Conference was all but formally completed. Mr. Dulles had opened the proceedings in a speech presenting the three-power conclusions. These were later embodied in a draft declaration which asserted the principle of international control, recognized the sovereign rights of Egypt, guaranteed her a fair return for the use of the canal, and proposed the negotiation of a new convention. Under the new convention the operation of the canal would be entrusted to a board:

> The members of the board, in addition to Egypt, would be other states chosen in a manner to be agreed upon from among the states parties to the convention with due regard to use, pattern of trade and geographical distribution; the composition of the board to be such as to assure that its responsibilities would be discharged solely with a view to achieving the best possible operating results without political motivation in favour of, or in prejudice against, any user of the canal.

Provisions were to be laid down in the convention for the arbitration of disputes, for sanctions in case of violation and for some form of association with the United Nations. This declaration was perfectly satisfactory to us and it was reassuring that the Americans presented it. If its terms had been maintained, all would have been well.

Eighteen nations* subscribed to this declaration, though Spain made a minor reservation. India, Soviet Russia, Indonesia and Ceylon supported a proposal for a purely advisory international board which would enjoy no powers of control. We were sorry that India was out of step with the majority of the Conference, which

---

* The eighteen nations were: Australia, Denmark, Ethiopia, France, Federal Germany, Iran, Italy, Japan, Netherlands, New Zealand, Norway, Pakistan, Portugal, Spain, Sweden, Turkey, United Kingdom, United States.

represented more than 95 per cent of the tonnage passing through the canal. In an attempt to persuade the Indian delegation to come nearer to us, we asked them whether they could endorse the principles upon which eighteen of the powers had agreed, even though they reserved their position as to the methods to give effect to them. This they felt unable to do.

Meanwhile, Her Majesty's Government had decided upon the action which must follow. The declaration of the Conference should be put before the Egyptian Government by a small committee. If Colonel Nasser accepted it as a basis, negotiations would follow. If not, we must reserve our position. My desire was to send a small, strong, and highly representative committee to Cairo, determined to reach a quick conclusion. At my appeal and that of the Conference, Mr. Menzies undertook the leadership. He did so despite political inconvenience at home, the Australian Parliament being due to debate the Budget on August 30. I telegraphed to Sir Arthur Fadden, the Deputy Prime Minister in Canberra, to say:

> The Commonwealth of Australia will be rendering a signal service to the solution of this vexed problem if you and your colleagues can spare your Prime Minister for a few more days to give his personal help. . . . The experience and counsel brought to our proceedings by Mr. Menzies during these anxious days has proved quite invaluable.

Sir Arthur agreed to our request.

On August 23 the Declaration of the London Conference was published. Mr. Menzies was appointed by the eighteen powers to convey their proposals to the Egyptian Government accompanied by the representatives of Ethiopia, Iran, Sweden and the United States. The first three countries were represented by their Foreign Secretaries, and the United States by Mr. Loy Henderson, in whom we had confidence, although we were sorry that Mr. Dulles could not attend himself. Thus the five continents were associated in this new mission.

A few days later I telegraphed to the President:

> This is a message to thank you for all the help Foster has given. Though I could not be at the Conference myself, I heard

praise on all sides for the outstanding quality of his speeches and his constructive leadership. He will tell you how things have gone. It was, I think, a remarkable achievement to unite eighteen nations on an agreed statement of this clarity and force.

Before he left, Foster spoke to me of the destructive efforts of the Russians at the Conference. I have been giving some thought to this and I would like to give you my conclusions.

I have no doubt that the Bear is using Nasser, with or without his knowledge, to further his immediate aims. These are, I think, first to dislodge the West from the Middle East, and second to get a foothold in Africa so as to dominate that continent in turn. In this connection I have seen a reliable report from someone who was present at the lunch which Shepilov gave for the Arab Ambassadors. There the Soviet claim was that they "only wanted to see Arab unity in Asia and Africa and the abolition of all foreign bases and exploitation. An agreed unified Arab nation must take its rightful place in the world."

This policy is clearly aimed at Wheelus Field and Habbaniya, as well as at our Middle East oil supplies. Meanwhile the Communist bloc continue their economic and political blandishments towards the African countries which are already independent. Soon they will have a wider field for subversion as our colonies, particularly in the West, achieve self-government. All this makes me more than ever sure that Nasser must not be allowed to get away with it this time. We have many friends in the Middle East and in Africa and others who are shrewd enough to know where the plans of a Nasser or a Musaddiq would lead them. But they will not be strong enough to stand against the power of the mobs if Nasser wins again. The firmer the front we show together, the greater the chance that Nasser will give way without the need for any resort to force. That is why we were grateful for your policy and Foster's expression of it at the Conference. It is also one of the reasons why we have to continue our military preparations in conjunction with our French allies.

We have been examining what other action could be taken if Nasser refuses to negotiate on the basis of the London Conference. There is the question of the dues. The Dutch and the

Germans have already indicated that they will give support in this respect. The Dutch may even be taking action in the next few days. Then there is the question of currency and economic action. We are studying these with your people and the French in London and will be sending our comments soon. It looks as though we shall have a few days until Nasser gives Menzies his final reply. After that we should be in a position to act swiftly. Selwyn Lloyd is telegraphing to Foster about tactics, particularly in relation to United Nations.

Meanwhile I thought I should set out some of our reflections on the dangerous situation which still confronts us. It is certainly the most hazardous that our country had known since 1940.

I was so glad to see such excellent photographic testimony of your growing health and abounding energy. That is the very best news for us all.

4

THE MENZIES MISSION
August 23–September 9

Meeting with Nasser fixed — Question of Security Council —
Economic pressure — Oil supplies — Problem of using force —
We resolve to appeal to U.N., if Menzies mission fails — Issue
raised with N.A.T.O. — M. Spaak's warning — Our draft resolu-
tion for Security Council — "Ganging-up" — Mr. Dulles proposes
Users' Club — My letter to President Eisenhower — The Suez
Canal Company's staff — Failure of the mission — Mr. Menzies'
letter

MR. MENZIES' COMMITTEE spent some time in London preparing
their case and arranging their meeting with Colonel Nasser. Every
consideration was shown for Egyptian convenience. A meeting
was eventually fixed for September 3 in Cairo, and the interchanges there lasted six days. Little more than a fortnight passed
between the declaration of the eighteen powers and the comple-
tion of Mr. Menzies' mission, but it was a critical fortnight in the
development of the Suez crisis.

The United Kingdom Government had to determine what
action to take if Nasser turned down the proposals of the
eighteen powers. The United States was not in agreement with
France and ourselves on the nature of this action and its timing.
We wished to refer the issue to the Security Council, if Nasser
declared his unwillingness to negotiate. We also desired as many
powers as possible to exert financial and economic pressure upon
Egypt. The United States discouraged us in both these initiatives.

While Mr. Dulles was still in London we had again urged upon
him the importance of denying the canal dues to Nasser. Each
year some 55 per cent of the dues were paid by British and
French ships, and these were already being withheld from Egypt.

American-owned ships were the third largest payers. After them came the ships of Italy, the Netherlands and Norway. The Dutch, Norwegians and Germans were willing to take steps in line with our policy. Mr. Dulles was not forthcoming. He side-stepped the point by telling us much that we already knew about the disadvantages of sailing round the Cape and the undesirability of petrol rationing.

On dues, the United States Government never agreed to effective action. This made it impossible to put pressure upon Nasser by a means which was ready to hand, depriving him of the revenue of the canal he had seized, until a new settlement was made.

The United States Government were not helpful about other forms of financial restraint. The French and ourselves had blocked all Egyptian sterling and franc accounts a month before. The United States had merely frozen the dollar balances of the Egyptian Government and the National Bank of Egypt, as they stood on July 31. New receipts in these accounts were not affected, nor were privately owned dollar accounts. This meant that maximum pressure was not being exerted on Egyptian finance and commerce.

Our policy was to persuade as many powers as we could, and especially the United States, to take the same action as we had done. A number of them were already in line. Dulles, however, felt that he had first to pave the way with the American public for any further steps. In the event, no paving was ever done. On his return to Washington, Dulles spoke to our Ambassador of keeping a number of alternatives in view. In principle, he was in favour of economic measures, but all he could promise was that the United States Government should prepare to take them. In fact, they never took them.

While the United States was in a hesitant mood, we had to face the dilemma of our oil supplies. All would be well if the Americans continued to uphold the declaration which Menzies was taking to Cairo, and played their part in getting it accepted by Egypt, but time was not on our side. To allow discussions to drag on was more likely to diminish than increase the chances of a satisfactory settlement. Her Majesty's Government accepted that every diplomatic method must be employed and exhausted, and shown to be exhausted, before resorting to military action. We agreed that we should put our case to the United Nations. The Security Council had to be given a full and genuine opportunity to debate the situation. On the other hand, means had to be found to prevent the endless circumlocution and eventual disregard which usually befell resolutions coming before the Council.

There was always a danger that the passage of time and the multiplication of talk would weaken the resolve of the eighteen powers. The risk of letting Nasser keep his prize might in the end be greater than the risk of using force. The question was, how long we could pursue diplomatic methods and economic sanctions, which very likely would not succeed, before the possibility of military action slipped from our grasp. Winter was approaching, when action would be more difficult and other plans would be called for. On August 28 French forces took up their stations in Cyprus. In a few weeks we should be poised to strike, if we had to strike. It would be very costly to keep up this position indefinitely.

During these days in late August, the Government discussed the wisdom of taking the issue to the United Nations. There was no binding obligation to do so at this stage, for the Charter of the United Nations itself allows latitude. The threat to peace in 1948 at Berlin was not referred to the United Nations until some months after the Russian blockade and the answering airlift began. Nothing happened then but talk.

There were risks in going to the United Nations. All kinds of suggestions might be put forward at the Security Council for solving our differences with Egypt which would only prolong them. The State Department had so far shown itself against any such step on our part. One of Mr. Dulles' advisers described the Security Council to us as a quicksand. Once in it, one did not know how deep it would prove, or whether one would ever get out. Pineau had remarked that the power possessed by the United Nations was one of "suspensive action." All this was true but, as signatories to the Charter, we had undertaken not to resort to military action without first going to the United Nations. We were pledged and we intended to keep our word. The questions before us were when and in what form we should do so.

We thought that advantage lay in an early appeal. It was important to take the initiative before Egypt or any other power did so. Our concentration of forces in the Mediterranean might be used as a pretext against us. On the other hand it would be unwise to go to the Security Council before Mr. Menzies' committee had elicited a reply from Nasser. We must not weaken the committee's position by giving the impression that the ground was being cut from under its feet, or that we expected its proposals to be rejected by the Egyptian Government. Nor should we give Nasser the pretext to withhold his answer until the Security Council had considered the matter. There was still a chance that the Egyptians might accept outright, or at least with qualifications which would not rule out further negotiations.

The Government decided on August 28 to go to the United Nations, only after we had heard from Mr. Menzies. This in turn had its parliamentary consequences. I wished to summon Parliament from the summer recess at the earliest possible moment, but it was desirable to give Members something concrete to debate. Parliament is not at its best when asked to discuss general situations; it is wiser, if possible, to give solid fare. We agreed, after consulting Mr. Menzies while he was in Cairo, that Parliament should be called together immediately after his return. The report of his committee would then be available for debate.

The form of our appeal to the Security Council was our next problem. A possible course was to introduce a resolution seeking support for the principles of the eighteen-power declaration and inviting Egypt to accept them. France and Australia, as members of the Council, would certainly join with us in this. The United States could hardly do otherwise in view of its leading part in drafting and sponsoring the declaration. A resolution would in all likelihood evoke a Russian veto, but we hoped it would be possible to show that a large majority in the Security Council endorsed the London proposals. There were other risks besides the Russian veto. During the Council's debates some amendments might be moved by one of the less friendly powers, in an attempt to shackle our freedom of action. If we had the firm co-operation of the United States, such amendments would probably fail to pass. These were the Government's conclusions and the Foreign Secretary was authorized, on August 28, to convey them to Mr. Dulles and enlist his aid.

At the same time I wanted to give the countries of free Europe a chance to consider together the situation facing us all. It was these countries which had most to lose if the Egyptian Government were not checked. It was they who would become dependent for the security of their oil supplies upon the decisions of one man. I suggested that we should raise the matter at N.A.T.O. This would accord with the broader political character which we wished that organization to assume. It was decided that the Foreign Secretary should deliver a report to the council of N.A.T.O. on the discussions at the London Conference.

This he did on September 5. He found a vigorous ally in the Netherlands Foreign Minister, M. Luns, who urged that the North Atlantic powers should refuse to recognize the seizure of the canal, withhold dues from the new authority and join in a reference to the Security Council. The Canadian Foreign Minister, Mr. Lester Pearson, endorsed these views. Though he was averse to military sanctions, he did not exclude them in the last resort. Mr. Selwyn Lloyd considered that the meeting of the Council had been a success and that its discussions of Suez would have a useful influence.

M. Spaak, the Foreign Minister of Belgium, who had been paying a visit to the Congo in August, came back to Europe fully alerted to the danger of Colonel Nasser's *coup*. It would have ramifications throughout Africa, not only in the north but deep in the central tropics. M. Spaak was firm on the importance of re-establishing international control over the Suez waterway, but he was convinced that the question was even larger than this. If the Western powers quailed, he foresaw a long series of retreats before them, in Africa and the Middle East. He strongly favoured enlisting the support of the North Atlantic Treaty powers, and declared himself haunted by the mistakes committed at the outset of the Hitler period. He feared that they might now be repeated. So did I.

Our information tallied with M. Spaak's. We had received reports from West and East Africa, Somaliland and Aden. Taken singly, these might not be alarming, but in sum they foreshadowed widespread unrest in the Muslim world. We knew that the Egyptian Government were laying plans for a revolutionary upheaval in Iraq. There was also an underlying threat to the Government of Iran. The Foreign Secretary and I were much encouraged by M. Spaak's determination that this menace must be faced, even if the United States was not squarely behind us. Belgium, he told us, would agree to pay her canal dues into a blocked account, and she would be at one with us in any proceedings at the United Nations. He was as good as his word.

★ ★ ★ ★ ★

The course of the Suez Canal crisis was decided by the American attitude toward it. If the United States Government had approached this issue in the spirit of an ally, they would have done everything in their power, short of the use of force, to support the nations whose economic security depended upon the freedom of passage through the Suez Canal. They would have closely planned their policies with their allies and held stoutly to the decisions arrived at. They would have insisted on restoring international authority in order to insulate the canal from the politics of any one country. It is now clear that this was never the attitude of the United States Government. Rather did they try to gain time, coast along over difficulties as they arose and improvise policies, each following on the failure of its immediate predecessor. None of these was geared to the long-term purpose of serving a joint cause.

The reality of the issue was clearly put by a Communist, Milovan Djilas, in his remarkable book, *The New Class*.* He saw the struggle for what it was: "a dispute between Egyptian nationalism and world trade, which, by a coincidence, happened to be represented by the old colonial powers of Britain and France."

Unhappily for the future of Asia and Africa, no such clarity of vision advantaged the Administration in Washington. The old spoor of colonialism confused the trail.

★ ★ ★ ★ ★

* Eds. Morton Puner and Konrad Kellen (New York: Praeger, 1957). Quoted by permission of Frederick A. Praeger, Inc.

At the end of August we began to receive American views on our proposed approach to the United Nations. Dulles agreed in general that the Security Council should be consulted before any decision was taken on military action, but he expressed a number of doubts. He drew attention to technical difficulties. On August 29 he asked whether our problem in the language of the Charter was a "dispute" or a "situation." If the former, he said we might be faced with a considerable adverse vote, and if the latter, we could not, under the procedure we had suggested, ask the Council for any effective resolution. We met Dulles on this point by choosing a different procedure, but we did not satisfy his doubts.

The Government decided that they must make their position clear beyond question. Accordingly we sent to Washington the next day the terms of the draft resolution which we proposed to submit. This found "that a threat to peace exists," and, in the name of the United Nations, invited Egypt to negotiate on the basis of the eighteen-power proposals. We pointed out that we could go forward with this resolution only after we had got a clear answer from Egypt on the proposals of the Menzies mission.

Mr. Dulles at first sight liked our draft, but he was preoccupied with counting heads in the Security Council and worried by the question of the number of votes on which we could depend. He declared that we could naturally rely upon the support of the United States at the Council, on the understanding that our move was an honest attempt to reach a solution and not "a device for obtaining cover." Mr. Dulles thought that our proposition implied the possible use of force. The United States did not necessarily want to be committed to this. We could not ourselves see any signs of this implication in our draft, which was as follows:

Draft Security Council Resolution

Recognizing that the arbitrary and unilateral action of the Government of Egypt in relation to the operation of the Suez Canal has disturbed the *status quo* and has created a situation which may endanger the free and open passage of shipping through the canal, without distinction of flag, as laid down by the Suez Canal Convention of 1888, and has thus given rise to a threat to the peace;

Noting that a conference to discuss this situation was called in London on August 16, 1956, and that eighteen of the twenty-two states attending that conference, who between them represent over 95 per cent of the user interest in the canal, put forward proposals to the Egyptian Government;

Regretting the refusal of the Egyptian Government to negotiate on the basis of the above-mentioned proposals, which appear to offer means for a just and equitable solution;

Considering that such refusal constitutes an aggravation of the situation;

Recalling the Egyptian Government's failure to comply with the Security Council's resolution of September 1, 1951:

1. Finds that a threat to the peace exists;

2. Reminds the Government of Egypt of its continuing obligation, under Article 25 of the Charter, to accept and carry out the above-mentioned resolution;

3. Reaffirms the principle of the freedom of navigation of the Suez Canal in accordance with the Suez Canal Convention of 1888;

4. Considers it essential that, in order to guarantee this principle, the canal should be operated on the basis of the above-mentioned five-power proposals;*

5. Calls on the Government of Egypt to negotiate on the basis of these proposals.

In further discussions, the American officials questioned the time-table which we had in mind. They did not think that a week of debate would be sufficient. If a lot of amendments were tabled, it would take much hard work in the lobbies to dispose of them. In London we were well aware of this characteristic defect in the United Nations' machinery, hence our determination to try to speed it up. But the Americans were particularly anxious to avoid creating the impression of what they called railroading

* Those carried to Cairo by Mr. Menzies' mission on behalf of the eighteen powers.

tactics. They also did not want us to add Belgium, or any other power which had not been represented at the London Conference, to our list of sponsors. Belgium was a member of the Security Council and in our view nothing was more natural than to call on the support of our friends, but the Americans considered that this looked like "ganging-up."

This term "ganging-up" requires some explanation. It has a melancholy history. I think that I first heard it in connection with the Yalta Conference. There it was interpreted as meaning that we and the United States must not get too close together for fear of arousing the suspicions of the Russians whom we were to meet. It certainly was an obstacle in the way of close understanding at the highest level, though Mr. Stettinius, then Secretary of State, did not share a love for this phrase. Neither at Yalta nor later at San Francisco did he ever use it or lean upon it. However, it plagued our discussions at Yalta, where the Conference would have had better results for the world had it not prevailed.

Negotiators with the United States from many of the Western powers have since become more accustomed to this unhappy frame of mind, though I have never heard the phrase used when representations were made to induce them to align their policies with those of the United States. Nobody suggested, for instance, that acquiescence by Britain and France in the repeated refusal to admit Communist China to the United Nations was in any sense ganging-up.

★   ★   ★   ★   ★

So, for a few days, matters rested on the issue of the appeal to the United Nations. Our draft resolution was in the hands of the United States. The French had approved it, the Americans held back. The next move came unexpectedly. Mr. Dulles returned on September 4 from a week-end holiday on Duck Island, Lake Ontario, with some fresh thoughts. He now declared that we did not need a new convention with Egypt, though this was precisely what had been asked for by the eighteen powers in the London proposals, which he had himself put forward.

Mr. Dulles told our Ambassador that he regarded our position as a weak one judicially. Although we were not infringing Egyptian sovereignty by asking them to accept a new treaty, we were threatening force if they refused. This implied, he said, that we did not possess adequate rights under existing treaties and needed to acquire them. But, in fact, the Convention of 1888 gave us all the rights we required.

He suggested that the users should club together, hire the pilots, organize navigation, and themselves manage the canal. This might be inconvenient, but it was quite feasible and would probably lead in time to some settlement with Egypt. If we could show that, in the event of Nasser refusing our proposals, we had an alternative to war, we would be in a far stronger position. The Convention gave Nasser no right to make a profit out of the operation of the canal. He would now see the money vanishing from his grasp and this, so Dulles argued, would deflate him more effectively than the threat or use of force. By thus relying on the rights which we possessed under the Convention, rather than asserting fresh ones, we would be much better placed in regard to the United Nations.

This account was amplified next day at the State Department when Her Majesty's Minister was told that, in the opinion of the United States Government, the users, including the United States, should issue an announcement rehearsing their rights and declaring their intention to set up a new organization. They must define exactly what it would do, and make clear that all ships passing through the canal would have to use the services of this organization.

Such was the first exposition of the idea of a Users' Club, which was to deflect the course of events. It marked a turning point. As reported, we thought this a promising plan, but we were doubtful of its legal basis. Our advice in London was that though the Convention imposed obligations on Egypt, there was nothing in it which gave the users any such rights as Dulles claimed. The signatories of the Convention could make certain that it was observed only by diplomatic and economic pressure and in the last resort by force. Moreover, we were faced with the same difficulty as at the summoning of the London Conference. There were far more user nations than there were surviving signatories of the Convention.

On September 6 we had news from Mr. Menzies that his mission was near deadlock. We decided to pursue our appeal to the United Nations, at the same time exploring the meaning of Mr. Dulles' latest idea. The Government regarded resort to the Security Council as a further attempt to persuade Egypt to accept a solution on the lines agreed at the London Conference. We suggested to the United States that our representative at the United Nations should deliver a message to the President of the Security Council requesting him to summon a meeting. The French Government agreed with this course of action. We knew that the Egyptian Government wanted to prolong the palavers while they strengthened their hold on the canal. Admittedly our move at the United Nations would give them still further time. However, Mr. Dulles' Users' Club, we hoped, would provide a method of denying Egypt any profit from her act of nationalization, until a settlement was reached.

Canal transit dues, the Foreign Secretary insisted in his communications with Washington, must be paid to the Users' Club. This was the key to the whole business. Meanwhile Nasser must not get the dues. The body proposed by the United States Government, he told them, might for the time being fulfil most of the functions of the international authority proposed by the London Conference. I reflected that the United States would be fully committed to take part in it.

I still believed that the United States Government held firmly to their determination that Nasser must be made to "disgorge." This being so, I considered that they must be allowed as free a hand as possible in selecting methods. The Users' Club could be the American choice. It was true that the club would take some time to constitute. We therefore proposed to make our approach to the United Nations at once while Mr. Dulles' ideas were still being clarified. In the event, we were frustrated, and the Users' Club assumed a different form from that which we had been led to expect.

In the meantime I had received a disquieting message from Mr. Eisenhower on September 3. Hitherto he and his officials had always given us to understand that the United States would not take exception to the use of force, if all peaceful means of

settlement had been exhausted. The fact that we had taken
military precautions had, furthermore, been approved from time
to time. Now the President told me that American public opinion
flatly rejected force. He admitted that the procedures of negotiation on which we were then engaged would probably not give
Nasser the set-back he deserved. But he advised that we should
sharply separate the question of the canal from our general
policy towards the Egyptian dictatorship and the menace under
which Africa and the Middle East lay. The latter he considered
a long-term problem.

I found this most disturbing. I felt that we had to deal with
the canal not only for its own importance, but because Nasser's
seizure of it affected the whole position in the Middle East and
Africa. The canal was not a problem that could be isolated
from the many other manifestations of Arab nationalism and
Egyptian ambition.

I replied to the President on September 6 in a message on which
I had spent much care:

> Thank you for your message and writing thus frankly.
>
> There is no doubt as to where we are agreed and have
> been agreed from the very beginning, namely that we should
> do everything we can to get a peaceful settlement. It is in
> this spirit that we favoured calling the twenty-two-power con-
> ference and that we have worked in the closest co-operation
> with you about this business since. There has never been
> any question of our suddenly or without further provocation
> resorting to arms, while these processes were at work. In
> any event, as your own wide knowledge would confirm, we
> could not have done this without extensive preparation last-
> ing several weeks.
>
> This question of precautions has troubled me considerably
> and still does. I have not forgotten the riots and murders in
> Cairo in 1952, for I was in charge here at the time when
> Winston was on the high seas on his way back from the United
> States.
>
> We are both agreed that we must give the Suez committee
> every chance to fulfil their mission. This is our firm resolve.
> If the committee and subsequent negotiations succeed in get-

ting Nasser's agreement to the London proposals of the eighteen powers, there will be no call for force. But if the committee fails, we must have some immediate alternative which will show that Nasser is not going to get his way. In this connection we are attracted by Foster's suggestion, if I understand it rightly, for the running of the canal by the users in virtue of their rights under the 1888 Convention. We heard about this from our Embassy in Washington yesterday. I think that we could go along with this, provided that the intention was made clear by both of us immediately the Menzies mission finishes its work. But unless we can proceed with this, or something very like it, what should the next step be?

You suggest that this is where we diverge. If that is so I think that the divergence springs from a difference in our assessment of Nasser's plans and intentions. May I set out our view of the position.

In the nineteen-thirties Hitler established his position by a series of carefully planned movements. These began with occupation of the Rhineland and were followed by successive acts of aggression against Austria, Czechoslovakia, Poland and the West. His actions were tolerated and excused by the majority of the population of Western Europe. It was argued either that Hitler had committed no act of aggression against anyone, or that he was entitled to do what he liked in his own territory, or that it was impossible to prove that he had any ulterior designs, or that the Covenant of the League of Nations did not entitle us to use force and that it would be wiser to wait until he did commit an act of aggression.

In more recent years Russia has attempted similar tactics. The blockade of Berlin was to have been the opening move in a campaign designed at least to deprive the Western powers of their whole position in Germany. On this occasion we fortunately reacted at once with the result that the Russian design was never unfolded. But I am sure that you would agree that it would be wrong to infer from this circumstance that no Russian design existed.

Similarly the seizure of the Suez Canal is, we are convinced, the opening gambit in a planned campaign designed by Nasser to expel all Western influence and interests from Arab countries. He believes that if he can get away with this, and if he can successfully defy eighteen nations, his prestige in Arabia will be so great that he will be able to mount revolutions of young officers in Saudi Arabia, Jordan, Syria and Iraq. (We know that he is already preparing a revolution in Iraq, which is the most stable and progressive.) These new Governments will in effect be Egyptian satellites if not Russian ones. They will have to place their united oil resources under the control of a united Arabia led by Egypt and under Russian influence. When that moment comes Nasser can deny oil to Western Europe and we here shall all be at his mercy.

There are some who doubt whether Saudi Arabia, Iraq and Kuwait will be prepared even for a time to sacrifice their oil revenues for the sake of Nasser's ambitions. But if we place ourselves in their position I think the dangers are clear. If Nasser says to them, "I have nationalized the Suez Canal. I have successfully defied eighteen powerful nations including the United States, I have defied the whole of the United Nations in the matter of the Israel blockade, I have expropriated all Western property. Trust me and withhold oil from Western Europe. Within six months or a year, the continent of Europe will be on its knees before you," will the Arabs not be prepared to follow this lead? Can we rely on them to be more sensible than were the Germans? Even if the Arabs eventually fall apart again as they did after the early Caliphs, the damage will have been done meanwhile.

In short we are convinced that if Nasser is allowed to defy the eighteen nations it will be a matter of months before revolution breaks out in the oil-bearing countries and the West is wholly deprived of Middle Eastern oil. In this belief we are fortified by the advice of friendly leaders in the Middle East.

The Iraqis are the most insistent in their warnings; both Nuri and the Crown Prince have spoken to us several times of the consequences of Nasser succeeding in his grab. They would be swept away.

[I then gave the President an account of three other warnings which we had received, each from a different Middle Eastern country; as the authors of these warnings are still alive, I do not propose to make their names public.]

The difference which separates us to-day [my message continued] appears to be a difference of assessment of Nasser's plans and intentions and of the consequences in the Middle East of military action against him.

You may feel that even if we are right it would be better to wait until Nasser has unmistakably unveiled his intentions. But this was the argument which prevailed in 1936 and which we both rejected in 1948. Admittedly there are risks in the use of force against Egypt now. It is, however, clear that military intervention designed to reverse Nasser's revolutions in the whole continent would be a much more costly and difficult undertaking. I am very troubled, as it is, that if we do not reach a conclusion either way about the canal very soon one or other of these Eastern lands may be toppled at any moment by Nasser's revolutionary movements.

I agree with you that prolonged military operations as well as the denial of Middle East oil would place an immense strain on the economy of Western Europe. I can assure you that we are conscious of the burdens and perils attending military intervention. But if our assessment is correct, and if the only alternative is to allow Nasser's plans quietly to develop until this country and all Western Europe are held to ransom by Egypt acting at Russia's behest it seems to us that our duty is plain. We have many times led Europe in the fight for freedom. It would be an ignoble end to our long history if we accepted to perish by degrees.

★   ★   ★   ★   ★

Syria was one of the lands we were watching. Communist agitation was active there. The neighbouring Lebanon was small, but stoutly led by its President, Mr. Chamoun, whom I knew personally. Libya was another country where Nasser's agents were busy, and in Jordan elections were due whose outcome might result in closer association between that country and Egypt.

While we exchanged messages with Washington, we kept our eyes on Cairo. Our Ambassador held many conversations with Egyptian Ministers before Mr. Menzies arrived. He reminded them that only a few months earlier they had been speaking of an enlarged canal as a further link to strengthen relations between Egypt and the West. They had then told him that they would do nothing to infringe the rights of the old company. They had now changed all that. The Egyptians made no excuses; they waited to see what would happen.

Egypt was not seriously hit by the economic measures which a number of countries, including France and ourselves, had taken. Nasser was getting help from Communist countries, from uncommitted states and from India. Such sufferings as Egypt had so far experienced were falling upon the opponents of the dictatorship. This confirmed my scepticism about the effect of economic sanctions. It strengthened the need for speed in our diplomacy and in any possible military sequel.

The problem of the Suez Canal Company's staff gave us much trouble. Many of the pilots had wished to quit the service as soon as the canal had been nationalized, even though the Egyptian Government threatened to imprison them if they did not continue at work. The French and British Governments urged them to stay at their posts, first until the end of the London Conference and then until Mr. Menzies' mission was finished.

Despite our efforts, about sixty pilots had either left Egypt or failed to return from leave by early September. Only two-thirds of the original number were still on duty. A Swede who had made good his escape, declared:

> I have no intention of going back to Suez so long as the canal is under Egyptian administration, and the same applies to my sixty colleagues who are at present in Europe. . . . I have no confidence in the Egyptians. I was there during the days of terror in 1952. For my part I hope no sea-captains get caught on Nasser's hook.

Colonel Nasser himself told the American Ambassador at this time that if the pilots left, he would get others from elsewhere, if necessary from Russia. This he did. The replacements, drawn from many lands, did their job much better than the company or we had been led to expect.

Mr. Menzies and his committee had arrived in Cairo on September 3. His plan was to keep discussions with the Egyptians short. He presented Colonel Nasser with an *aide-mémoire* describing the London proposals, and explaining to him the spirit in which he and his colleagues were approaching their task. He kept the conversations strictly to the point in his determination to get an answer within a week. Mr. Menzies' *aide-mémoire* was cogent. In it he said:

> The nations for whom we speak . . . have a clear belief that, if the canal is to be maintained and developed as a waterway open to the use of vessels of all nations, it should be detached from politics, and the management of its operations should be placed on such a basis as to secure the maximum of international confidence and co-operation. . . . There is a long history of friendly relations with Egypt. . . . We have all welcomed Egypt's attainment of complete self-government and we would desire that anything done or proposed now should be regarded as containing no derogation from Egypt's sovereignty and national dignity. These two points of view were indeed clearly illustrated by the whole temper and tone of the discussions at the London Conference.

Mr. Menzies conducted his talks with customary candour and lack of cant. He said that his mission was to expound the London proposals and that he was not empowered to consider alternatives. His committee showed unity and gave him firm support. During the first talks with Nasser, Menzies felt that he had made a considerable impression. At their conclusion, in a private interview, Menzies warned Nasser that he would be mistaken if he supposed that the London Conference had ruled out the use of force. It had not addressed itself to that question. But France and Britain took a very serious view of the situation and had taken the precautions of which he was aware.

Nasser did not contest this, and Menzies left the meeting with some confidence, believing that the Egyptian Prime Minister had taken his warning to heart. Perhaps he had, but at this moment a stroke of bad luck befell us. Overnight came a statement from Mr. Eisenhower. He said, at a press conference: "We are determined to exhaust every possible, every feasible method of peaceful settlement." This was well enough, then he added in answer to a question asking him what he would do if Egypt refused the London proposals: "I am still very hopeful that the London proposals will be accepted; but the position of the United States is not to give up, even if we do run into obstacles." This sentence gave encouragement to Nasser, who did not need much, to raise those obstacles. The Egyptians began to feel it safe to say no. Such was the impression gained by Mr. Menzies.

Thinking aloud about the next move is a dangerous practice. It almost inevitably destroys the chances of success for the present move. It is also a process which causes acute embarrassment to friends. Often in these weeks we longed for the crisp "No comment," so firm an ally of American diplomacy in the past. Alas, it never came.

This was not the first occasion upon which we had suffered from episodes of this kind. Already, while Mr. Menzies was on his way to Egypt, Mr. Dulles, in answer to a question from the press, had said that the canal was not of primary importance to the United States. No doubt he hoped thus to reassure American opinion; he also reassured Nasser.

Two days were spent by Nasser in reflection on the eighteen-power proposals and on the impression he had derived from the United States. Then he said no. He said that the idea of insulating the canal from politics was unreal, it could never be sundered from Egypt's political life. He also talked of sovereignty and declared several times that an international authority would mean "the restoration of collective colonialism."

All the members of the committee responded promptly to the taunt of colonialism. The Ethiopian, Iranian, and Swedish members were outspoken in rejecting it as ridiculous. Mr. Henderson joined them by pointing to the anti-colonial record of the United States. The Egyptians put forward no counter-proposals to Mr.

Menzies and his committee. They confined themselves to vague generalities. There was nothing to be gained by discussing these and Mr. Menzies held firmly to the position that he was not authorized to do so. He carried his colleagues with him.

The committee's next step was to agree upon the terms of a letter to Nasser, recounting the course of the conversations and drawing attention to the principle of international authority on which these had broken down. The letter stressed the sovereign position which Egypt would continue to hold under the London proposals. It stated:

> Our discussions have been conducted in an atmosphere of courteous frankness and responsibility. But they have, in our opinion, disclosed deep differences of approach and principle which it seems clear that no repetition of debate can affect. . . . The whole essence of what we have put forward is (to use a homely illustration) that, Egypt's position as the landlord of the canal being completely accepted, she should proceed by international agreement to install a tenant so constituted that the future of the canal would be satisfactory both to its owners and to those many nations who use it. We believe, as we have pointed out, that it cannot seriously be maintained that when a landlord grants a lease of premises that lease derogates from his ownership. . . . Indeed, as the "tenant" in this analogy would be a body which includes Egypt herself, the position of Egypt would be even stronger.

The committee finished their work on September 9. They then dispersed and Mr. Menzies flew back to Australia by way of London and Washington. On arrival in Melbourne, he sent me the following personal letter:

> You have about as difficult a task over Suez as mortal man ever had. I am sorry that we have not been able to get it solved for you in Cairo. Our report and, in particular, our *aide-mémoire* to Nasser will give a pretty fair picture of the arguments that we were using and of those we encountered. There are some aspects of this matter, however,

which no committee could officially mention but which I would like to put down for your personal assistance.

Egypt is not only a dictatorship but it has all the earmarks of a police state. The tapping of telephone lines, the installation of microphones, the creation of a vast body of security police — all these things are accepted as commonplace.

I was told that Nasser was a man of great personal charm who might beguile me into believing something foreign to my own thought. This is not so. He is in some ways quite a likeable fellow but so far from being charming he is rather *gauche*, with some irritating mannerisms, such as rolling his eyes up to the ceiling when he is talking to you and producing a quick, quite evanescent grin when he can think of nothing else to do. I would say that he was a man of considerable but immature intelligence. He lacks training or experience in many of the things he is dealing with and is, therefore, awkward with them. He will occasionally use rather blustering expressions, but drops them very quickly if he finds them challenged in a good-humoured way. His logic does not travel very far; that is to say, he will produce a perfectly accurate major premise and sometimes an accurate minor premise, but his deduction will be astonishing. I will give you a powerful example of this which I think you might usefully have in mind. I will put it in the form of a substantially verbatim account of one passage in one of the arguments which I had with him.

NASSER: You say in your proposals that you are "concerned by the grave situation regarding the Suez Canal." I agree that there is. But who created it? We didn't create it, for all we did was to nationalize the Suez Canal Company and this was a matter which we had a perfect legal right to do. Therefore that action of ours could not have created the grave situation. It was the subsequent threats of Great Britain and France which created the grave situation.

MENZIES: But don't you see that the critical atmosphere in the world began at the very moment that you nationalized? It was that announcement which brought me back from America to the United Kingdom. It was that announcement which took Dulles from the United States to London. It was that announcement which brought the representatives of twenty-two nations to London. What you are overlooking is that the actual thing you did was to repudiate (and I use that expression because plain language will be appreciated) a concession which had twelve years to run.

NASSER: But how could anybody complain about that, if it was within our power?

MENZIES: I don't concede it was within your power. In fact I think it was not. But can't you see that if your attitude is that merely because it was within your power you can repudiate a contract binding upon you, this, in one hit, destroys the confidence that the world has in your contractual word?

NASSER: I don't understand this. The concession would have expired in twelve years anyhow and then I suppose the same uproar would have occurred, if you are right.

MENZIES: Not at all. If you had not interfered with the concession, I have no doubt that the company itself would have quite soon begun negotiations with you for some future organization for the canal. But those negotiations would have been conducted in an atmosphere which was not one of crisis, and sensible and fair conclusions might well have been arrived at without the heated exchanges on such matters as "sovereignty."

NASSER: But this ignores the fact that we had the right to do what we did, and if we have the right to do something we can't understand how people can take exception to it.

This will explain the kind of logical mess which exists in his mind. It is just as if one said that, as the Parliament of the United Kingdom has power to pass any laws it thinks fit to pass, nobody should ever be at liberty to complain about its law, to resent it, to seek to alter it.

With frightful reiteration he kept coming back to the slogans. Our proposal was "collective colonialism" which we were seeking to enforce; he constantly came back to "sovereignty"; to our desire for the "domination" of the canal; to our proposed "seizure" of the canal. I exhausted my energy and almost wore out my patience in explaining to him that he was surely underestimating his own significance as the political head of Egypt. What we were seeking was *an agreement;* and any scheme for the actual control and management of the operations of the canal, while leaving Egypt's sovereign rights untouched, was the kind of working arrangement which was an exercise of sovereignty and not a derogation from it, and could be described as "domination" or "seizure" only if he made his agreement under actual duress.

I pointed out that many countries in the world had willingly granted concessions to foreign enterprises to explore and develop national resources, and that so far from thinking that these represented foreign domination, the nations granting such concessions granted them willingly because they were convinced that their own resources and position would be thereby strengthened. To this he replied that he saw no analogy, because the grantees of these concessions remain entirely subject to national law (and, therefore, no doubt could have their concessions revoked at will).

Mr. Menzies had not won success, though he had deserved it. Thanks to his efforts, and those of his committee, the difference which was revealed was on clearly defined issues.

5

THE USERS' CLUB
September 10–17

Illegality of Nasser's seizure — American doubts — Mr. Dulles
discourages appeal to Security Council — We confer with French
Ministers on September 10 — Their loyalty and understanding —
Details of Users' Club — Its possibilities — American proposals on
oil supplies — Our doubts about the Users' Club — Our decision
— Debate in the House of Commons — Criticism of Users' Club
— Effect of Mr. Dulles' statement — I wind up the debate —
Nasser rejects the Users' Club — A letter from Marshal Bulganin
— My reply

ON SEPTEMBER 7, when Mr. Menzies' talks in Cairo broke down,
we informed Washington that we might, within twenty-four hours,
wish to announce our decision to go to the Security Council.
News of our plans had already begun to appear in the press,
though in garbled form. At the same time, our ambassadors
and high commissioners accredited to the eighteen powers were
asked to take action on the refusal we now expected from Egypt.
We wished as many governments as possible to state publicly
that they did not consider the nationalization of the canal to be
valid, that they did not recognize the new Egyptian authority
and that they would deny it transit dues.

There was a strong legal argument to advance, based upon the
close link between the Convention of 1888 and the Concession of
the Suez Canal Company. The Concession was the earlier and had
been granted in 1856 by the Khedive of Egypt, with a life of
ninety-nine years after the opening of the canal to navigation.
It was not due to terminate until 1968. The Sultan of Turkey
in 1866 had issued an Imperial Firman sanctioning the Khedive's
concession. The Convention of 1888 had set out to "guarantee at

all times and for all powers the free use of the Suez Maritime Canal and thus to complete the system under which navigation of this canal had been placed" by the Imperial Firman.

It was implicit in the Convention that the operation of the canal should not be entrusted to any single power. The canal had an international character, commonly assumed in the various agreements made between the Canal Company and the Egyptian Government. Egypt had never hitherto dissented from this view. Moreover, as a member of the United Nations, she had undertaken "to establish conditions under which justice and respect for obligations arising from treaties and other sources of international law can be maintained." By nationalization, by peremptorily ending the concession, the Egyptian Government had destroyed all assurance that the rights guaranteed by the Convention to users of the canal would continue to be enjoyed. Nasser had himself stated that he intended to use the canal revenues to build the Aswan Dam. This was clearly illegal.

Here were good grounds for our stand, in terms of law, which we wished to proclaim formally and in public. The United States Government, however, now took a different view, although at the first London Conference they had expressed no such doubts. They questioned our basis in law. They were opposed to any immediate pronouncement. They also let us know that they would not join in sponsoring the draft Franco-British resolution to the Security Council. What is more, they would not even support it. As Mr. Dulles expressed it to our Ambassador on September 7, "he would find it very difficult to go along with the operation in its present form." He accused us of trying to enlist the aid of the Security Council to force a new treaty on Egypt which would bestow new rights on the users of the canal. In fact, we simply wished to reaffirm old rights and make certain that they would be observed.

The French and ourselves were determined that an appeal to the United Nations must be firmly based on two conditions. First, that the United States and our two countries should agree in advance not to accept any solution which fell short of the eighteen-power proposals. Secondly, that together we should resist any move by less friendly powers to limit our freedom of action. The United

States Government now told us that they could not be bound in advance by either of these conditions. This was extraordinary, since the United States Government had themselves tabled the proposals which the eighteen powers had endorsed.

Mr. Dulles urged us, for the time being, merely to inform the Security Council of the situation by letter and ask for no action. One of the French leaders described this procedure contemptuously as "leaving a visiting card." He saw no harm in it, but no good either. Given the lack of American support for a stronger move, we were obliged to adopt it. Even then, the United States Government declined to add their signature to our letter. We were told that they did not wish to create an identity of interest, which might prove embarrassing to the French and ourselves.

We found the American response to our proposals disappointing and the Foreign Secretary said so. Our two countries, he told the United States Government on September 8, seemed farther apart in their thinking than at any time since the crisis began.

Mr. Lloyd expressed his grave anxiety at the present state of our consultations and urged the absolute necessity for effective action. Delay would be disastrous for a number of reasons. Every day Nasser was strengthening his hold on the canal. The Western powers would lose face unless they could react clearly and speedily to his rejection of the eighteen-power proposals, which now seemed certain. Meanwhile the friendly Arab states were in great and ever-increasing peril.

Her Majesty's Government, Mr. Selwyn Lloyd said, did not believe that the canal issue could be separated from the general Egyptian menace to the friendly governments of the Muslim world. At that moment, the Foreign Secretary told Washington, we could not make out where the United States stood. They had poured cold water on our suggestions without so far putting forward any alternative.

Such was the position until September 10. That day we were concerting our ideas with the French Prime Minister and Foreign Minister, who had come to London. I was to have many other meetings with M. Mollet in the next few weeks. I always found him, as on this occasion, cool, resolute and reasonable. His convictions were firmly held but argued with calm. He understood that others could differ from him in equal good faith. We had met before we each became Prime Minister, but I had not known him as intimately as other leading French political figures. The times we lived through together were tense and tough. Our association could have been very difficult; it was not. I have never enjoyed more completely loyal understanding with any man. In the hours of strain there was never a harsh word, a reproach or a recrimination between us.

We knew that we were approaching a situation in which there was no good course, though some were less bad than others. We were eager for a solution by negotiation, even when we were least hopeful of one. Whatever the cost, we were determined not just to drift. Those who have held high responsibility know how enervating that temptation is, and the higher the responsibility the more persuasive it becomes. We both felt this many times, but we knew that to yield to it was to make disaster certain, and in the worst conditions. We also knew that if we took positive action at any time in these months, it would make us many enemies.

It is the nature of things that those who clamour for strong action are often the first to condemn it when it is taken. This they do on the specious pretext that the intention is right, but the circumstances or the execution are wrong. They excuse themselves by demanding a perfection into which events are not malleable. We knew, too, that one of the consequences of action is that no one can finally determine what would have been the consequences of inaction. The immediate results can be criticized, the worse results that would have befallen can be ignored or shrugged off.

All these things we knew and something else as well. A Minister's final responsibility is to his own convictions, sharpened by his own experience.

While M. Mollet and M. Pineau were with us, the latest formulation of Mr. Dulles' thought on the proposed Users' Club arrived. We at once turned our minds to this and studied it together. The telegrams which reached us showed that the United States Government had now worked out their scheme in some detail. They also made plain that they regarded the scheme as the answer to our immediate requirements.

The American draft, describing the purposes of the club, emphasized co-operation between users and its legal and historical justification. "It has become appropriate and necessary," the draft ran, "that the Governments of the users should organize as among themselves for the most effective possible enjoyment of the rights of passage given by the 1888 Convention." These were unexceptionable words, so long as action was taken at once. The proposed association would "promote safe, orderly, efficient and economical transit of member-controlled vessels" through the canal. Membership would include, it was hoped, all the eighteen powers and such others as might qualify by virtue of their pattern of trade and tonnage. The club would have its headquarters in Rome and be governed by an elected executive group. In the first instance, this body might consist of nations which had been represented on Mr. Menzies' committee. This was agreeable to us, provided that the principal users of the canal, the French and ourselves, were added to the group.

The association was to appoint an administrator to supervise the passage of its members' ships. He was to co-operate with Egypt, in so far as co-operation was forthcoming, on matters of pilotage, scheduling, signalling and the manipulation of bridges. Full use was to be made of the pilots and technical staff of the old Suez Canal Company, and all those still at their posts were to be encouraged to remain there. Not much time was left, since most of the pilots and staff were at the end of their tether and eager for release, unless they could transfer their services to the Users' Club at once.

If Egypt made difficulties, the administrator was to carry out his task from two ships stationed at either end of the canal, which would serve as his marshalling centres. He was to collect dues from all ships convoyed under the auspices of the club, at rates to be determined by it, without profit to any member. Egypt was to be compensated for the facilities she afforded, but the main purpose of collecting dues was to defray the expenses of the association.

Despite the various practical drawbacks which were evident in it, even as outlined to us, this appeared to the United Kingdom Government to be a possible interim scheme. We proposed only a few modifications. We urged that the Users' Club should set up immediately a separate bank account, into which dues would be paid. We also asked the United States to take steps to see that all American-owned ships, whatever flag they flew, should comply. We were to be disappointed on both points.

The French Ministers viewed the plan with misgiving from the start. They did not particularly mind the delay in appealing to the Security Council, since public opinion in France had little confidence anyway in the efficacy of the United Nations. But they were concerned at Mr. Dulles' general procrastination in dealing with the canal, and they suspected that the Users' Club was a device to prevent Britain and France from bringing matters to a head with Nasser. M. Pineau frankly regarded further talk with the United States Government about the Users' Club as a waste of time. We were ourselves perturbed at the extent to which successive American modifications had already watered down the original plan. On the other hand, it was still presented to us by Mr. Dulles in one of the messages we received that day as something that "Egypt would like much less" than the eighteen-power proposals which Nasser had rejected, Dulles' argument being that the Egyptians, having refused these, could not expect such good terms again. The plan would also provide a means of withholding the canal dues. Both of these were capital considerations for us and without them we would not have contemplated the scheme. Above all, it provided a means of working with the United States. I was prepared to lean over backwards to achieve this.

For these reasons, and with the reluctant agreement of the French Ministers, we accepted the Users' Club. We tried to make it work in the weeks that followed, only to find that the vital assurances on which the offer rested did not exist in substance at all. Her Majesty's Government fell in with the idea in order to keep unity with the United States. It was to lose us unity in the House of Commons. The paradox was that the United States Government made this lack of unity at home an increasing reproach against us.

Putting Mr. Dulles' plan into effect was to be accompanied, he told us, by two further prongs of attack. One prong was provided by the financial measures which the French and ourselves had already taken, but in respect of which the United States continued to lag behind. The other prong was the rerouting of oil traffic. The object of this, in American eyes, was to decrease our dependence upon the canal. Much thought had been given to this proposal by the State Department, in conjunction with the American oil companies. It was an ambitious plan and meant sending round the Cape of Good Hope about half of the one and a half million barrels of oil a day which usually passed through the canal. The other half of the normal Western consumption of canal-borne oil was to be obtained from expanded production in the Gulf of Mexico and the Caribbean.

The plan had two unwelcome implications for us. First, friendly countries in the Middle East would have to be asked, while this emergency lasted, to cut back their oil production, though their stability largely depended on its revenues. Second, Britain would have to spend many dollars to replace her supplies by Gulf and Caribbean oil. Even if we were granted a loan from the Export-Import Bank to finance this oil transaction, as had been promised, that loan would eventually have to be repaid in dollars with interest. Since we and the French were not paying dues to Nasser, and did not intend to do so, to send our oil round the Cape would injure us more than Nasser. The Cabinet decided against this project as an immediate means of pressure upon Egypt.

Our meeting with the French Ministers in London was concluded on September 11. In the next forty-eight hours a sheaf of telegrams passed between ourselves, Washington and Paris, which seemed to clarify the Users' Club idea. The form and the actual words in which it should be announced were carefully agreed between us.

The President was asked at a press conference on September 11 whether the United States would back France and Britain, should these countries be obliged to resort to force. He replied by a reference to his constitutional powers as United States Commander-in-Chief:

> I don't know exactly what you mean by backing them. As you know, this country will not go to war ever while I am occupying my present post unless the Congress is called into session and Congress declares such a war. And the only exception to that would be in the case of unexpected and unwarranted attack on this nation, where self-defence itself would dictate some quick response while you call Congress into action.

A fair comment on this statement in the international context of the time was made by a correspondent at Mr. Dulles' conference two days later. He asked the Secretary of State: "With the United States announcing in advance that it will not use force, and Soviet Russia backing Egypt with its propaganda, does not that leave all the trump cards in Nasser's hands?"

The decision whether to endorse the American users' plan was one of the most crucial we had to face during the whole Suez crisis. Its consequences were far-reaching. If we had told the United States Government that we did not consider the Users' Club a workable proposition and that we preferred to go direct to the Security Council in support of the kind of resolution we had already shown them, and they had declined to approve, we would, I suppose, have forfeited, for the time being at least, something of their goodwill. On the other hand, we would have avoided the long and dismal trail of negotiation in which we became involved in an effort to set up this Users' Club. I have to bear a large part of the responsibility for this decision myself. A number of my colleagues were uneasy, some because they doubted whether the scheme could be made to work, others because they doubted whether the United States Government were in earnest in the assurances they had given and would see the scheme through. Disturbed as I had been by some recent events, I was still in a temper to endorse an American initiative which had a hope of success, and take a chance upon it. Close co-operation with the United States had been a guiding principle throughout my political life. On this account I had differed gravely from Mr. Chamberlain in 1938, and later, during the war, had accepted decisions which, on a cold calculation, I would not have endorsed.

I believed in our common interest and I had no thought of abandoning this conviction now. If the benefit of the doubt had to be given, I would give it. The Government took their decision on the evening of September 11, my colleagues concurring with varying degrees of confidence.

Looking back over the run of events, I think that I probably underestimated the parliamentary consequences of the action I was going to advocate in the House of Commons. If I did, it was because I was eager to maintain an Anglo-American front on this issue of respect for agreements, which must decide all our futures. On another count, I now think that this decision on the Users' Club may have been wrong. The future of the canal was, among the great powers, primarily our concern and that of the French; American interest was secondary. We might have done better to adhere to our own plan, refusing to be side-tracked from it, even by the new ideas of a powerful ally, however strongly urged upon us. The United States might or might not have given us full support at the United Nations. But we would have been acting in fulfilment of our conviction and would at least have been spared a disastrous chapter of disillusion.

The next morning I was busy with the speech I was to make in the House in a few hours' time, when the Foreign Secretary asked to see me. He told me that he had had a night of indifferent sleep, during which he had turned over and over again in his mind this question of the Users' Club. Should we go ahead, or should we not? On reflection he had come to the conclusion that we had better not. He felt convinced that the scheme was not really workable. He had come round to tell me so and to ask me whether I had had the same reflections. I was naturally a good deal shaken by the view now expressed by the Foreign Secretary. I put aside the notes for the speech and we talked the matter over. Eventually we decided, with a full consciousness of the risks we were taking, that we should go on with the policy which the Cabinet had decided upon the night before.

On September 12 I opened the Suez debate in the House of Commons. As I took my seat the Chief Whip, Mr. Heath, murmured to me, "There will be no division if you announce that you are going immediately to the United Nations." This, in view of our acceptance of the Users' Club, I could not do. I reminded the House that our last debate five weeks earlier

> ... had revealed a remarkable measure of unanimity of opinion in the House and in the country. ... There was wide acceptance of the proposition that to prevent any interference with the free use of the canal, and to maintain the efficiency of its operation, the canal should be placed under an international system designed to secure the rights of the users. There was

also acceptance of the view that the precautionary military measures taken by the Government had been justified. . . . Nothing which the Government have done since that debate took place has in any way changed the policy which the Foreign Secretary and I described in our speeches on that occasion.

Having rehearsed the arguments for restoring an international character to the canal, I then gave an account of the London Conference, the Menzies mission and the Egyptian rejection of the offer which it carried. Mr. Menzies was himself in the gallery.

I told the House that we had informed the President of the Security Council of the situation and we certainly did not exclude referring the dispute to the United Nations, if it became necessary. But we were setting up immediately a Suez Canal Users' Association, which I then described, concluding in the exact words agreed upon with the United States and French Governments:

> I must make it clear that if the Egyptian Government should seek to interfere with the operations of the association, or refuse to extend to it the essential minimum of co-operation, then that Government will once more be in breach of the Convention of 1888. In that event, Her Majesty's Government and others concerned will be free to take such further steps as seem to be required either through the United Nations, or by other means for the assertion of their rights.

I was at once interrupted with a request to explain the meaning of these words. This I declined to do, the words having been deliberately chosen by the three powers.

Sir Robert Boothby wound up the debate on that evening in words which expressed my own thoughts. He said:

> We went through all this in the nineteen-thirties, and it was not much fun. Shameless appeasement does not really pay. . . .
> As I listened to the Prime Minister this afternoon, I thought of what Nasser had been saying about what he was going to do to establish an Arab Empire from Morocco to the Persian

Gulf, and how he was going to eliminate Israel altogether. That is all in his speeches, and in a horrible little book called *A Philosophy of Revolution,* which is like a potted edition of *Mein Kampf.* As I heard the Prime Minister speaking, I said to myself, "Well, thank goodness, at any rate we shall not have to go through all that again," and we shall not.

Though there were some difficult moments on the first day of the debate and some encouraging shouts of "provocation" and "resign," all went reasonably well. On the morning of the following day, M. Mollet made his parallel statement in Paris in the agreed terms. This aroused no critical comment. Mr. Dulles did the same in Washington, but in answer to questions afterwards, he made a remark which caught world-wide attention and entirely submerged the identity of our original statements. "We do not intend," he said, "to shoot our way through. It may be we have the right to do it but we don't intend to do it as far as the United States is concerned." The alternative for the United States, he admitted, was to "send our vessels round the Cape." On being asked whether there was a conflict between British and American views on this point, Mr. Dulles replied:

> I think that each nation has to decide for itself what action it will have to take to defend and if possible realize its rights which it believes it has as a matter of treaty. I do not recall just exactly what Sir Anthony Eden said on this point. I did not get the impression that there was any undertaking or pledge given by him to shoot their way through the canal.

It would be hard to imagine a statement more likely to cause the maximum allied disunity and disarray. The Americans having themselves volunteered that the new arrangements would be less acceptable to the Egyptians than the eighteen-power proposals, Mr. Dulles proceeded to make plain at this juncture that the United States did not intend to use force, even though it had the right to do so. The words were an advertisement to Nasser that he could reject the project with impunity. We had never been told that a statement of this kind was to accompany the announcement of the

Users' Club. Had we known that they were to be used as an accompaniment to the American announcement, we would never have endorsed it. To us, the emphasis had been that the Egyptians, having rejected reasonable eighteen-power proposals, could not expect to do as well. To the public, the emphasis now was that, whatever happened, the Egyptians had nothing to fear. The Users' Club was an American project to which we had conformed. We were all three in agreement, even to the actual words of the announcement. Yet here was the spokesman of the United States saying that each nation must decide for itself and expressing himself as unable to recall what the spokesman of a principal ally had said. Such cynicism towards allies destroys true partnership. It leaves only the choice of parting, or a master and vassal relationship in foreign policy.

In the House I had, in fact, said nothing to suggest that we would shoot our way through. I had used the formula agreed upon with the United States Government, which M. Mollet had also used, that we would seek our rights "through the United Nations or by any other means." This left the course of future action deliberately vague so as to strengthen pressure on behalf of the Users' Club. The whole purpose of the Users' Club had been, by a display of unity in association with the United States, to avoid having recourse to force. American torpedoing of their own plan on the first day of launching it left no alternative but to use force or acquiesce in Nasser's triumph.

Mr. Dulles' words, as headlined in the press, helped to create a considerable storm on the second day of our debate. This was not allayed by the speech of a former Conservative Attorney-General, Sir Lionel Heald, in which he maintained that force could not be used unless we first went to the United Nations. I was asked to say that the Government endorsed this. I could not do so. I could not foretell what emergency might arise, as had occurred in Korea and was to occur later in the Lebanon and Jordan. Moreover, the French had asked us not to undertake publicly that we would go to the United Nations at this moment, just as the Users' Club was being formed. They felt, quite rightly, that the Egyptian Government would then be able to ignore the club, arguing that, as we were going to the United Nations, they would make their case there. Nor could I explain that we were taking account of the

United States wishes in deferring our approach to the United Nations.

In our Parliament, the Government spokesman on foreign affairs is often hampered by being unable to tell the whole story of the reasons for the policy he advocates publicly in debate. This is a greater embarrassment in Britain, for instance, than in the United States, where neither the President nor the Secretary of State is called upon publicly to explain his attitude to Congress. It is true that they have to face press conferences from time to time, but these are neither so closely reasoned nor have as much authority as debate in Parliament.

In France the use of all-party committees reduces the embarassment, for though there may be leakages there is no official reporting, and more information can be given. This also applies to the powerful Foreign Relations Committee of the United States Senate.

In my winding-up speech, amidst much interruption, I said:

> I want to deal with the question: Would Her Majesty's Government give a pledge not to use force except after reference to the Security Council? If such a pledge or guarantee is to be absolute, then neither I nor any British Minister standing at this Box could give it. No one can possibly tell what will be Colonel Nasser's action, either in the canal or in Egypt.
>
> Nevertheless, I will give this reply, which is as far as any Government can go: it would certainly be our intention, if circumstances allowed, or in other words, except in an emergency, to refer a matter of that kind to the Security Council.

The Government hoped they had proved the strength of their case, while retaining essential powers and doing what they could to hold the alliance together. In the division we had a majority of seventy, which was satisfactory.

The *Star* newspaper, generally liberal in its views, printed a leading article on the evening of the 12th approving the Users' Club. "Unless Nasser is quite regardless of his country's interest," it said, "and is merely a power-crazed dictator, he must surely agree to negotiate on the basis of this Western plan." However, members of the Opposition in the debate, while endorsing the broad aims of the plan, denounced some important aspects of it as provocative. They insisted that it would be a provocation towards Egypt for the Users' Association to employ its own pilots and to collect its own dues. They did not explain what effective purpose the club would serve if it did not do this.

Our own shipowners, whom the Minister of Transport frequently consulted, took the practical view that the club would be of no value unless it actively managed the transit of the canal, as Mr. Dulles' original proposal had provided.

We applied ourselves now to the next immediate step. There was a danger that shipping would pile up at either end of the canal because the pilots could no longer be held at their posts under the Egyptian authority. The users' agency must begin its work with all speed, otherwise it would lose its customers. Some would divert their ships around the Cape, while others might be tempted to reach a compromise with Nasser. The British shipping industry urged us to ask the United States to request Egypt for minimum facilities forthwith on behalf of the agency. This approach would be made in the spirit of the 1888 Convention and on the basis of the agency's willingness to co-operate with Egypt.

Any hopes we entertained of this suggestion were at once destroyed by the Egyptian reaction to the users' plan. Colonel Nasser made a speech on September 15 in which he accused the eighteen powers of "international thuggery and imperialism." He declared that "not only the Egyptian Government but also the whole of the Egyptian people will resist any attempt on the part of any nation or group of nations to have an international body exercise Egypt's sovereign rights." He described the Suez Canal Users' Association as an "association for waging war," and flatly announced that he would resist force with force. After the assurances volunteered by Mr. Dulles, this bravado was both safe and popular.

The association for waging war was meanwhile being peacefully prepared. Invitations had been sent out on September 14 to the eighteen powers for another meeting in London to consider the report of the Menzies' mission, to take note of the Egyptian memorandum of refusal and to discuss arrangements for the Users' Club. Thus the stage was set for the second London Conference.

★   ★   ★   ★   ★

While we were debating our policy at Westminster and concerting plans for the Users' Club, the Russians, who had for some time been silent on the subject of Suez, made a new move. Marshal Bulganin wrote me a long letter. He went out of his way to deny reports that the Soviet Government were inciting Egypt. Far from it, he maintained, Russia was eager to contribute to a peaceful settlement with due regard to the interests of all the states concerned. Nevertheless, Russia stood by Egypt's side. How could the Soviet Union, Marshal Bulganin asked, not treat favourably Egypt's position when she was defending her sovereignty and her national territory? He then accused France and Britain of threatening Egypt's inalienable rights with the use of force and spoke of official declarations of the readiness of Britain and France, on the pretext of defending their interests, to lead their forces on to Egyptian territory and infringe Egypt's territorial integrity and inviolability.

I pointed out in my reply to Moscow on September 17 that no such declarations had ever been made. On the contrary, we had publicly stated many times that our aim was to seek a peaceful solution. I told the Soviet Premier of the successive steps we had taken to secure this. As to our military measures, which he criticized, I added:

I must tell you frankly that these precautionary military measures are fully justified by the circumstances. In the first place the ruler of Egypt is a militarist who glories in the fact. In his book, for example, he says "Throughout my life I have had faith in militarism." Secondly, Colonel Nasser not only preaches militarism but employs it. Thus the premises of the Universal Suez Canal Company were occupied by troops, its assets were forcibly seized and the foreign employees of the company were threatened. This act of force which has created a state of tension in the Middle East has not yet evoked any expression of disapproval on the part of the Soviet Government.

Finally I reminded Marshal Bulganin that:

In 1946 the Soviet Government proclaimed their support for the international control of the canal. That is what we seek and it is of course fully consistent both with Egypt's sovereignty and with the Charter of the United Nations.

A fortnight went by before Marshal Bulganin wrote again. By then he had critical views to express on the Suez Canal Users' Association. So had we, but from a different standpoint.

6

THE UNITED NATIONS
September 19–October 13

American reluctance to withhold dues — Suez Canal Users' Association set up — Indian opinion — Deterioration of our position in Middle East — France and United Kingdom decide to appeal to the Security Council — Mr. Macmillan's visit to Washington — Mr. Menzies' speech — Mr. Selwyn Lloyd and I meet French Ministers in Paris — Some thoughts on U.N.O. — Anglo-French decisions announced — Marshal Bulganin's objections — My telegram to President Eisenhower — America and "colonialism" — Users' Association meets — Mr. Krishna Menon's views — Mr. Dulles and Mr. Selwyn Lloyd — The Security Council — Russia uses the veto

THE SECOND London Conference was convened to meet on September 19 with the Foreign Secretary once again in the chair. In the meantime, the Egyptians were handling the traffic of ships through the canal by various expedients. The remaining pilots of the old company were working overtime and new ones were being recruited from all over the world. Russia, Yugoslavia and the United States were among the contributors. An early breakdown in the operation of the canal, which had been one of our fears, was not now expected by our shipping advisers. This in its turn had certain consequences.

One of the main purposes of the Users' club in its original form had been to convoy the ships of its members through the canal if the Egyptians refused or proved unable to do so. The second contingency was now unlikely to arise. Should this modify the object of the club, and if so how? Obviously it was all the more important that the agency should now withhold the dues from Egypt until a general settlement was reached, and that this should be set forth clearly and accepted by as many maritime powers as possible. The British draft declaration, which was to be considered at the Conference, therefore firmly proposed that the Suez Canal Users' Association should:

> . . . hold in trust the surplus revenues accruing from the pay-ment of canal dues to the association as a fund for allocation in accordance with such permanent arrangements as may be made for the operation of the Suez Canal.

The French were equally strong on this point and judged the issue with admirable clarity. They held that we must persuade the countries, representing at least 80 per cent of the traffic passing through the canal, either to join the new association or at least to deny dues to Egypt. This was the only sure weapon, short of force, which we could bring to bear on Colonel Nasser. If we did not use it effectively, the world would clearly see that he had got away with his prize. All the consequences in Asia and Africa, forecast by ourselves and the French two months earlier, would begin to come to pass.

The American delegation at the second London Conference were less precise in their expressions. Mr. Dulles in his opening speech stated:

> Membership of the association would not involve the as-sumption by any member of any obligation. It would however be hoped that members of the association would voluntarily take such action with respect to their ships and the payment of canal dues as would facilitate the work of the association and build up its prestige and authority, and consequently its ability to serve.

This was a further weakening of the Users' Club. An organization towards which members had no obligations could hardly be ex-pected to show greater firmness than the eighteen-power proposals. Yet this was the basis on which the Users' Club had been traded to us.

After debate, the Conference issued a statement on September 21 reaffirming its belief in the reasonableness of the eighteen-power proposals as presented to Egypt by Mr. Menzies' committee. These, it declared, "still offer a fair basis for a peaceful solution of the Suez Canal problem." It also published a declaration proposing the setting up of the Suez Canal Users' Association, to which Governments represented at the Conference were invited to adhere.

In the main, this document followed the lines already agreed upon in three-power talks between Britain, France and the United States. But the British draft had been considerably modified in the course of negotiation. The clause defining the purpose of the Suez Canal Users' Association on dues now read as follows:

> . . . to receive, hold and disburse the revenues accruing from dues and other sums which any user of the canal may pay to the association without prejudice to existing rights, pending a final settlement.

There were pitfalls in this which later became apparent. The words "may pay" did not commit the subscribing countries to withholding dues from Egypt. Moreover, the word "disburse" would allow the association to hand over to Egypt any proportion it chose of the dues it collected.

At the time, we accepted the assurances given us by the United States delegation. They declared their Government ready to take action to prevent payment to Egypt. They could not, however, compel their shipowners to pay to the new association. Nor, we acknowledged, could we. But Britain and other countries were already denying dues to Egypt, whereas the United States was not. It was agreed that once the association had been constituted, had set up a separate bank account, and made some interim arrangement with the former Canal Company, the voluntary consent of shipowners to pay to the Users' Club, and the Users' Club only, should be sought and obtained. The shipowners were likely to work closely together so long as there was no discrimination between them.

This was the best that our delegation, and those who thought like us, could get at the second London Conference. The declaration was undoubtedly marked by some ambiguity and it had a cool, though not unfavourable, public reception. The results could be made effective if the machinery of the association was established at once and set to work in the way that the French and ourselves wanted, for which we thought we had United States' backing. It became clear to us only gradually that the American conception of the association was now evolving so fast that it would end as an agency for collecting dues for Nasser. Perhaps this was not clear to the United States delegation themselves at the time.

★ ★ ★ ★ ★

From the start, the Suez crisis was never a problem between Egypt and two, or even three, powers only: it concerned a very large part of the world. We realized that the repercussions of the crisis ranged wide and we naturally took heed of the advice offered.

The Indian Government, for instance, were constantly urging a negotiated settlement upon us. As we repeatedly explained to them, this was what we were seeking. This had been our aim in Korea, in Indo-China, in Trieste and in Iran, and we had gained it in all cases, sometimes with Indian help. We had no need to be ashamed of our record. Our difficulty now was that there could be no negotiation with Egypt unless there were some basis on which to negotiate. Mr. Menzies' committee had carried their fair proposals to Cairo, but Nasser had turned them down. Still we persevered in pursuit of an international solution, hence the Canal Users' Club. Meanwhile, Mr. Krishna Menon made a number of journeys between Cairo, London and eventually New York. Her Majesty's Government considered fully and at length all suggestions put to them by India, but Delhi did not then share our view of the importance of keeping international agreements in the interest of all nations, or of the need to restore them when broken.

The Egyptian Government showed no readiness to compromise, though they had at first been apprehensive of the Users' Association. They feared for a while that it might be really effective. Reassured on this point, they were content to stand pat.

Our information from the Middle East at this time confirmed the gloomy views we had been forming in London about the effects of the second London Conference. We had telegraphed for reports. Opinion in Cairo, we were told, had been encouraged to think that Nasser had succeeded, that the affair was practically over and that the threat of sanctions by the Western powers no longer existed. From elsewhere in the Middle East we learnt that the second London Conference had given an impression of far less firmness and unanimity than the first. Several Arab leaders were still perturbed by Nasser's declarations against the West and by his co-operation with Russia, and they were beginning to fear that time might be on his side. They mistrusted the forces that he represented, and the ambitions he entertained to enhance Egypt's position at the expense of her neighbours. If Nasser could not be obliged to accept some form of international control of the canal, he would have won the game.

The negotiations at the second London Conference, like those of the first, were handled exclusively by the Foreign Secretary, and he did all a man could do. He saw me often and we talked over the situation, but I took no part in the detailed work of the Conference. An attempt to do so could only have led to confusion. I did meet the principal delegates informally from time to time, often at Number 10, or with the Foreign Secretary at his house in Carlton Gardens. On one of these occasions, Mr. Dulles told us that Mr. Gaitskell had asked to see him, and Mr. Dulles inquired whether we had any objection to his doing so. I replied that we certainly had none.

It had always been a principle with me, since I became Foreign Secretary in 1935, to encourage meetings between foreign visitors and the Opposition or other leading figures in our country. I thought this useful on many counts and in no sense embarrassing to the Government. Any good embassy has contacts with the leading political figures in a free country, and the Government does itself no harm by encouraging what is likely to happen anyway. I used to invite Mr. Churchill, when he was out of office before the war, to meet visitors when they came to London. He told me long afterwards how much he had valued this, and I have no doubt that he did my visitors good too.

On an informal occasion Mr. Dulles spoke several times of the state of public opinion in Britain, which he maintained was not in support of the Government's policies over Suez. In the end I had to contest this myself. I still believe that American opinion underestimated the firm sentiments of our country at that time, and that this underestimate had a debilitating influence on their policies.

The United States Government were still reluctant to approach the United Nations, and we tried to meet them on this for a while longer. But the closing stage of the London Conference brought increasing pressure upon us to go to the Security Council. This was publicly voiced at the last meeting; privately the pressure became even stronger. Several representatives of the eighteen powers emphasized to the Foreign Secretary that it would be easier for them to join the Users' Association if an appeal to the United Nations were under way at the same time. This was repeatedly put to me at a luncheon which I gave on the last day to the leading delegates of New Zealand, Iran, Norway and Portugal, the Foreign Secretary being also present. They wanted us to help them to help us. My colleagues and I felt that they were right. The indifferent outcome of the Conference lent support to the pressure for further action by us. Finally the repercussions in the Middle East showed that if we waited longer our position would slip. Therefore, even though the United States still favoured delay, we felt we could no longer hold our hand.

The French were now ready for United Nations action, so was our own public opinion, and there was some danger that the Russians might anticipate us at the Security Council. Our plan was to inaugurate the Suez Canal Users' Association in London on October 1 and to ask for a debate at the Council on October 3, a full ten days after the conclusion of the London Conference. We held up our move for a day, so that Mr. Dulles might be informed in advance. He expressed himself unhappy at our timing, but he did not seek to dissuade us. The United States Government, however, would not sponsor our letter to the President of the Security Council, which we despatched on September 23, requesting that the Suez problem be placed on the Council's agenda. This was therefore an Anglo-French document.

The Chancellor of the Exchequer, Mr. Harold Macmillan, at this time paid a visit to Washington. He found the American attitude reassuring in a number of respects. He reported that the United States Government definitely undertook to make it unlawful for their ships to pay canal dues to Egypt. This was an important decision of principle if it were carried out, but, to have any real effect, American-owned ships flying the flags of Panama and Liberia must be included. Mr. Macmillan also told us that the American Administration was prepared to use its influence on these countries, but was doubtful of their co-operation, especially in the case of Panama, which the United States regarded as virtually lined up with Egypt. I was sure from past experience that, if the Americans had the will, they would find a way. The Chancellor of the Exchequer said that he found Washington confident that six months of economic pressure upon Nasser would accomplish all we wanted. On this point I was less hopeful, especially as nearly two months had passed since the canal had been seized and user nations were still as far as ever from applying any effective pressure, economic or otherwise.

Mr. Dulles now returned to a more resolute line about the use of force. In a television interview he said:

> I do believe that peace and justice and international law are two sides of the coin, and you can't always count on nations not using force unless there is some alternative which conforms to international peace and justice.

On September 25 Mr. Menzies, speaking in the Australian House of Representatives, surveyed the history of the Suez crisis in lucid and forcible language. In his conclusion he summed up the alternatives which faced us:

> First: Negotiation for a peaceful settlement by means of an honourable agreement. So far, we have tried this without success. Our failure, let me repeat and emphasize, has not been due to any unfairness or illiberality on our side, but to a dictatorial intransigence on the other. Should we continue to negotiate on a watered down basis in a spirit which says that any agreement is better than none? I cannot imagine anything more calculated to strengthen Colonel Nasser's hand or weaken our own.
>
> Second: Putting on of pressure by a co-operative effort on the part of user nations. Colonel Nasser must be brought to understand that his course of action is unprofitable to his country

and to his people and that he is abandoning the substance for the shadow. This is one of the great merits of the Users' Association now established by the second London Conference. The more canal revenue is diverted from the Egyptian Government the less will the Egyptian people believe that it pays to repudiate.

Third: Should the United Nations, by reason of veto, prove unable to direct any active course of positive action, we may find ourselves confronted by a choice which we cannot avoid making. I state this choice in stark terms:

(a) We can organize a full-blooded programme of economic sanctions against Egypt, or

(b) We can use force to restore international control of the canal, or

(c) We can have further negotiations, provided we do not abandon vital principles, or

(d) We can "call it a day," leave Egypt in command of the canal, and resign ourselves to the total collapse of our position and interests in the Middle East with all the implications for the economic strength and the industrial prosperity of the nations whose well being is vital to ours.

This, I believe, is a realistic analysis of the position.

It has been for me an astonishing experience to find that there are people who reject force out of hand, reject economic action on the ground that it is provocative and so, being opposed to action of either kind, are prepared to accept new tyranny with regret, perhaps, but without resistance. Such an attitude is so inconsistent with the vigorous tradition of our race that I cannot believe it commands any genuine and informed public support.

★   ★   ★   ★   ★

On September 26 the Foreign Secretary and I flew to Paris to consult the French Government. M. Mollet and M. Pineau were firm in their belief that we must stand by the eighteen-power proposals and resolutely oppose negotiation on any other grounds.

At this moment the United Nations was buzzing with projects for negotiating committees, some based on Indian proposals for compromise, others arising from attempts by Russia and her satellites to weaken the Western position, and still others from the readiness of the United Nations' Secretariat to devise means of negotiation at any price, whatever the cost to the sanctity of international agreements.

The United Nations was founded as a means to an end, to keep the peace. Armed conflict will not be avoided unless international agreements are respected. The chief purpose of the United Nations should be to uphold these engagements. We sought the best method by which the Security Council could do this. The League of Nations always set much store by the preservation of international agreements. There is less taste for this in the present United Nations, because some of the newly created states among its members still feel expansive. They have not yet understood that the rule of law is important to them as to others.

The United Nations is built round the Security Council, which should be its Cabinet, and the Assembly, which should be its forum for general discussion. These were to be its executive and debating components. The abuse of the veto in the Council has restricted the opportunities of the greater powers to exercise diplomatic leadership. As a result, totalitarian states can hope to get away with illegal acts, especially if they raise a clamour of anti-colonialism. Two standards of conduct are being evolved. One for the free nations who wish to be law-abiding. The other for Communist powers who see no incongruity in denying the authority of the United Nations to influence their own actions, while noisily demanding sanctions against others. Satan rebuking sin is a modest moralist beside them.

At our meeting in Paris, the French and ourselves were agreed that we must not allow our case to be submerged or manoeuvred into a backwater at the United Nations. I wanted to reassure our allies that we would not abandon our main objective, to remove the canal from the control of a single Government or man, and to secure enforceable guarantees for efficient navigation and maintenance. The French were sceptical about the United Nations and more sceptical still about the Users' Club, which had been even less well received by their public opinion than by ours. They felt that the American Administration was not fulfilling its promises, that some of the utterances of the President and Mr. Dulles would make the Russians believe that they could back Nasser with impunity, that the delay was allowing Nasser to build up an ever stronger position, thanks to a continuous supply of Russian arms. Finally, there was a danger of the whole Middle East coming under the dominance not so much of Egypt as of Russia. For all these reasons the French favoured action at an early date.

I had much sympathy with their views, but I was sure that we must first have recourse to the United Nations and do our best there. The Foreign Secretary and I undertook, however, that, if the Security Council showed itself incapable of maintaining international agreements, Britain would not stand aside and allow them to be flouted. If necessary we would be prepared to use whatever steps, including force, might be needed to re-establish respect for these obligations. The French Ministers agreed, though with some reluctance, to try out all the resources of the Security Council, on the strict understanding that there should be no abandonment of the original proposals approved by the eighteen powers. This was an attitude with which we were ourselves in full agreement. We issued the following statement at the end of our meeting:

> The primary purpose of this meeting, the importance of which has been greatly increased by the latest international developments, was to strengthen Franco-British solidarity in every respect. This result was fully achieved.
>
> In particular the Ministers defined their common position in the United Nations as a result of the recent British decision to place the question of the Suez Canal before the Security Council. They were fully agreed on the line to be followed by them in the forthcoming debate.
>
> The Ministers expressed their determination to continue, in respect of any further developments, the close co-operation which has characterized the policy of the two Governments since the beginning of the Suez Canal crisis.
>
> The Ministers then reviewed the course of the relationship between France and the United Kingdom in recent years, and reaffirmed the identity of aim and community of interests of the British and French peoples. To this end they agreed on

further studies designed to eliminate such minor points as may be outstanding between the two countries.

Finally they recalled the action taken by both countries since the war to strengthen political, military and economic co-operation between the nations of Western Europe. They agreed to pursue this policy and to study, in the European organizations to which they belong or by other means, the new forms which it might take.

They expressed their determination to ensure that constructive results should flow from these initiatives.

Further ministerial meetings between the two countries will be arranged as may be necessary.

On leaving Le Bourget, I added these words:

> We have during these two days had some very useful talks, in the course of which we have established a common Franco-British policy on many points. In particular, we have agreed upon a common action in the United Nations during the forthcoming debates. . . .
>
> This crisis, or rather the *coup de force* of Nasser, has not only endangered the economic interests of many nations, but has constituted an attack on the traditional respect of treaties, and gnawed at the very basis of international confidence. This was a lesson before the war, and is also one to-day. It is our duty to work together, French and English, to find a just solution to the present difficulties.

On my return to London, I received a further long letter from Marshal Bulganin, who now objected to every action upon the Suez problem that the maritime powers had ever proposed or taken. The future of the canal was of little practical concern to Russia, but the Soviet Government saw an opportunity to fish in troubled waters and fish they did. This letter prompted me to telegraph President Eisenhower:

> You can be sure that we are fully alive to the wider dangers of the Middle East situation. They can be summed up in one word — Russia. . . .

There is no doubt in our minds that Nasser, whether he likes it or not, is now effectively in Russian hands, just as Mussolini was in Hitler's. It would be as ineffective to show weakness to Nasser now in order to placate him as it was to show weakness to Mussolini. The only result was and would be to bring the two together.

No doubt your people will have told you of the accumulating evidence of Egyptian plots in Libya, Saudi Arabia and Iraq. At any moment any of these may be touched off unless we can prove to the Middle East that Nasser is losing. That is why we are so concerned to do everything we can to make the Users' Club an effective instrument. If your ships under the Panamanian and Liberian flags would follow the example of those under your flag that would greatly help.

I feel sure that anything which you can say or do to show firmness to Nasser at this time will help the peace by giving the Russians pause. As usual I send you my thoughts in this frank way.

This message was despatched to the President on October 1. The next day a damaging statement came from Mr. Dulles at a press conference. This, however unintentionally, was likely to make Nasser believe that if he held fast, the United States would fall apart from France and Britain over the seizure of the canal.

The United States [the Secretary of State said] cannot be expected to identify itself 100 per cent either with the colonial powers or the powers uniquely concerned with the problem of getting independence as rapidly and as fully as possible. There were, I admit, differences of approach by the three nations to the Suez dispute, which perhaps arise from fundamental concepts. For while we stand together, and I hope we shall always stand together in treaty relations covering the North Atlantic, any areas encroaching in some form or manner on the problem of so-called colonialism, find the United States playing a somewhat independent role. The shift from colonialism to independence will be going on for another fifty years, and I believe that the task of the United Nations is to try to see that this process moves forward in a constructive, evolutionary way, and does not come to a halt or go forward through violent, revolutionary processes which would be destructive of much good.

He then spoke of the Suez Canal Users' Association:

> There is talk about teeth being pulled out of the plan, but I know of no teeth: there were no teeth in it, so far as I am aware.

The representatives of the Users' Association countries were then assembled in London confidently awaiting the United States decision to pay the canal dues to their organization. These were the teeth. Mr. Dulles' statement was in conflict with the users' understanding of the United States Government's intentions. Our representative on the committee, Lord John Hope, reported exasperation and dismay in their ranks. The dispute over Nasser's seizure of the canal had, of course, nothing to do with colonialism, but was concerned with international rights. If the United States had to defend her treaty rights in the Panama Canal, she would not regard such action as colonialism; neither would I. Yet her rights in Panama are those of one nation, not of many nations, as at Suez.

★   ★   ★   ★   ★

It would be foolish to pretend that Mr. Dulles' remarks on colonialism did not represent his feelings and those of many of his countrymen. These sentiments certainly played their part in the reaction of some Americans to the Anglo-French intervention at Suez. It is worth while to probe deeper into the causes for the frequent divergences on colonialism, which have presented a continuing problem in Anglo-American relations and still do so, despite official denials.

With the passage of nearly two centuries since 1776, this issue should vex us less. George III has much to answer for. But it is too easy an explanation merely to take refuge in that monarch's mistaken judgments. Britain has had her share of responsibility for the instinctive American reaction to any question of colonialism. What is disturbing is its tendency to reappear at any critical moment in the relations of the United States with one of her Western allies. I have no doubt that in part these sentiments are due to a difference of approach to the general problem of relationship with what are often called "dependent peoples." The United Kingdom has, for a century or more and in an increasing degree, applied herself to the trustee conception of her responsibilities towards colonial territories. As a result, we have for years past fostered and admired the growth of countries which were once colonies and have since become partners in the Commonwealth. Great nations like Canada and Australia, countries growing apace like New Zealand and the Union of South Africa are the earliest examples. More have followed.

At the Peace Conference after the first world war, there was a characteristic tussle, from which Mr. Lloyd George emerged victorious, to secure a fair representation for the Dominions. Later, during the inter-war years, when the League of Nations was in the heyday of its power, these Commonwealth countries were prominent. One of them was always a member of the Council of the League of Nations, which, unlike the Security Council, was regularly manned by the Foreign Secretaries of the countries composing it. As a result, the British Foreign Secretary of the day experienced a continuing and most helpful contact. I enjoyed working very closely in those years with men like Stanley Bruce, of Australia, who had been Prime Minister of his country, and William Jordan, of New Zealand.

Our personal relations were so happy in our countries' friendship that they occasioned comment which was sometimes envious. The states of the Little Entente, which were active at Geneva, did not always find their relations with their ally France quite so easy. I remember in particular one luncheon at which both M. Titulescu, the brilliant Foreign Minister of Roumania, and the French Foreign Minister of the day, were present among others. While Stanley Bruce and I were having some friendly exchanges across the table, M. Titulescu, who had been crossed in some argument with his French colleague earlier in the day, galvanized the assembled company with a sudden exclamation: *"Moi, je veux être dominion."*

The United States point of view on trusteeship tends to differ from our own. In her judgment, there is nothing wrong in expending large sums of capital in the development of a country and deriving much gain from the process, the American companies or individuals accepting no responsibility for the administration of the country. This point of view is strongly held and there can be no doubt that in many parts of the world the results are satisfactory, both to the countries concerned and to the United States. On the other hand, this practice can also have unexpected consequences which seem less laudable. It remains a fact that two of the more backward countries in the Middle East and in Africa, Saudi Arabia and Liberia, are also two where American interests play a conspicuously large part.

Much of the sparring between the United States and Great Britain on colonial issues could certainly be removed if more was understood of the record of this country in the colonial sphere, especially since the beginning of the century. But the orderly development of self-government in an important territory, like Malaya or Nigeria, is not sensational news; a riot in Cyprus is. As a consequence, understanding grows slowly.

★   ★   ★   ★   ★

On October 1 the Foreign Secretary presided over the inaugural meeting of the Suez Canal Users' Association in London. Then, at long last, all was set for an approach to the Security Council of the United Nations. Mr. Selwyn Lloyd flew over to New York to state our case. Throughout this period he worked closely and effectively with his French colleague, M. Pineau, and with the Australian representative on the Security Council, Dr. Walker. M. Spaak also lent valuable aid. We were, in fact, fortunate in the composition of the Council at this time. Australia, Belgium, Cuba, Iran, Peru and Yugoslavia were the elected representatives. Except for Yugoslavia, which took a line akin to that of Moscow, this was as friendly a membership as we could wish. Nevertheless, we had our anxieties.

The Foreign Secretary and M. Pineau made clear in their preliminary consultations with other representatives that they were determined to hold fast to the eighteen-power proposals as a basis for any negotiation with Egypt. Between the declared position of the eighteen users of the canal and Nasser's refusal of any international authority, there was no place for committees of mediation. The issues were clear cut, a decisive pronouncement was called for. From the outset, however, there had been in all countries those who were not prepared to see this dispute for what it was, the denial of an international engagement, recently reaffirmed by the Egyptian Government, and the seizure by force of international property. They preferred to look upon it as the expression of a nationalist mood in a country recently emancipated, for which, therefore, benevolent allowances must be made.

This was broadly the Indian view. The Government of that country looked to the West for repeated concessions and found no difficulty in urging this course, while refusing the slightest concession to Pakistan over Kashmir. The Indian Government were canvassing their scheme, which they now put in writing, for attaching an international advisory body, which would only have vague powers of supervision, to the Egyptian nationalized canal authority. Mr. Menon had found ears in Cairo ready to listen to such a proposal, naturally enough, for this meant that any effective international element was eliminated. It might be that the Indians had sincerely convinced themselves that Nasser would not accept the eighteen-power proposals. Certainly the Indian Government had not supported them, but this did not seem a sufficient reason why all eighteen powers should, in deference, abandon their position. We had already considered Mr. Menon's ideas in London and found no substance in them. Thanks to the staunchness of the principal users of the canal, he now failed to sway the deliberations of the Security Council, but his activities still caused a superficial flurry.

Meanwhile, in New York Mr. Selwyn Lloyd had found the United States Secretary of State in a cordial frame of mind. It is true that Mr. Dulles had once more alluded to the "suddenness" of the Anglo-French decision to have recourse to the Security Council, but he had seemed convinced by Mr. Lloyd's assurance that this move was indeed a genuine effort to reach a settlement on the part of France and Britain. He also appeared to accept our argument that time was running out and that there was every need for decision.

At international conferences rumours, ill-founded and other-wise, are apt to find their way into the press. This is all the more likely to happen when great cities are chosen as their setting. It is one of the reasons why Geneva would have been a better head-quarters for the United Nations than New York. The newspapers in New York now reported that the American delegation were openly talking of "rifts" between themselves and their French and British colleagues. It was also written that the United States was thinking of accepting the Indian proposals. The Foreign Secretary took this up direct with the Secretary of State.

Mr. Dulles strongly denied having given any support to ideas of compromise, or having taken any part in putting these rumours about. He declared that he was with Britain on every point, except the use of force. Even force he did not rule out as an ultimate resort, and he once more recognized our right to maintain the threat of using it. Nevertheless, he felt that to employ force in the immediate future would be a mistake, since in his view Nasser's position was deteriorating. There seemed no grounds for this last estimate.

Direct talks with the Egyptian Foreign Minister, Dr. Fawzi, began on October 9. They were conducted with firmness and patience by the French and British Foreign Secretaries. The Egyptian counter-proposals offered vague hopes for negotiation, but as the days went by they lost what little precision they had. In particular the Egyptians accepted no international authority and they offered no effective sanction for any breach of the principle of free naviga-tion.

Meanwhile, a number of developments were serving, at least in appearance, to weaken the position of the eighteen powers in Egyptian minds. There were delays in setting up the Suez Canal Users' Association for effective work. Fifteen members had so far joined, but no administrator had yet been appointed. As late as October 10 the American representative in London was still with-out authority to open a bank account into which canal dues could be paid. It had not even been firmly laid down and accepted that dues must be paid to the association. Unless the association had the power to withhold dues from Egypt, it would possess no safe-guard against Egyptian interference with its members' ships. There was still a disturbing lack of unanimity within the Users' Club as to how dues should be apportioned; how much for the maintenance and development of the canal, how much in compensation to the Suez Canal Company and how much for payments to the Egyptian Government. The United States were inclining to the view that a considerable part of the dues ought to be paid to Egypt. We had never been willing to agree to this in advance of the settlement and felt growing exasperation at the constant whittling away of our position.

After ten days of discussion at the United Nations, a vote was now due in the Security Council. The resolution before the Council was substantially the one to which we had agreed with the French and the United States. By skill and hard work, various weaker or vaguer alternative resolutions had been set aside, yet the outcome gave us only partial satisfaction. It confirmed our standpoint, but it brought us no nearer the solution we sought. The resolution under debate on October 13 consisted of two parts, the first part of which was passed unanimously. This laid down six principles by which it was agreed that any settlement of the Suez question must abide. At my suggestion these principles, largely coinciding with those outlined by Mr. Dulles in his speech at the first London Conference, had now been renamed "requirements." They ran as follows:

1. There should be free and open transit through the canal without discrimination, overt or covert.

2. The sovereignty of Egypt should be respected.

3. The operation of the canal should be insulated from the politics of any country.

4. The manner of fixing tolls and charges should be decided by agreement between Egypt and the users.

5. A fair proportion of the dues should be allotted to development.

6. In case of disputes, unresolved affairs between the Suez Canal Company and the Egyptian Government should be settled by arbitration.

The second part of the resolution declared that the proposals of the eighteen powers corresponded to these requirements and invited the Egyptian Government to put forward its proposals to give effect to them. It requested the Governments of Egypt, France and the United Kingdom to continue their interchanges. It also laid down that in the meantime the canal should offer free passage to all shipping. Thus we hoped to open a way for a test case on the banning of Israeli ships. It further declared that the Users' Association should receive the dues payable by the ships of its members, and that the association and the Egyptian nationalized authority should co-operate to ensure the satisfactory management of the canal. This part of the resolution was what mattered to us; it obtained nine votes. There were two against, those of the Soviet Foreign Secretary, Mr. Shepilov, and the Yugoslav representative. Mr. Shepilov's vote was a veto and so the operative part of the resolution was killed.

This was as far as our appeal to the United Nations took us. We were left with six principles, and principles are aimless unless translated into action. The Soviets having vetoed the part of the resolution which set out the action to be taken, no method was left for harnessing the principles. They just flapped in the air. Nor had a time limit been set to the interchanges expected of the French, British and Egyptian Governments. The way was open to endless procrastination by Egypt. Worse, it also lay open to her to renew her aggressive designs in other fields.

These discussions bowed out the practical proposals of the eighteen powers, which were our minimum requirement for the security of the canal. They were never allowed the limelight again. Though the Americans had been the first advocates of these proposals, the Administration showed no concern at the American defeat by the Communist veto. Beaming through rose-coloured spectacles, it acclaimed the six principles in their place. I soon learnt that the Soviet Government regarded the proceedings at the United Nations as a victory for Egypt and for them. In this they were undoubtedly right. I was not surprised when messages from our friends in the Middle East showed dismay at Nasser's swelling success.

It was clear enough to me where we were. The powers at the London Conference had worked out, with care and forethought, a scheme which would have made the Suez Canal part of an international system giving security for all. The United States had put its

whole authority behind the scheme and her Secretary of State had
introduced the proposals himself before the London Conference.
Now all this was dead. It was of no use to fool ourselves on that
account. We had been strung along over many months of negotiation from pretext to pretext, from device to device, and from
contrivance to contrivance. At each stage in this weary pilgrimage
we had seen our position weakened. Now we had gone to the United
Nations itself. It was not at our wish that we had been so late to make
an appeal there. Here was the result. Two Communist powers,
Yugoslavia and Soviet Russia, had voted against the only practical
scheme in existence for the creation of an international system for
the Suez Canal. As a consequence of the Soviet veto, the free
world had recoiled, some with reluctance and some with relief.
There was no one in that room at the United Nations, at the conclusion of the vote, who supposed for an instant that any life was left
in the work of the London Conference. The Soviets had had their
way and no amount of soothing optimism could conceal the truth.

Yet the notion gained currency that the Security Council had
prepared the terms for a peaceful and just settlement of the
dispute. Those who wished to assure themselves that the easy path
is also the wise one, pointed to the six principles, which all the
members of the Council had endorsed. Six principles, when it had
taken us three months of negotiation to carry practical working
proposals for the future of the canal to the United Nations, only to
have them smothered. At the end of that time we were to rejoice at
being offered six principles in their place. The truth was starkly
clear to me. Plunder had paid off.

Perhaps the most disturbing feature of all these discussions was
the utter indifference shown by the United Nations to the international aspects of the crisis. The Suez Canal was the greatest international waterway in the world and had been internationally
owned and administered. The founders of the United Nations
believed that they were building an international order. It might
be thought that one of the first duties of that order would be to
protect the international organizations which already existed in the
world, and to promote others. The guardian of internationalism
might have been expected to defend this successful experiment.
Nothing of the kind. From the start to the end of the business,

not one single syllable of censure or regret was uttered by the United Nations, or on its behalf either by the Security Council or by the General Assembly, at the seizure of a great international waterway by force. It is inevitable that there will be a reckoning for this moral backsliding.

7

PRELUDE
October 13–23

My speech to Conservative Conference at Llandudno — Meeting
with Mollet and Pineau — Course of our discussions — We decide
to stand by eighteen-power proposals — Our despondency about
the Users' Club — Danger of an Israeli attack on Jordan — Our
joint communiqué — The *fedayeen* — Nasser's threats to Israel
— Russian arms supplies to Egypt — The two world wars — Arab
joint command established — Ministerial changes — Steadfast
attitude of my colleagues

ON OCTOBER 12, towards the end of the proceedings at the Security
Council, I travelled to Llandudno to address the public meeting
which by tradition closes the Conservative Party Conference. As
not infrequently happens, there had been gloomy forebodings in
the press about the state of the party. These had not been fulfilled
and the conference had shown itself vigorous and united. I found
its members more lively and enthusiastic than they had been a year
before in the wake of victory. I also found them in agreement
with our foreign policy. Lord Salisbury, who was to have spoken
during the foreign-policy discussion, was unfortunately not well
enough to come to the conference and take part. His speech was
delivered for him by Mr. Anthony Nutting and warmly acclaimed.

Early on the morning of October 13, the day of my speech to the
conference, a message came through from the Foreign Secretary in
New York, telling me of an optimistic statement made by the President
of the United States in a television interview the day before.
He had said that progress on the Suez Canal dispute had been "most
gratifying" and that it looked as though "a very great crisis is behind
us." This confidence was ill-timed, for on the next night Soviet
Russia vetoed the operative part of the resolution at the Security

Council, thus denying the eighteen-power proposals and those of the Users' Association, which the United States Government had themselves sponsored. The Foreign Secretary was much concerned at this American attitude, which was remote from reality and would fortify the Egyptian position still further. We had hoped, at the least, for a grave statement about the serious position threatening at the Security Council and an exhortation to the United Nations to give effect to the agreed views of the eighteen powers.

The difference in time between London and New York created a constant problem during these negotiations, the morning in Wales was still night in New York. The Foreign Secretary had got to bed late after a strenuous day and I was most reluctant to wake him. Yet I had to speak at 2 P.M. our time, only 9 A.M. in New York. I left him to sleep as long as I could and, a little over an hour before I had to begin my speech, telephoned to him about the situation. We both wished to avoid an open divergence and I told him of my intention to seize on the least optimistic of the President's phrases, underline it, and point out once again that force could not be excluded. We also agreed that he should speak plainly to the United States Government, expressing our concern at the consequences for us of these repeated and unjustified flights of hopeful fancy. I spent luncheon rewriting my speech and glumly reflecting on the disturbing precedent which had been set for the future.

In my speech I gave an account of the Suez crisis and of the position as it then stood. I first warned the delegates not to indulge in hasty or over-optimistic judgment. I continued:

> President Eisenhower in his press conference on Thursday is reported to have said that you must have peace with justice, or it is not peace. I agree with those words. We should all take them as our text. That is why we have always said that with us force is the last resort, but it cannot be excluded. Therefore, we have refused to say that in no circumstances would we ever use force. No responsible Government could ever give such a pledge.

When we drove to the overflow meetings, it took my wife and me quite a while to make our way through the cheering throngs.

I came back to London encouraged by the loyalty of the conference. The testing time for our policy was at hand. The veto fell that night.

When the Foreign Secretary returned from New York, my colleagues and I talked things over. There had been a suggestion at the United Nations for a meeting between representatives of French and Egyptian Governments and ourselves at Geneva. There was never any hope that the Egyptians would agree to this on the basis of the eighteen-power proposals, or on any that restored international control over the canal. Perhaps we could have found a pretext for going to Geneva. We might even have persuaded the French to come along too and negotiate with Nasser an agreement of sorts about the canal. It might have been dressed up to look fairly reasonable, even though I knew that it did not mean much. This was in fact approximately what happened when the Americans were later entrusted with the task, after I had resigned.

It might be said that such a policy would have led to postponing the crunch with Nasser, and would have been advantageous to us. I did not believe this and, not believing it, I could not pursue such a course. I could not return from Geneva with a piece of paper and commend it to the House of Commons, when I knew it had no real value. This would have lulled people at a time when I thought they should be alerted. It would have reassured the world about a dictator whose intentions were, I was sure, predatory. Those who did not wish to face unpleasant realities would have been encouraged, and by an agreement which I had brought about and commended. Such action would have been false to everything I had learnt in thirty years of foreign policy. Nor would it have insulated the canal from the control of one man. If we did not ensure this we were laying up certain trouble for the future, first with Israeli commerce, later with that of others.

I had been through so much of this before. I had not been willing to commend to Parliament an agreement with Mussolini which I had not believed would be fulfilled. Having resigned rather than do this twenty years ago, in the lesser responsibility of a Foreign Secretary, I was not prepared to reach and proclaim another agreement as a step to peace, when I did not believe that it was any such thing. As I said two years later in a speech at Leamington:

In external affairs a democratic state has to be on its guard against certain dangers. The most insidious of these is to take the easy way, and to put off decision. Drift is the demon of democracy. Democracies should rather consider, in any step they take in world affairs, whether what they do will serve only to relax tension for a while, or whether it is in the true interest of lasting peace. That is the difference between appeasement and peace.

The Government agreed that they must await the proposals which the Egyptian Government had been told to produce, though with little expectation that they would provide a basis for discussion. The Security Council was no sooner over than the Egyptians began to plead excuses against even the principles which they had accepted. The Government decided meanwhile to align their views with the French Government, who were their partners in these talks. It was all the more necessary to do so because the Middle Eastern scene began to look threatening again; the immediate consequence of weakness.

★   ★   ★   ★   ★

The Foreign Secretary and I flew to Paris on October 16 to see M. Mollet and M. Pineau. There was no lack of material for discussion, little of it encouraging. We had to deal with three principal topics. The first was the state of general negotiations about the future of the canal. We had to assess the position as it was left after the Security Council meeting and the conversations in which M. Pineau and Mr. Selwyn Lloyd had taken part with the Secretary-General and the Egyptian Foreign Minister. The second was the progress, if such it could be called, of the Users' Club and what our next step should be. In the third place we had to pool our information and consider the action we must take in the light of developments in the Middle East itself and, in particular, the growing menace of hostility by Egypt against Israel. The moment that the Security Council acquiesced in the Russian veto, and relieved Colonel Nasser of any anxiety at the United Nations, tension began to grow in the area again. The *fedayeen* raids on Israel were started up afresh.

We began with a discussion of the position at the United Nations. We felt that the proceedings of the Security Council had decided nothing, the Soviet veto having crushed the effective part of them. We agreed that the general principles which had been endorsed were impeccable, but they had been accepted because they were not a serious commitment. When it came to detailed action like the eighteen-power proposals, all was held up.

We and the French reviewed alternatives. The more we examined these the more we came back to the proposals, which seemed to us to improve in usefulness when set against the confusion of the present situation. We decided we must stand by them. As regards the tactics to employ in negotiation, these were reasonably clear. The Egyptians had been instructed by the Security Council to produce proposals to conform to the six principles. They had not yet done so. Therefore the ball was firmly in their court. We would examine what they might put forward and use as our criterion the extent to which they approached the eighteen-power proposals on which the nations who used the canal were agreed.

The next point which we discussed was the Users' Club. Here was much disappointment. Communications had been exchanged only the day before between Mr. Dulles and the Foreign Secretary; their messages had, in fact, crossed. The general American complaint was that we were concerned with the punitive character of the Users' Club proposals, whereas the United States Government regarded them as a means of co-operating with Egypt. This was not how they had been originally described to us. Our cause for disappointment was more particular. We saw the Users' Club being increasingly organized as an agency to forward dues to Egypt. There was a danger of absurdity in this. At that time 60 per cent of the canal dues was being denied to Nasser by the ships of Britain, France and others who had followed our lead. From what Mr. Dulles had told the Foreign Secretary, it appeared that nine-tenths of this 60 per cent was to be handed over to Egypt when the Users' Club was in force. The only gain to the users would be that they would retain one-tenth of the 3 per cent of canal dues paid by ships flying the American flag. Nasser would have every reason to be grateful to the Users' Club if he could so much increase his proportion of dues. But all hope of Egyptian agreement to the eighteen-power proposals, or anything like them, would be dead.

The American assurance, on which the whole of this discussion began, was that Nasser could not expect anything so good, having rejected the proposals of the eighteen powers. He was now to be paid infinitely more than anything he had been offered before. Both the French and ourselves felt that we could not continue with proposals of this character. The French in particular were without illusions and clearly had no confidence in American support for our negotiations.

Finally, at our meeting we discussed the situation in the Middle East, its dangers and what we could do. The line-up between Jordan, Egypt and Syria was becoming ever closer. There were reports of the establishment of a joint command under Egyptian direction, which in fact soon came into existence. Cairo radio blared with increasing vehemence against Israel, menacing her with destruction. Unless Israel was prepared just to sit and wait until it suited her enemies to strangle and finally destroy her, it was clear that before long she would have to take some counter-action, at least to put an end to the *fedayeen* raids. If directed against Jordan, from which some of the *fedayeen* raids were said to be mounted under Egyptian leadership, then the position for us would be terrible indeed. We had a treaty obligation to defend Jordan. The Jordanians had no effective air force, our fighter squadrons provided their only protection. Already there had nearly been an incident when, in some counter-raid, an Israeli aircraft had for the first time been engaged. Our help had been called for and our aircraft were on the point of going up, when a wise and rapid exchange of cautionary messages on the spot avoided catastrophe.

Nevertheless, the danger was there. If an attack were launched against Jordan, the Israelis would be using their French Mystères, the delivery of a number of these having previously been agreed by the United States, France and ourselves, the three partners to the Tripartite Declaration. The Royal Air Force would be in action for Jordan, the United States would be on the sidelines. This was a nightmare which could only too easily come true; Jordan calling for support from Nasser and ourselves, Nasser calling for support from Russia, France lined up with Israel on the other side.

As long ago as January, our Ambassador had warned Jordan that Egyptian interference was highly dangerous for her. Egypt was manoeuvring to embroil Jordan with Israel. If Israel were to act against one of her encircling enemies, the choice lay between Jordan and Egypt. Syria was insufficiently important. Jordan had provided the one effective Arab military force, the Arab Legion, in the fighting of 1948–49. Despite the large supplies of Soviet equipment which the Egyptians had received, the Legion was probably still the most formidable military formation which Israel's neighbours could put into the field. It might be thought imprudent to act against Egypt while leaving the Legion intact. As against this, Egypt was the political source and inspiration of the threat to Israel. It was the Cairo radio which blared out the daily hatred and the incitement to kill. It was Nasser who had thought out the horror of the *fedayeen*. In the event, Israel found the answer by keeping her best troops in position to cover the front against Jordan, while using less experienced forces for the incursion into Sinai. They proved brilliantly equal to the call upon them.

My colleagues and I were acutely aware of the consequence of action by Israel against Jordan, which we had to do all in our power to avert. Our relations with Israel were not close or intimate, there were constant arguments about the supply of arms. Therefore, at this meeting in Paris, we asked the French Ministers to do everything they could to make clear to Israel that an attack on Jordan would have to be resisted by us. This they undertook to do. It was not only our own treaty engagements which concerned us, but the effect upon Iraq of events in Jordan. To fail to carry out our engagement would be the end of our position in the Middle East, to have to carry it out would be disastrous to Western unity. No dilemma could be more difficult. If Israel were to break out against Egypt and not against Jordan, this dilemma would not arise. For this reason, if there were to be a break-out it was better from our point of view that it should be against Egypt. On the other hand, if the break-out were against Egypt, then there would be other worries, for example the safety of the canal. We discussed these matters in all their political and military aspects. In common prudence we had to consider what our action should be, for our two countries were, as we knew, the only powers to have effective military forces at our command in the area. During recent months we had been mounting our military preparations to deal with any interference or other act by Nasser against our ships or our people. Now Nasser's policies were provoking Israel beyond endurance and this also we had to prepare for.

We four Ministers, M. Mollet and I, M. Pineau and Mr. Lloyd, after talking for an hour or so, dined together. After dinner we adjourned to another room, where our advisers were waiting, and in due course started to draw up our communiqué. It is an old maxim of conferences that if you do not want to waste time at the end, you should start drafting the communiqué at the beginning, or even have it ready in advance. We broke this excellent rule, with the result that we sat later than we need have done.

As agreed at the last meeting [we announced] between the French and British Ministers in Paris on September 25, a meeting was held to-day at the Hôtel Matignon between Sir Anthony Eden and Mr. Selwyn Lloyd on the one hand, and Monsieur Guy Mollet and Monsieur Christian Pineau on the other.

They examined the situation resulting from the recent votes in the Security Council on the Anglo-French resolution.

They resolved to adhere to the requirements set out in the first part of the resolution and unanimously approved, and noted with regret that these were already being questioned in certain Egyptian quarters.

As regards the implementation of these requirements they also resolved to stand by the second part of the resolution, which received nine votes but was vetoed by the Soviet Union. According to the resolution, the eighteen-power proposals, including the international operation of the canal, should constitute the basis for a settlement, unless the Egyptian Government produce other proposals for a system meeting the requirements and affording equivalent guarantees to the users.

The two Governments are ready to consider together any proposals of this nature.

They also had a general exchange of views on the other

problems of the Middle East and decided to maintain constant contact on these questions in the spirit of the closest Anglo-French friendship.

On October 18 at a meeting with our Cabinet colleagues in London, the Foreign Secretary and I went over the ground we had covered in our discussions in Paris. We reported the exchanges of views we had had with French Ministers on the stage which the negotiations had reached in the Security Council, and the direction in which the Users' Club proposals were developing. We described the increasing tension in the Middle East, with the growing danger that Israel, under provocation from Egypt, would make some military move. The position was indeed serious, but at this stage Her Majesty's Government decided they must await the proposals they had been told to expect from the Egyptians.

★   ★   ★   ★   ★

The clouds were lowering and menacing in October 1956. The storm could not be far ahead. No record of events at that time can be true which does not take account of this.

One set of circumstances might have countered this rising tension. Britain, France and the United States had signed an agreement in 1950, declaring that they would prevent any violation of the armistice lines in Palestine either by Israel or by the Arab states. If the signatories of this agreement had not only declared their intention to fulfil it, but had taken military precautions together publicly, to make action effective, then there might have been sufficient comfort in such preparations to give confidence to Israel. I had made this proposal when I was in Washington in January. It had not been possible to agree upon it. Ever since I had been increasingly concerned at what the outcome must be.

I had seen so many of these situations before, deteriorating rapidly, even menacingly, yet with no new element to seize and use, and nobody prepared to inject one. Trieste had been such another a year or two back. Then we and the Americans had intruded the new ingredient and it had flashed and flared in our faces. We had been much blamed at the time and for a while it looked as if we had only made matters worse. But we had not; we had made everyone realize the reality of the dangers Europe was running. The alternative to composition was collision, which meant war. Composition was to be preferred. It might be necessary to treat the Middle Eastern menace by the same methods.

★ ★ ★ ★ ★

Nasser's seizure of power from General Neguib brought with it a new essay in frightfulness against Israel, the *fedayeen* commando raids directed against the civil life of the nation in the night hours. "Wait and see," he said, "soon will be proven to you the strength and will of our nation. Egypt will grind you to the dust." These raids began in the spring of 1955 and for some months Cairo disclaimed responsibility. Then, on August 31, an official communiqué informed the world of this new military technique: "Egypt has decided to despatch her heroes, the disciples of Pharaoh and the sons of Islam, and they will clean the land of Palestine." And then again, on September 2, Cairo broadcast: "The forces of the Egyptian *fedayeen* moved towards Israel, approached her capital and caused heavy casualties along the border between Gaza and Tel Aviv."

In the spring of 1956 the campaign grew more furious and more dangerous. The United Nations attempted to negotiate a cease-fire which was promptly broken by Egypt. On May 15 Cairo radio announced: "The war is not now confined to attacks along the border, but has reached the heart of Israel and places which were believed to be safe from danger. The quiet reigning in the villages and towns remote from the armistice lines has turned to terror." Israeli casualties were heavy and war drew nearer.

The seizure of the Suez Canal in July brought a marked relaxation of raids across the Israeli frontier, a fair indication of where the guilt lay. After the Security Council had pronounced in October and diplomatic discussions of seemingly unlimited duration had begun, the danger signals were out again. The *fedayeen* resumed their activities with increased intensity. The main recruiting area and headquarters were in the Gaza strip. Later the raiders began to operate from Syria and Jordan as well, sometimes under the command of Egyptian officers, sometimes under the supervision of the Egyptian Military Attaché.

In the last days of October the Egyptians declared that it was they who would choose time and place for the final assault, that it was for Israel to wait passively the moment of their selection. Months before this, General Burns, the head of the United Nations Truce Supervisory Organization, had written to the Foreign Minister of Israel, "I consider that if Egypt has ordered these *fedayeen* raids, she has now put herself in the position of the aggressor."

All evidence pointed one way. Egypt was gathering her allies, piling up Soviet arms and enlisting Soviet technical help, sharpening her propaganda and intensifying her raids. The risks entailed in the seizure of the canal having been safely negotiated, all was being got ready for the next objective. When later the Israeli armies captured El Arish, they found huge supplies of equipment, stores and petrol which could only have been assembled in such a forward position for an imminent offensive. Was Israel to wait for it, and if so, how long? Her country and her cities were vulnerable, especially to air attack. Egypt was strong in modern Russian bombers and growing stronger. Egypt had fifty, Israel had none.

Syria as well as Egypt was now receiving a steady flow of arms, equipment and technicians from behind the Iron Curtain. In the past fifteen months Egypt had been supplied with equipment to the value of £150 million. Syria had been given arms to the value of £20 million. There were a thousand technicians and instructors from the Soviet bloc in Egypt. However unskilled those who received it were, the cumulative effect of so much Communist aid and instruction must in time increase their offensive power. It certainly raised Egyptian confidence; so had Western failure to obtain any concession from Nasser in the negotiations over the canal. The dread began to grow in the Middle East that nothing could check the swelling authority of the Egyptian dictator. Warning after warning came from friendly Arab states of the consequences of allowing this fear to become a conviction.

★   ★   ★   ★   ★

We are all marked to some extent by the stamp of our generation, mine is that of the assassination in Sarajevo and all that flowed from it. I was on the river at Eton, being coached near an elbow in the Thames we called "sandbanks," when I heard the news.

Is it imagination, or did I really feel that for a moment our young world stood still in something like fear, before it resumed its course? My tutor was gloomy when I got back to rafts. I had reached seventeen a few days before, and for the first and last time in my life I kept a regular diary. I have it still, with its school entries and the careful day-to-day account, mainly gleaned from the newspapers, of events as they grew in ugly shape.

The Archduke was murdered on June 28, the Austrian ultimatum was delivered on July 23, Europe was at war less than a fortnight later. In the last days the Foreign Office was strenuously active though hobbled most dangerously, as France and Russia repeatedly protested, by an inability to tell what we would do, because we did not know. The Foreign Secretary did all he could at that late hour. Sir Horace Rumbold, one of the best Ambassadors this country has ever had, and counsellor in Berlin at the time, was a stout defender of our official action. Yet he wrote: *

> The Entente statesmen had shown the maximum of good will, resource and patience. Events had been too much for them, however, and they had always been a lap behind in the march of events.

Therein lies the tragedy. It is impossible to read the record now and not feel that we had a responsibility for being always a lap behind. A month passed between the murder of the Archduke and the despatch of the Austrian ultimatum to Serbia. In that time we made no move. We hoped that the emergency could be localized, as between Austria and Serbia; we had no authority to intervene. How could it be localized except by Austria being left to deal with Serbia as she wished? How could Slav stand quiet while Teuton seized Belgrade? Even the wary Stalin rumbled when a like threat menaced Yugoslavia in 1941.

We should have learnt the Russian mood in those long weeks in 1914 and warned Vienna of the dangers of asking too much, and done so in advance of the publicly stated demand, from which retreat was so difficult. If this was not an earlier example of "a little country far away," there was certainly a wishful hope that we might not be involved, with all the debilitating conse-

* *The War Crisis in Berlin* (London: Constable, 1940), page 287.

quences. Stranger still, even after the Austrian ultimatum we addressed all our wise projects for restraint *via* Berlin, not using the direct channel also, even in the last emergency. The post office was sluggish in delivery and not always accurate, as might have been foreseen. Always a lap behind, that fatal lap.

When the nineteen-thirties came the problem was the same under another guise. In our country some thought that methods of diplomacy which were suitable when dealing with democracies controlled by free parliaments could not be applied without reserve to militant dictatorships. These dictatorships were not subject to the restraints of an elected chamber. Their word alone did not suffice, because it need not be kept. Therefore precautions must be taken. Others took a different view. They thought it important not to build up suspicion of the dictators or in the minds of the dictators. They thought that they must be met as honourable men and dealt with as such, and that the papers they signed and the assurances they gave must be accepted as having a validity comparable to those signed by elected governments. Not only must this be the form in which negotiations with them were conducted, but it must be the spirit and the faith.

As a consequence of all this, the dictators themselves were led to underestimate the temper of the people with whom they had to deal, on account of their experience in dealing with the leaders. Success in a number of adventures involving the breaking of agreements in Abyssinia, in the Rhineland, in Austria, in Czechoslovakia, in Albania had persuaded Hitler and Mussolini that the democracies had not the will to resist, that they could now march with the certitude of success from signpost to signpost along the road which led to world dominion. They were deceived. The second world war resulted.

★ ★ ★ ★ ★

As my colleagues and I surveyed the scene in these autumn months of 1956, we were determined that the like should not come again. We had seen how insidious was the excuse, how difficult the action. There might be other mistakes, there would not be that one. Drift spelt certain disaster for the West's authority and meant an Arab-Israeli war, fought under conditions most perilous for the peace of the whole area. Intervention by the Western powers, with all its risks, was clearly to be preferred. Nasser was well aware of this and guarded all the more carefully against a direct provocation. He was not ready for that, yet. It would not be good to act only at the time of his choosing. Unchecked over Suez, he set to work upon the next projects, needful to realize his proclaimed ambitions of Empire. These were to increase his supply of armaments from Communist sources, to undermine those Arab leaders who were in his way, and to tighten the noose around Israel, whose destruction in his own time was his declared objective.

In existing circumstances it was idle to hope for effective action by the United States or the United Nations. Left to itself, the United Nations would never move, as its melancholy record in Middle Eastern events clearly showed. If led or goaded by others, it might do so.

Meanwhile, pro-Nasser parties had won the election in Jordan. This was immediately followed by the establishment on October 23 of a joint command between Egypt, Jordan and Syria, under Egypt's leadership. Israel could not depend upon the United Nations coming to her aid in time, or expect that Nasser would not carry out his threats against her. The first was too nebulous a hope, the second too careless. The world knew that approval by the United Nations of action by the United States in Korea was an accident, due to Soviet absence from the Security Council and the non-application of the veto. The Soviets were not absent now. In the dispute over the canal we had seen the eighteen-power proposals vetoed and no action follow, except an invitation to talk over principles instead. Israel could not await the culmination of her enemies' preparations on a scale she knew she could not equal. No government of a small, free nation could rest on such frail hope. Some may doubt the wisdom of Israel's action, none can deny her courage nor the provocation offered her. For my part, if the responsibility had been mine as the head of the Israeli Government, I hope that I would have taken just such action as Israel took.

★   ★   ★   ★   ★

As was to be expected, the strain of these months on the Ministers who had to bear the principal directing and administrative responsibilities was very heavy. When I had appointed Sir Walter Monckton to the Ministry of Defence, I had admittedly not foreseen anything of this kind and I was made anxious by the effect upon his health, which was clearly suffering. I was therefore not surprised when he felt compelled to ask for his release. I was loath to lose his advice in the Cabinet and he readily agreed to stay as Paymaster-General.

In deciding upon his successor, I had no doubt that Antony Head was the man for the job. Earlier in the life of the Government I had suggested to him that he might take an office outside the Service Ministries. I did this not because I was critical of the work he was doing, but because I thought that, from the point of view of his own career, he would be wise to gain some experience in a civil department. He preferred to remain with the Army, where his life and loyalty had always lain. In the hazards of political selection it is always pleasing when a Minister grows to fill his responsibilities. I have never known any man do this so naturally and completely as did Antony Head. I have no doubt that he would have proved to be the best Minister of Defence this country has had since the close of the war, had he been continued in office after I resigned. Mr. John Hare succeeded Mr. Head at the War Office. These appointments, which had been decided before my visit to Paris, were announced on the evening of October 18.

I had interviews with a number of colleagues individually, during the weeks which passed after the seizure of the canal. There was no friction of any kind between us. When we were in council, no marked divergencies were revealed. I have been a member of many Governments in times of nominal peace. I have not known one more united on an issue of the first importance. There were, of course, shades of opinion, but these did not obtrude. The points of view ranged from that of the Minister who fervently informed Mr. Dulles at the United States Embassy that we would go through with the business, even if it meant "pawning the pictures in the National Gallery," through those who were quietly determined, to the more cautious characters who, whether from conviction or loyalty, were there all the same.

This calm passage during a period of many months was probably due to our having talked over the situation fully in its earliest phases. We had grown to know each other's minds; every senior member of the Government realized this and remembered the mood in which we had taken our first decisions. The others were their consequence.

8

THE CRUNCH
October 23–31

Hungarian rebellion — Israel mobilizes and moves into Egypt —
Our reasons for intervention — Anglo-French note to Egypt and
Israel — Question of consulting U.S. and Commonwealth — My
messages to President Eisenhower — My statement to the House
— U.S. resolution in Security Council — The veto — Russian
resolution — Sir Pierson Dixon's warning — "Uniting for Peace"
Debate in Parliament — Israel accepts and Egypt rejects — The
military situation and plans — Soviet "technicians" — Disorder in
the House — Victory for Israeli arms

FOR SOME DAYS after the return of the Foreign Secretary and myself
from Paris, conflicting reports reached us on Israeli intentions. In
the meantime an incident sparked between Egypt and France. The
French had intercepted a ship carrying arms from Egypt to the
Algerian rebels. They withdrew their Ambassador from Cairo in
protest and lodged a complaint with the Security Council.

It was now, on October 23, that the first reports of disturbances
in Hungary began to come in. They were soon to swell into fearful
tragedy. Here certain historical facts must be recalled. In 1945,
when the principal allies in the war against Hitler were gathered
in Yalta, the future of Europe was decided between them. The
Yalta Agreements have often been severely criticized as giving too
great an advantage to Soviet Russia. I have always thought that
it was not the Agreements themselves but Russia's failure to observe
them which led to so much grief and suffering.

The Agreements should be examined in the light of the Hungarian situation as it developed in the early autumn of 1956. Soviet
Russia, by her own declaration at Yalta, by her own signed statement, can only station troops in Hungary as a corridor, for so

long as she maintains an occupation force in Austria. Once Soviet contingents had been withdrawn from Austria, then Soviet Russia has no right, on her own showing at Yalta, to maintain troops in Hungary. It was my knowledge of this condition which had made me doubt whether the utmost pressure which the West could use would induce Russia to withdraw from Austria. In the event, after the long Berlin Conference, Russian policy underwent a change.

It is quite true that Russia claims to be in Hungary now by virtue of the Warsaw Pact. But the Yalta Agreements also declared that the Hungarian Government must be chosen by free election. The Soviet Government broke this stipulation too. The Warsaw Pact was made by an imposed Communist Government. In both these respects, and in others, the presence of Soviet troops in Hungary has no shadow of justification.

Agitation against the unpopular Communist Government in Budapest had long been growing. The example of Poland, which seemed to be winning some degree of national freedom within the Soviet orbit, provided a further inspiration to the Hungarians. In October, demands were voiced all over the country that Hungary should withdraw from the Warsaw Pact and declare herself neutral, as Austria had done, that free elections should be held and democratic liberties restored and that Russian troops should leave. Russian troops not only stayed, they shot.

Towards the end of the month a new Government was formed by Mr. Imre Nagy, himself a Communist who had at one time been expelled from the party. Mr. Nagy drew into his administration representatives of the non-Communist parties and attempted to form a coalition Government, pledged to a programme of free elections. This was supported by a widespread nationalist revolutionary movement directed against the presence of Soviet troops and the activities of the Communist security police. Events moved towards a climax on October 24. On that day a column of Russian troops, stationed in Hungary, intervened in Budapest and fired upon a crowd of demonstrators. Worse was to follow. During the previous night fresh Russian forces had been entering Hungary from Roumania.

★   ★   ★   ★   ★

On October 25 a report came that Israel was about to mobilize. She did so on the 27 and moved against Egypt on the evening of the 29th. I thought then, and I think now, that the Israelis had justification for their action. It is at least a grim possibility that they would not be a free nation to-day had they not taken it. The marked victim of the garrotter is not to be condemned if he strikes out before the noose is round his throat.

If we were not prepared to condemn Israel, we could not stand aside and watch events. In an Israeli-Egyptian conflict our military advisers expected the Israelis to win; their quality, intelligent training and dedicated courage outmatching the Egyptian advantage in numbers and equipment. The chief peril to us lay not in the conflict but in its extension by the intervention of other Arab states. The best way to halt that was by intervening ourselves. These considerations decided our course of action.

Ministers had already considered at several meetings the ways in which the situation might develop. These had also been canvassed with the French. On October 25 the Cabinet discussed the specific possibility of conflict between Israel and Egypt and decided in principle how it would react if this occurred. The Governments of France and the United Kingdom should, it considered, at once call on both parties to stop hostilities and withdraw their forces to a distance from either bank of the canal. If one or both failed to comply within a definite period, then British and French forces would intervene as a temporary measure to separate the combatants. To ensure this being effective, they would have to occupy key positions at Port Said, Ismailia and Suez. Our purpose was to safeguard free passage through the canal, if it were threatened with becoming a zone of warfare, and to arrest the spread of fighting in the Middle East.

To realize this we would put into operation the plan for occupation of the Suez Canal zone, prepared by the joint Anglo-French military staff which had been studying the problem since the end of July. An advantage of this course was that we did not need to recast our military preparations. The same plan that had been intended to deal with Nasser's seizure of the canal fitted equally well with our new objective. Critics asked why we landed so far behind the combatant area. The answer is that to land anywhere except as planned would have involved delay and we could not afford delay. We were also limited by shortage of landing craft and had to have the use of a port.

Of course there were dangers in this policy. But there were dangers in any policy which we might have chosen, not least in that of complete inaction. Political decisions, especially when they concern the Middle East, usually involve a choice of evils. I am convinced that we chose the lesser evil.

It was still necessary to be as certain as possible of the facts. For some time we had been keeping occasional and informal watch on the canal and Egyptian troop movements. We had done this by means of Canberras flying high and often a little way out to sea. There had never been any attempted interference with these flights and we believed them to be unperceived. Late on the evening of the 29th I had a talk with the Minister of Defence and the Chief of the Air Staff. I told them how important it was for us to have information upon which we could depend for certain, as early as possible the next day. A dawn reconnaissance was ordered by four Canberras flying at a great height, thirty to forty thousand feet. They would locate and, if possible, photograph the opposing forces. The Canberras carried out their instructions. Despite their altitude, all four were located and intercepted and some were fired on. All returned safe to base, but one machine was damaged. This interception was a brilliant piece of work by any standards, and when it was reported to me the next day it gave me grim cause for thought. I kept my own counsel. In the later fighting the Egyptian air force was, by contrast, completely ineffective. I do not know the explanation. Maybe the pilots of another nation were flying the M.I.G.'s that dawn.

On the morning of October 30 the Cabinet were informed that Israeli troops had entered Egyptian territory on the evening of the 29th and during the night had reached a point half way between their frontier and Ismailia. A second Israeli force was reported to be striking towards Suez. Other swift Israeli actions were also unrolling, though we only learnt details of these later. This was the situation the Cabinet had considered five days before.

The Cabinet was sternly conscious of the importance and urgency of the decisions it had to take. Now that the situation had actually arisen, it confirmed its readiness to act as had been decided, subject to the agreement of the French Ministers, who were flying to London for consultations. It now considered the actual terms of the note in which this demand was to be addressed to Egypt and Israel; these would be discussed with M. Mollet and M. Pineau on their arrival.

The Cabinet examined the wording of the statement I was to make in the House that afternoon and endorsed it. We also discussed the attitude of the United States. The American Administration were urgently proposing to have Israel branded as an aggressor by the Security Council. They were unmoved by the history of the dispute or Egypt's aggressive attitude and declared intentions against Israel. Our hope was that the United States would take some account of those events and be watchful of Soviet moves. The Cabinet then approved the terms of a message to President Eisenhower inviting his general support. I sent two telegrams to Washington that day. In the first I said:

> We have never made any secret of our belief that justice entitled us to defend our vital interests against Nasser's designs. But we acted with you in summoning the London Conference, in despatching the abortive Menzies mission and in seeking to establish S.C.U.A.* As you know, the Russians regarded the Security Council proceedings as a victory for themselves and Egypt. Nevertheless we continued through the Secretary-General of the United Nations to seek a basis for the continuation of the negotiations.
>
> Egypt has to a large extent brought this attack on herself by insisting that the state of war persists, by defying the Security Council and by declaring her intention to marshal the Arab states for the destruction of Israel. The latest example of Egyptian intentions is the announcement of a joint command between Egypt, Jordan and Syria.
>
> We have earnestly deliberated what we should do in this serious situation. We cannot afford to see the canal closed to or lose the shipping which is daily on passage through it. We have a responsibility for the people in these ships. We

* Suez Canal Users' Association.

feel that decisive action should be taken at once to stop hostilities. We have agreed with you to go to the Security Council and instructions are being sent this moment. Experience however shows that its procedure is unlikely to be either rapid or effective.

My second message was sent after our talks with the French Ministers and the delivery of our jointly agreed notes to the Egyptian Ambassador and the Israeli Chargé d'Affaires. It informed the President of the requests we were making to the belligerents, and continued:

My first instinct would have been to ask you to associate yourself and your country with the declaration. But I know the constitutional and other difficulties in which you are placed. I think there is a chance that both sides will accept. In any case it would help this result very much if you found it possible to support what we have done at least in general terms. We are well aware that no real settlement of Middle East problems is possible except through the closest co-operation between our two countries. Our two Governments have tried with the best will in the world all sorts of public and private negotiations through the last two or three years and they have all failed. This seems an opportunity for a fresh start.

. . . Nothing could have prevented this volcano from erupting somewhere, but when the dust settles there may well be a chance for our doing a really constructive piece of work together and thereby strengthening the weakest point in the line against communism.

A message from President Eisenhower crossed my telegrams. He expressed his disquiet upon a number of points, but considered it of the greatest importance that the United Kingdom and the United States should quickly and clearly lay out their present views and intentions before each other, so that they might not in any real crisis be powerless to act in concert because of misunderstanding. That had been my purpose also at the January meeting in Washington, and all through this drawn-out business.

The question of consultation before action with the Commonwealth countries and the United States was one that troubled us
greatly. Of course we would have preferred to do this. Whatever
the outcome of such consultation, it would have smoothed our
path. On the other hand, however sharply pressed, such consultation was not possible within a matter of hours; it must take
days at least. Nor was there any chance that all concerned would
take precisely the same view of what action must follow the consultation. As a result there would be attempts to modify our
proposals, to reach some compromise between several divergent
points of view and, before we knew where we were, we would be
back at an eighteen-power conference once more. This was the
last thing in the world we wanted, because we knew quite well
that once palavers began, no effective action would be possible.

The chief danger, especially for us, was that the conflict would
spread. A localized war between Israel and Egypt, while troublesome, should not be highly dangerous internationally. The same
could not be said of a war which had spread to include Syria
and Jordan, with Iraq morally compelled to take a hand too. If
this were to happen, the Jordan commitment would raise its head
again, not in so acute a form, but alarming enough. Two events
could be counted on to encourage Jordan and Syria to inaction,
swift Israeli military success and the knowledge that British and
French forces were on the way and would be used to localize the
dispute. If that restraint was to be effective it must be applied
at once. Twenty-four hours might well be too late, forty-eight
certainly would.

The choice for us was stark and inescapable, either act at once
to bring about the result we sought, the localization of the conflict, or involve ourselves in consultations. This would mean
the same inaction as in the last three months. We chose to act.

I can imagine no conditions in which this conflict, so long
expected, could have taken place with less risk of wider consequences for the world. Among these conditions Anglo-French
presence and action signified most. It may be that our intervention brought the conflict "prematurely" to an end, to use the
adverb which the Leader of the Oppcsition employed. It is evident
that intervention stopped its spreading.

Our consultations with the French Ministers began the moment they arrived and continued over luncheon. As soon as these had been concluded and all points of action and timing settled, the Foreign Secretary, Mr. Butler, who was Leader of the House, and I saw the leaders of the Opposition. We gave them in advance a copy of the statement I was about to make in the House of Commons.

I thought it my duty to tell the House of the decision we had taken at the earliest moment. This led me into what I now consider was an error in timing. If I had done so two hours later, the Opposition would have been given time to consider the statement I was to make. The Commonwealth and the United States would have had time to reflect upon the messages we had sent them. However, I informed the House at 4.30 P.M. that the French and British Governments were agreed "that everything should be done to bring hostilities to an end as soon as possible." I announced the terms of our notes to Israel and Egypt and described the action we proposed to take if those countries did not comply. Our purpose was "to separate the belligerents and to guarantee freedom of transit through the canal by the ships of all nations."

I emphasized that if Anglo-French forces were obliged to move into key positions on the canal, this occupation would be temporary. At the same time I told the House that our representatives at the United Nations had been instructed to join with the United States in seeking an immediate meeting of the Security Council.

Later in the evening I intervened again in the House:

> Naturally, we hope that compliance by both sides with our appeal will enable those two objects to be secured rapidly, and then there would clearly be no need for anything more than token forces to make sure that what was accepted by both sides was, in fact, carried out, and they would, of course, be withdrawn the moment an agreement, a settlement, was arrived at.

I was questioned upon our obligations under the Tripartite Declaration of 1950. I pointed out that the Egyptian Government had never accepted this declaration. They did not regard it as giving rise to contractual duties and they had made it plain that it did not apply to them in the event of conflict with Israel. I added:

> In any case, there is nothing in the Tripartite Declaration nor in the Charter of the United Nations which abrogates the right of a Government to take such steps as are essential to protect vital international rights such as are here at stake.

At that very moment the Security Council was meeting in New York. When the House divided about ten o'clock in the evening, giving us a majority of 52, we did not know what the United Nations would decide.

On the night of the 30th I received a further telegram from the President. Mr. Eisenhower had now learnt the terms of our notes to Egypt and Israel. He was deeply concerned at the prospect of drastic action and he expressed the belief that peaceful processes could and should prevail. I was not surprised at this sentiment, but we had no reason at this moment to suppose that the United States would oppose us at the United Nations upon almost every point. The substance of the President's message to me was published in the United States that night. In consequence, I asked him if I could use in the House of Commons the two telegrams I had sent him earlier that day. The President at once agreed, but in fact I did not have to quote from the texts of the telegrams themselves.

Further reports were reaching us from Washington and New York of the reactions of the United States Government. They were unfavourable. Few officials concealed the irritation they felt that we and the French should at last have taken the action which we had long forecast. All United States opinion did not share this view. The *New York Times,* on November 1, was critical of our action but not deceived by Nasser. The newspaper wrote, explaining our attitude:

> It would be ridiculous to permit Colonel Nasser to pose before the United Nations or the world as the innocent victim of aggression, or to hold a protecting hand over him.

On the contrary, in so far as there is any one man guilty of aggression it is the Egyptian President, for he has waged war against Israel, Britain and France by propaganda, by gun-running, by infiltration of murderous bands, by stirring up rebellion in French North Africa, by seizing the Suez Canal by force and scrapping a treaty in the same manner in which Hitler marched into the Rhineland, by blocking the canal for Israeli shipping in defiance of United Nations orders — finally, by his whole loudly proclaimed program of throwing Israel into the sea in alliance with other Arab states and creating an Arab empire under his own hegemony which would expand his influence in concentric circles to all Africa and the whole Moslem world.

Ridiculous or not, this is precisely what happened. The Security Council met on the morning of October 30 and its debates continued throughout the day. From the start the United States delegation were determined simply to condemn Israeli action in forthright terms, without laying down any principles for a general settlement. They refused to amend the letter summoning the Security Council so that the French and ourselves could also sign it. To denounce and neither to offer nor to accept any constructive suggestions was the core of American policy.

We and the French pointed out that the long history of Israeli-Egyptian relations must be taken into account. We also considered that the Israeli action must be viewed in the light of the Egyptian threat to peace and security in the Middle East. This had been growing alarmingly in the past three years. All our diplomatic efforts in recent months had failed to secure redress for the seizure of the canal.

Our arguments were not heeded. The United States took the lead. Its representatives at the Council meeting put forward a resolution demanding an immediate cease-fire and the withdrawal of Israeli forces behind the armistice lines. The resolution also urged all members to refrain from the use of force, or even threat of force, in the area and to avoid giving any assistance to Israel so long as she did not comply with the resolution.

The object of this move was to take the initiative out of the

hands of the French and British Governments and to render
our joint summons to Egypt and Israel unnecessary. The United
Nations itself possessed no means of securing compliance with
the resolutions which it passed. Therefore the effect of the
American proposal would have been to condemn Anglo-French
initiative, while substituting nothing for it. We urged a short
delay at the Security Council, at least until there had been time
in New York to consider the text of my statement in London.
The Australian and Belgian representatives were understanding
and helpful about this. The former added that his Government
accepted none of the objections raised to the action undertaken
by Britain and France, which he hoped would achieve its objective.

Mr. Henry Cabot Lodge, the American representative, pressed
his resolution to a vote with all speed and included in it phrases
explicitly directed against Anglo-French action. His only reply to
the arguments of the British representative, in public and in
private, was to ask the Council to take the vote at once. As a
result, Britain used her veto for the first time in her membership
of the United Nations. The American resolution secured seven
votes, we and the French voted against it, Australia and Belgium
abstained.

The Russians then moved a resolution substantially the same
as the American draft, but without its most offensive paragraph
directed at the French and ourselves. We were willing to abstain
on this vote, in the hope of taking some of the heat out of the
debate and inducing reflection on the wider issues at stake.
It would certainly have been helpful if this had been possible, but
here we were up against the difficulties of rapid consultation
between the capitals and New York, and the insistence on immediate decisions by the United States delegate. The French
delegation were under instructions to use their veto and no time
was allowed for further discussion between the Governments. For
the sake of solidarity, therefore, we acted together. Tension
mounted at the United Nations and our friends among the maritime powers were appalled at the rift which was revealed between
us and the United States.

★   ★   ★   ★   ★

During this period Parliament was in almost continuous session for long hours at a stretch. In addition, as military operations developed, I had to hold frequent meetings with the Ministers concerned and the Chiefs of Staff. It was therefore not possible for the Foreign Secretary to be present at U.N.O. in person. Fortunately this was not as serious a handicap as it might have been, for our representative in New York was Sir Pierson Dixon, one of the ablest diplomatists I have ever known. It was said of him when the period of the Suez crisis was over, "He went through the whole business without ever missing a trick and without making an enemy."

I had known Sir Pierson since the days of the war when he was my Principal Private Secretary at the Foreign Office. He figured prominently in many events and in the taking of critical decisions. He has a remarkable sense of diplomacy and played a leading part in the Iranian oil negotiations and those concerning Trieste. There is something of the renaissance in the suppleness of his methods. Though a scholar of repute, there is nothing academic about the thrust of his mind. In this situation I might have been unhappy at leaving an official in such a position, but I was quite sure that if this had to be, no better choice was possible.

Sir Pierson warned the Council that the danger of a major war between Israel and her Arab neighbours had never been so imminent. The Anglo-French intervention was designed to prevent a disastrous conflagration from spreading. We were also exercising our right to defend our vital interests in the canal, which was now threatened by fighting. Our intervention was a temporary measure and in no way aimed at the sovereignty or territorial integrity of Egypt. The Security Council had spent ten years attempting to grapple with the problem of Palestine, to little effect. Owing to persistent Russian opposition, the United Nations had never been equipped with an armed force of its own which would see to it that the resolutions of the Security Council were observed. The absence of such a force had made Anglo-French action essential.

The next move, by the Yugoslav delegation, was fateful in its consequences. Prompted from the sidelines by the Indian representative, Yugoslavia sought to transfer the dispute from the

Security Council to a special session of the General Assembly, under the procedure known as "Uniting for Peace," originally devised at the time of the Korean conflict. In a General Assembly of eighty members, any chance of examining these events dispassionately, or of using them to bring about a Middle Eastern settlement, would be infinitely less than in the smaller Security Council. The authors of the Charter knew what they were about when they charged the Assembly with the power to debate and recommend, and the Council with the power to take decisions. Now the Assembly was to be invited to give orders.

The resolution to give effect to the Yugoslav proposal could be adopted only if it received at least seven votes in the Security Council. As the resolution concerned procedure, it was not subject to the veto. For the purpose of voting, abstentions had the same consequence as votes against. The French and ourselves voted against the resolution. Australia and Belgium abstained. The seven in favour were Nationalist China, Cuba, Iran, Yugoslavia, Peru, the Soviet Union and the United States. The United States vote decided the issue.

★   ★   ★   ★   ★

On October 31 the Cabinet decided that, Egypt having rejected the Anglo-French note, the Commander-in-Chief of the Allied Forces should be authorized to put into operation the approved plan. At dusk that evening the attack on the Egyptian air force began.

On the same day I explained in the House of Commons why Her Majesty's Government could not associate themselves at the United Nations with a condemnation of Israel:

It is not possible to pronounce in this way against one of the parties in the dispute for the action which they have taken, regardless of the cumulative effects that went before. . . . The Security Council resolution simply called upon the Israeli Government to withdraw within their frontiers. That seems to us in all the circumstances that have preceded these events to be a harsh demand, if it is to stand alone. It cer-

tainly could not be said to meet in any way the guarantees
for Israel's security, which were asked for by several Honourable
Members in the course of yesterday's debate.

I announced Israel's acceptance of the terms of the Anglo-
French note, and Egypt's rejection.

We have no desire, nor have the French Government, that
the military action that we shall have to take should be more
than temporary in its duration, but it is our intention that
our action to protect the canal and separate the combatants
should result in a settlement which will prevent such a situation arising in the future. If we can do that we shall have
performed a service not only to this country but to all users
of the canal.

Some Members during these debates expressed concern about
our relations with the United States. I gave the House the substance of the messages sent to President Eisenhower on the previous day. Apart from the exchanges between the President and
myself upon the Middle Eastern problem, my colleagues had held
numerous consultations with the American Secretary of State and
American Ministers and officials during recent months. We had
come to a conclusion which I then stated:

It is obvious truth that safety of transit through the canal,
though clearly of concern to the United States, is for them
not a matter of survival as it is to us and, indeed, to all
Europe and many other lands. Indeed, Mr. Dulles himself
made this clear on August 28 when he said the United States'
economy is not dependent upon the canal. Of course that is
true. We must all accept it, and we should not complain
about it, but it is equally true that throughout all these
months this fact has inevitably influenced the attitude of the
United States to these problems, as compared to that of ourselves and France.

If anyone says that on that account we should have held
up action until agreement could be reached with the United

States as to what to do, I can only say that this would have been to ignore what everyone here and in the United States knows to have been different approaches to some of these vital Middle Eastern questions. They know it. We know it. Of course, we deplore it, but I do not think that it can carry with it this corollary, that we must in all circumstances secure agreement from our American ally before we can act ourselves in what we know to be our own vital interests.

At the outset of the Suez crisis the Chiefs of Staff had been asked to prepare a plan of action for armed intervention against Egypt, should the need arise. The operation proposed had involved a build-up of forces at home and in the Mediterranean over a period of six weeks. Mid-September was the earliest date by which action could be taken.

From mid-September until the end of October our forces had been standing ready. During this period, Ministers had frequently examined the state of our precautions in conjunction with the Chiefs of Staff and with the Commander-in-Chief, Middle East Land Forces, General Sir Charles Keightley, who had been appointed Allied Commander-in-Chief for the operation. After much consideration, a plan had been drawn up, designed to secure our objectives with the utmost speed and the least possible loss of military or civilian life.

One Sunday in October, Sir Winston Churchill invited himself to luncheon at Chequers. On the three-hour journey by car from Chartwell he had dictated a series of queries and suggestions. We had a stimulating discussion which covered almost every eventuality. As he left, he said: "I must look up and see exactly where Napoleon landed."

Our planning had been complicated by various factors. The number of parachute troops and carrier aircraft available to us was limited by decisions taken some years before. There was also a crippling shortage of landing craft. The French 10th Airborne Division, allied to our own 16th Independent Parachute Brigade group, went some way to meet the first of our needs. The shortage of landing craft we met as best we could by requisitioning any that could be found including some which were being used for ferrying commercial vehicles to and from Northern Ireland. Even so, this shortage definitely ruled out certain types of operation. To land on a coast without a deep-water port to facilitate the unloading of heavy equipment and stores involves the use of a large number of landing ships and craft, particularly tank-landing ships. Shortage of suitable craft constricted us. Our advisers agreed that a deep-water port must be captured.

We also needed a deep-water port at which to embark. Cyprus has none. This meant that a seaborne assault in immediate support of an airborne landing had to be mounted from Malta, which lies more than nine hundred miles from Port Said. This is six days' steaming time. Further support troops to follow up the initial landing would have to be drawn from the United Kingdom, Libya and Algeria. These were inescapable strategic facts which had to be taken into account.

The plan was for an operation which could be launched at short notice, but which could also be held back for some time without loss of efficiency. The first phase was to consist of the elimination of the Egyptian air force, if possible on the ground, by bombing from Cyprus, Malta and Aden, and by fighter attacks from carriers and from Cyprus. We hoped also in this phase to put Cairo radio out of action and to sink as many Egyptian blockships as possible by pin-point bombing, before they took up blocking positions in the canal.

In the second phase, our air assault was to be switched to Egyptian military targets and installations, with the object of destroying the Egyptian capacity for organized defence. It had originally been estimated that these two phases might occupy from ten to fourteen days. In our discussions of the military plan we had, however, reduced the preliminary period of air bombardment to six days. In the third phase, the airborne drop from Cyprus would be made on Port Said, to be followed within twenty-four hours by the seaborne landing from Malta. It was not possible to be certain that the first two phases, with their strictly limited military targets, would succeed in their purpose. The military commanders had therefore prepared for the possibility of a tough and troublesome battle in the third stage.

There was one element in all these calculations which could not then be ignored, the part that the foreign technicians in Egypt would play. Would they remain technicians or become "volunteers," most incongruous of Communist phrases? It was to be expected that they would give good advice as to initial military dispositions and that their training would have brought about some improvement in the handling of their weapons by the Egyptians. We could not tell if this would be all. We knew what had happened in Korea, how, when the Communist forces were being worsted, Chinese "volunteers" had come to the rescue of the hard-pressed North Koreans. The same technique could be followed in Egypt. Even if this were not done on a considerable scale, the technicians could fly the aeroplanes and maybe man some of the tanks. If so, the nature of the opposition to be overcome would be far greater than that which the Egyptian forces themselves could offer.

There was another element. During September information had reached us of naval reinforcements to Egypt. These were of little account in themselves, but they might be taken as an indication of similar help being given in the air and on the land, where it would be much more serious. Two submarines had sailed for Alexandria under the Polish flag with Russian ratings and Egyptian officers on board. It was probable that an equivalent reinforcement had arrived by air.

In the event, when the Anglo-French intervention took place, the Soviet technicians were withdrawn to Khartoum.

★   ★   ★   ★   ★

On November 1 the Minister of Defence, Mr. Antony Head, gave the House details of the first raids on Egyptian airfields. There was much interruption and disorder and the Speaker was obliged to suspend the sitting for half an hour. When the House resumed, the Opposition moved a vote of censure.

In my reply to the debate I made the suggestion that a United Nations force should eventually be associated with the Anglo-French police action. This idea was taken up in the General Assembly the next day by Mr. Lester Pearson and others. I had put it in the following words:

We best avoid great wars by taking even physical action to stop small ones. Everybody knows that the United Nations is not in a position to do that. We and the French have the forces available. We must face the fact that the United Nations is not yet the international equivalent of our own legal system and the rule of law. ....

Effective action to re-establish peace will make easier an international solution of the many problems which exist in that area. Of course, we do not delegate to ourselves any special position in that respect. On the contrary we would welcome and look for the participation of many other nations in bringing about a settlement and in upholding it.

Israel and Egypt are locked in conflict in that area. The first and urgent task is to separate these combatants and to stabilize the position. That is our purpose. If the United Nations were then willing to take over the physical task of maintaining peace in that area, no one would be better pleased than we. But police action there must be to separate the belligerents and to prevent a resumption of hostilities.

This was no chance suggestion. I had always thought how much the League of Nations had suffered from lack of an international force to back its decisions. From the first conception of the United Nations, I had, as Foreign Secretary, been an advocate of the creation of such a force. Mr. Stettinius, Mr. Molotov and I discussed this at San Francisco in 1945, but the Russians were cool towards the idea. However, with the support of the French, we carried matters to the point where it was agreed that an international army would be created and placed at the disposal of the United Nations. The organization of this force should have been one of the first tasks of the United Nations in accordance with the terms of the Charter; Articles 43–48 provided for it. Mainly owing to Soviet obstruction, it never came into being.

Mr. Selwyn Lloyd and I, when together at the Foreign Office and later, had been concerned to strengthen the forces at General Burns's disposal against the evident dangers on the borders of Israel and the Arab states. There was little enthusiasm for this suggestion either, and to have proposed a United Nations force in advance of the outbreak of hostilities would have evoked no response. Now, however, there was a chance, not only to create a force, but to use it to bring about a permanent settlement in the Middle East.

In the division which followed, the Government had a majority of 69, but the most important outcome of the debate was that the idea of a United Nations police force had been implanted.

★   ★   ★   ★   ★

Meanwhile, the Israelis in Sinai had won a brilliant series of victories. Their objective was not to acquire territory, it was to forestall aggression. Their intention was to defeat the Egyptian army and to destroy its extensive equipment; to stamp out the nests of *fedayeen* raiders; to open the Gulf of Aqaba to international shipping. Egyptian forces in Sinai numbered some 45,000 men and the Israeli numbers were about the same. The Egyptians were better equipped and they held well-sited and well-fortified strongpoints. The Israelis were splendid in their courage and confidence. The mobilization caused no alarm, it even brought relief after the strain and tension and the raids of the last months.

There were four prongs to their attack. The first action at nightfall on October 29 was the dropping of a parachute battalion in the passes of the Mitla mountains forty miles to the east of Suez. This advance guard was speedily reinforced by the rest of the airborne brigade, which travelled overland from the Israeli frontier, a distance of a hundred and thirty miles through the centre of Sinai, taking fortified positions on the way.

Farther north a second task force of two brigades overcame formidable defences outside Abu Aweigla. These had been planned by the Egyptian army's German advisers. The task force then advanced by road to Ismailia on the canal, which they reached in four days.

In the north of the peninsula, near the Mediterranean coast, a third task force stormed the Egyptian bases of Rafa and El Arish. These were strong positions, with highly organized defences, which could have been expected to put up a stout resistance. Each fell within a few hours of a dawn attack. Here

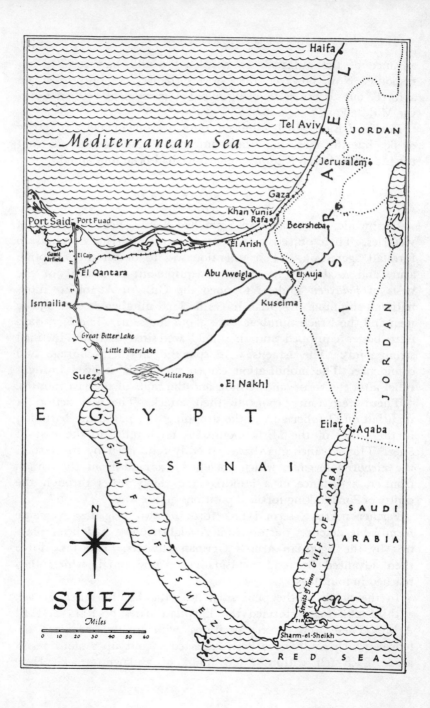

Haifa

Mediterranean Sea

Tel Aviv

JORDAN

Jerusalem

Gaza

Khan Yunis

Rafa

Beersheba

Port Said

Port Fuad

Gamil
Airfield

El Cap

El Arish

El Qantara

Abu Aweigla

El Auja

Ismailia

Kuseima

Great Bitter Lake

Little Bitter Lake

Suez

Mitla Pass

El Nakhl

EGYPT

SINAI

Eilat

Aqaba

I S R A E L

J O R D A N

GULF OF SUEZ

GULF OF AQABA

N

SAUDI

ARABIA

SUEZ

Miles

0 10 20 30 40 50 60

Straits of Tiran

TIRAN

Sharm-el-Sheikh

RED   SEA

the victorious Israelis found workshops, ordnance depots, stores and vast parks of the latest war material covering many square miles of territory. What was all this for?

The Gaza strip was thus sealed off and its surrender followed after a short struggle. Detachments of this northern force then moved westwards in the direction of El Qantara, on the canal. When their Government accepted the Anglo-French notes, all three of these Israeli forces withdrew from the neighbourhood of the canal.

The fourth Israeli column of one brigade plunged towards the south. It advanced along almost impassable tracks down the west coast of the Gulf of Aqaba and assaulted the fortified position of Sharm-el-Sheikh. The Egyptian Government had spent much money on the defence of this position, which was the key point from which they had been blockading the Israeli port of Eilat on the Gulf. Although its commander had 2000 men and was strongly entrenched, he surrendered after a brief fight. Like many Egyptian commanders, he explained that his men were "no good."

Thus after five days' struggle, the Israeli army had gained all its main objectives. The Egyptians were everywhere in retreat. Israeli losses were 180 killed and 4 captured. The Egyptians lost 1000 men killed in action and 6000 prisoners; others were killed by the unfriendly Bedouin.

While the Israelis were driving home these victorious thrusts against Egyptian forces with superior equipment, cries for help went out from Cairo, by code, and sometimes even *en clair,* to Amman and to Damascus. These were received with caution and returned with prudence, various pretexts being alleged to cover present inaction and a variety of assurances being offered of support to come. In reality, however, the knowledge that the allied expedition was on its way and the speed of the Israeli victories, strengthened those in Jordan and in Syria who wisely preferred discretion.

The outcome of this fighting casts an interesting reflection on the Egyptian revolution. Many had supposed that it had some resemblance to comparable upheavals in other lands, notably that of the Young Turks in the first Balkan war. The expectation was

that, while the senior officers might still be inefficient, the younger
ones at least, brought up in the atmosphere of the revolution,
would show themselves brave and determined in battle. The
reverse proved to be true. The older officers in some instances
fought well, the younger ones were the first to leave the battle.
The Egyptian revolution had clearly not affected the quality of
leadership in its armed forces. All of which was notched up by
watchful neighbours.

9

THE FIGHTING

October 31–November 7

THE GENERAL ASSEMBLY of the United Nations met on the morning of November 2. Sir Pierson Dixon rehearsed the case for our police action with his customary clarity and vigour. But the Assembly was in an emotional mood. There was talk of collective measures against the French and ourselves. Our friends were concerned lest some rash initiative should lead to a situation in which either the French and ourselves would have to abandon our purpose or leave the organization. Such was the frenetic atmosphere prevailing in New York. In London the Government had no intention of doing either.

It was not Soviet Russia, or any Arab state, but the Government of the United States which took the lead in Assembly against Israel, France and Britain. Their Secretary of State said he moved the resolution with a heavy heart. It took no account whatever of events preceding the action by Israel or France and Britain, nor did it propose any initiative by the United Nations to mend the dangerous condition of affairs which had existed in the area for so long. There was no suggestion of going to the root of the matter, or of using the Anglo-French intervention to good purpose, either to create an effective international force, or to negotiate a peace settlement for the area and an international agreement for the canal. There was no attempt to snatch opportunity out of trouble which is the stamp of statesmanship. This we had done when Trieste had brought Italy and Yugoslavia to the verge of war, and when the collapse of E.D.C. endangered the unity of Europe.

The resolution put peace in a strait-jacket. Directed against Anglo-French intervention as well as the fighting, it urged that all parties now engaged in hostilities in the Middle East should agree to an immediate cease-fire; it urged all members to refrain from introducing military goods into the area and asked the Assembly to remain in emergency session until the resolution was complied with. Mr. Dulles recognized that a resolution which merely sought to restore the *status quo* before the Israeli attack was neither adequate nor comprehensive. He hoped that the United Nations would strive to bring about a betterment of the conditions that had led to what he described as "this tragedy." He did not suggest how this could be done.

The Canadian Minister for External Affairs, Mr. Lester Pearson, explained why he could not vote for the United States resolution. In his speech he developed the idea, which I had advocated in the House of Commons the day before, of a United Nations police force. Mr. Pearson felt, as we did, that calling for a cease-fire and a withdrawal of forces was insufficient unless it were linked with proposals for a permanent settlement of the Israel and Suez problems. He declared that the resolution should have invited the Secretary-General to work out a scheme for a United Nations police force which would keep the peace on the frontiers of Israel. Canada was willing to contribute to such a force. The Norwegian Foreign Minister and other representatives were also attracted by this proposal, which they hoped would be approved.

Had the United States been willing to play a part as balanced as Canada's, the course of history must have been different, but this was not to be. The Assembly was in a mood to punish. The hunt was up after Israel and the "colonial" powers. Mr. Nixon, Vice-President of the United States, declared in a speech:

> For the first time in history we have shown independence of Anglo-French policies towards Asia and Africa which seemed to us to reflect the colonial tradition. This declaration of independence has had an electrifying effect throughout the world.

Mr. Dulles' resolution was adopted by the Assembly by 64 votes to 5. Australia, New Zealand and Israel voted with Britain and France. Canada, South Africa, Belgium, Laos, the Netherlands and Portugal abstained.

Her Majesty's Government had no doubt about their reply. We were not prepared to halt our action while the fighting continued. If an international force were created by the United Nations, we were willing, under certain conditions, to hand over to them. The terms of our note were agreed with M. Pineau in the course of the day and approved by the Cabinet that evening.

On November 3 I announced them to the House of Commons:

> The British and French Governments have given careful consideration to the resolution passed by the General Assembly on November 2. They maintain their view that police action must be carried through urgently to stop the hostilities which are now threatening the Suez Canal, to prevent a resumption of these hostilities and to pave the way for a definite settlement of the Arab-Israel war which threatens the legitimate interests of so many countries.
>
> They would most willingly stop military action as soon as the following conditions could be satisfied:
>
> 1. Both the Egyptian and the Israeli Governments agree to accept a United Nations force to keep the peace;
>
> 2. The United Nations decides to constitute and maintain such a force until an Arab-Israeli peace settlement is reached and until satisfactory arrangements have been agreed in regard to the Suez Canal, both arrangements to be guaranteed by the United Nations;

3. In the meantime, until the United Nations force is constituted, both combatants agree to accept forthwith limited detachments of Anglo-French troops to be stationed between combatants.

Our reply to the General Assembly also dealt with the future of the Suez Canal, as Mr. Pearson's speech had done the day before. We did this because we thought that the situation could be used to resolve the principal problems of the region. We defined our position accordingly.

It should have been clear that there would be no peace between Israel and the Arab states, unless the United Nations played an active physical part in the area, nor would there be security for world commerce in the canal unless freedom of passage were accepted as an international obligation. If these were insured by an international force, there would be confidence in the future. The gage which we and the French hoped to win at Port Said and along the canal might be exchanged for effective United Nations control. Financially, such an arrangement could be made attractive to an Egyptian Government bedraggled in authority by humiliating defeats in the field. Here was an occasion which could be used to negotiate an arrangement to ensure the future freedom of the canal for world commerce.

Nearly three years have passed since these events. I am more than ever convinced that an intelligent use of these opportunities would have resulted in an agreement of a lasting character for the Middle East. If Anglo-French action had been followed by the creation of an effective United Nations force, we would have made a reality of our attempts at international order. This would have sobered the whole area, discouraged imperialist ambition and interference in the affairs of other nations by radio and other methods of subversion. Much subsequent tragedy would have been averted, including the massacres in Baghdad.

While the majority of the United Nations was in haste to pillory France and Britain and Israel, not a mouse moved in Arab lands. As Israeli columns lunged victoriously across Sinai, and British and French sailed the Mediterranean, all was still from Morocco to the Persian Gulf. Cairo radio was successfully put out of action after a preliminary warning which avoided casualties.

Forecasts of universal hate for the Europeans who intervened were not borne out either then or later, because many were hesitant and some understood. The West has been as slow to read Nasser's *A Philosophy of Revolution* as it was to read Hitler's *Mein Kampf*, with less excuse because it is shorter and not so turgid. But Eastern rulers had read it, and there were many who knew that, if the Egyptian triumphed unchecked, his prowl to conquest would have wider scope and their turn in Syria, Saudi Arabia and elsewhere must soon follow. Nasser coveted their wealth and their empire, and whether they used their power for schemes of welfare for their people or for their own ends, if he won they would forfeit it.

★ ★ ★ ★ ★

Events in Hungary were now following their ruthless pattern. Real power in the country rested with the Soviet military authorities. They claimed, after the event, that their troops had been asked to restore order under the terms of the Warsaw Pact. The truth was that the Hungarian revolution was moving faster and farther than suited the Russians. They were determined not to let Hungary slip wholly from their grasp, and were fearful of the influence of the Hungarian movement upon other satellite states of Eastern Europe. The Hungarian army began to fraternize with demonstrators in the streets. When, on October 30, Mr. Nagy promised the people of Hungary that he would negotiate for the withdrawal of the Soviet forces, the Russian reaction was immediate. While sporadic fighting had been raging in Budapest, the Russians had built up their strength for a counter-attack.

Two days later, further Russian forces entered Hungary from the Ukraine with their tanks and heavy equipment. Nagy protested against this new Russian invasion. He proclaimed the neutrality of his country, appealed to the United Nations and asked for the aid of the four great powers in protecting Hungarian neutrality. While negotiations were going forward between Soviet and Hungarian officials, Budapest was surrounded by two Soviet divisions and five further Soviet divisions took up positions in the country. On Sunday, November 4, the Russians attacked the capital and an appalling struggle ensued. There were 50,000 casualties in Budapest alone.

The back of Hungarian resistance was broken in ten days of fighting. Guerilla warfare continued long after. There was a prolonged strike and demonstrations were frequent for months to come. Several times crowds assembled outside the British Legation, seeking Western sympathy. Our Minister gave them what comfort he could. On one occasion the crowd was surrounded by Russian tanks, their guns trained on the Legation door.

Nagy was kidnapped by the Russians and nothing more was heard of him for eighteen months, when the Russians executed him. Full-dress Communist government was reimposed upon Hungary. Before the end of the year some 150,000 refugees had fled the country, and many thousand fighters for freedom had been deported to Russia.

The pitiable failure of the United Nations to influence Hungarian events in the slightest degree lit up that tragedy in flaming colour. I had announced from 10 Downing Street on October 28 that in concert with our allies we were referring the Hungarian situation to the United Nations. The Security Council did not dally at the start. It considered the plight of Hungary on that same day. The Western powers indicted the Soviet Union for "violently repressing the rights of the Hungarian people," but the debate was inconclusive and the Council adjourned.

Five days passed without any further Council meeting upon Hungary, despite repeated attempts by ourselves and others to bring one about. The United States representative was reluctant, and voiced his suspicion that we were urging the Hungarian situation to divert attention from Suez. The United States Government appeared in no hurry to move. Their attitude provided a damaging contrast to the alacrity they were showing in arraigning the French and ourselves.

At length, on the night of November 3, the Council met while fresh Russian troops were speeding to Budapest. The Russians for the seventy-ninth time used their veto. Thereupon the issue was transferred to the General Assembly, which passed a resolution next day by 50 votes to 8, with 15 abstentions, calling upon the Russian Government to withdraw their forces from Hungary immediately. It also instructed the Secretary-General to visit Hungary and arrange for the entry of United Nations observers. The United Nations was not even treated to the pretence of ceremony, the Secretary-General was refused admission and its observers were never allowed into Hungary. The Russian forces remained and ruled. The General Assembly repeated its request to Russia on November 9, but to no effect. On that occasion India alone voted with the Soviet bloc.

The Indian reaction was remarkable. Mr. Nehru declared in a speech that whereas in Egypt "every single thing that had happened was as clear as daylight," he could not follow "the very confusing situation" in Hungary. He then proceeded to read out the excuses which Marshal Bulganin had sent him for the Russian intervention. These Mr. Nehru described as "facts." He displayed the same readiness to accept Russia's explanations as he had Nasser's.

★   ★   ★   ★   ★

The week-end of November 3–5 was tense and busy in London. On Sunday, November 4, a crowd of several thousand assembled in Trafalgar Square to hear Opposition speakers address them upon the slogan of "Law, not war." After the meeting a part of the audience attempted to make a demonstration by marching down Whitehall to Downing Street. There were scuffles with the police. Twenty-seven demonstrators were arrested and eight constables were injured. Eventually the crowd expended its energies in marching around the streets of the West End bearing banners abusing the Government. This rowdy demonstration won much notice in the newspapers of the following day. It took place at a time when the public opinion polls showed the nation to be almost evenly divided upon the Government's handling of the Middle Eastern crisis.

My wife was an eye-witness of the Trafalgar Square meeting. She had walked to it from Number 10 and stood on the edge of the crowd. She was wearing a scarf round her head but, in spite of this, onlookers began to recognize her. So many of them took the opportunity to congratulate her that she thought it prudent to return to Downing Street. A day or two later she received a letter from a London bus-driver who had been in the midst of the affair. He wrote of me:

> He's done the only thing possible — my opinion and also that of a great number of fellow bus employees — only a small proportion of London's multitudes — but if a bus driver agrees — he must be right — I personally thank God we've got one man who's not afraid to do the right thing. As regards the rioting of the other evening — as I was on a bus (driving) right in the middle of it — I saw possibly more than most people — Eighty per cent of the crowd were of foreign extraction so that was no true census of opinion and can be ignored.

During the days which passed after our decision to intervene I had little leisure to learn about any changes in public opinion. However, one's mail bag can give a fair indication. In the first few days after our decision the letters were heavily adverse, at the outset something like eight to one against. With the passage of time, this majority weakened and finally disappeared until, in the later stages and on the day before the cease-fire, the majority was heavily in favour of the action we had taken to the extent of about four to one. The *Daily Express* public opinion poll bears out this impression. Between October 30 and November 5 support for the Government's action rose from 48½ per cent to 51½ per cent and opposition dropped from 39 per cent to 30 per cent. During the next fortnight, until November 21, the same poll recorded that satisfaction with my leadership of the Government rose from 51½ per cent to 60½ per cent and that opposition fell away from 36 per cent to 30½ per cent.

The little I saw of public demonstrations confirmed this. Every day I drove in the early afternoon across to the House of Commons and, though the way was short, there were usually small crowds on the road. In the early days the booing about equalled the cheering. As time went on, the booing grew fainter and the cheering louder until in the last stages the booing had entirely disappeared; except in the House of Commons.

I have often known noisy interludes in the House, but never such a continuous abuse of the rules of order as during the Suez debates, if by any stretch of courtesy they can be so called. It was impossible to respect or heed the House in such conditions. One ambassador of a foreign power with a regard for democracy was seen to leave the diplomatic gallery almost in tears during one of these displays. Perhaps the most ludicrous scene took place one evening when, as the Speaker left the Chair, the Opposition leaders rose and booed me as I went out. What they hoped to gain by this demonstration I cannot tell.

There is one particular in which the habits of the House of Commons have recently deteriorated. Members wanting to interrupt used to jump to their feet and try to make the Member in possession of the House give way, if he was prepared to do so. This sometimes led to noisy exchanges, but at least the Member who was challenged, and the House, knew who the interrupter was. Now it is a frequent habit of Members to heckle as if they were at a public meeting, shouting insults at a Minister or other speaker while sitting or sprawling. This is a sloppy and not exactly courageous practice which Front Benchers should set an example in shunning. They do not.

One of the letters protesting against the Government's action which appeared in the newspapers at this time came from Oxford University and was signed by a number of professors and heads of colleges. It drew a powerful rejoinder from a number of equally eminent dons, which was published in the *Daily Telegraph* on November 7, 1956:

> The fact remains that after years of conflicting and often cynical attempts by Russia and other nations to influence, even confuse, political affairs in the Middle East and after the clear and repeated failures of the United Nations to act effectively in the Israeli-Egyptian dispute, a crisis was likely sooner or later to develop when one or more major powers would feel impelled to intervene to prevent a more serious war.

They appealed for "patient but, if necessary, critical support" of British and French action until the United Nations had itself taken on the task.

Dr. Gilbert Murray headed the list of signatories. This fine scholar, humanist and champion of the League of Nations wrote a further letter to the weekly paper *Time & Tide,* published in the November 10, 1956, issue. In it he said:

> The rather wild confusion into which people have fallen about the Middle East situation is, I think, due to two main causes. First, it is strictly a question of International Law, and our system of International Law is not complete. The U.N. was intended to have a means of enforcing the law; it has no such means. (See Articles 43–48 of the Charter.) Egypt and Israel have been breaking the law for nine years with no correction.
>
> Secondly, the Nasser danger is much more serious and pressing than a local friction consisting of Colonel Nasser's irregular nationalization of the canal and the perpetual war between Egypt and Israel, with which the U.N. has been unable to deal. The real danger was that, if the Nasser movement had been allowed to progress unchecked, we should have been faced by a coalition of all Arab, Muslim, Asiatic, and anti-Western States, led nominally by Egypt but really by Russia; that is, a division of the world in which the enemies of civilization are stronger than its supporters. Such a danger, the Prime Minister saw, must be stopped instantly, and, since the U.N. has no instrument, it must be stopped, however irregularly, by those nations who can act at once.
>
> So much for the immediate present; the next step, of course, is the creation of a police force for the U.N. Happily this has now been done. As soon as a cessation of hostilities has been imposed, that force should proceed to discharge its functions of maintaining the law afterwards. The Russian plan has actually been revealed on November 6. It is frustrated and indeed shown to be absurd; but we can see now what Russia and Nasser once intended and may possibly still make a desperate attempt to renew.
>
> The Prime Minister's policy may well prove to have been the only road to success.

I mentioned Dr. Murray's views because they were based upon long reflection on world affairs and a lifetime's devotion to the cause of international peace. The conclusion which he had reached at Oxford was the same as I had formed in Downing Street.

★   ★   ★   ★   ★

The pace was faster and the strain more intense upon the principal members of the Government during these days and nights than at any time during the second world war. It is true that we had held debates then of the first importance, the results of which were sometimes critical, but these had not been frequent. Now they were continuous. They took place virtually every day during the decisive period and lasted throughout the session. This always made it difficult, and often made it impossible, to deal with even the most urgent work while the House was sitting, which was at least from 2.30 P.M. to 10 P.M. and sometimes later. Added to this was the problem of the difference in time. During the war there was hardly any communication by telephone across the Atlantic. For one thing it was not safe, the Germans might listen in, and did. Now all this was changed. It was after midnight, our time, that the United Nations and Washington became most active, both by telegram and telephone. I had always to be available and so had the Foreign Secretary. My excellent staff did all they could to spare me and were organized to be at hand in relays, but frequent interruptions of a night's rest were inescapable.

Robert Allan was my Parliamentary Private Secretary. He was a member of Parliament with a brilliant war record as a naval officer. It was his task to keep in touch with the House of Commons and to report to me on moods and sentiment there. He also dealt as far as possible with members who wanted to see me or get messages to me.

My day ran something like this. While I was shaving, bathing and dressing, Mr. Allan would report to me and raise any points he wished. Sometimes one of the Private Secretaries would break in with an immediate telegram, or the Chief Whip, Mr. Edward Heath, with whom lay the responsibility for guiding and marshalling our forces in the House of Commons, would arrive with some suggestion or point for decision. Though Mr. Heath's service in Parliament had been short at that time, I have never known a better equipped Chief Whip. A ready smile concealed a firm mind. Downstairs in the Cabinet room at Number 10, where I always worked, as being more convenient than my study on the first floor, the morning was the only time we ever had for the urgent affairs of the nation. Into this period had to be crammed Cabinet sessions, special meetings to deal with the military, financial, economic or diplomatic aspects of the crisis, messages to and from Commonwealth Prime Ministers, consultation with individual colleagues, and a chance to think.

My critics wrote that I was calm under the strain. I felt at ease; there was a reason for this. From the first I was convinced that the course on which we had decided was the only acceptable one in a grim choice of difficulties. I did not expect it to be popular, but my colleagues and I had been grappling with the deteriorating situation for months and we were confident in our course. That makes for calm.

During these days private life ceased to exist. It was useless to fix engagements and unwise to invite guests to meals. Luncheon could be at any hour and dinner was often not eaten until far into the night. My wife somehow adapted our domestic arrangements to meet these unsteady requirements; my digestion took less kindly to them.

As a result of having no country home, except the cottage at Broad Chalke, we had moved our own pictures, furniture and books into Downing Street. I was never more happy at this arrangement than during these heavily charged days and nights. It was a refreshment to escape for a while from the official rooms and be able to reflect in an atmosphere which was part of my own personal life.

I do not have many pictures, for I have never been rich enough to buy much. A watercolour by Dunoyer de Segonzac, "Le Canotier," which is a sketch for a painting now hanging in one of the national collections in Paris, was the first picture I ever bought. My collection was made for the most part when on holiday in France. I also hung upstairs in Downing Street a number of my father's watercolours, which I like more and more with the passage of years. My admiration of them is not merely filial. On several occasions during the prolonged crisis I found time to sit in my wife's green drawing-room and enjoy the two Derain sanguines, and the Degas bronze of a girl in her bath which Sir Alexander Korda had given us as a wedding present.

★ ★ ★ ★ ★

On the noisy Sunday of November 4 we held two meetings of the committee of Ministers which had kept in constant touch with the situation throughout these anxious months. In the evening a full Cabinet considered the position. Our armada from Malta was nearing Port Said. The Minister of Defence, who had just paid a flying visit to allied headquarters in Cyprus, reported that Egyptian forces appeared to be withdrawing upon Cairo. The outlook for our action at Port Said was favourable and the allied commanders believed that they could occupy key positions in the town by immediate parachute drop. This air assault was due to be launched at first light next day. There were good hopes of success without recourse to naval bombardment.

When the Cabinet met, the next stage in military operations lay still some twelve hours in the future. We had to consider two further resolutions which had been adopted by the General Assembly of the United Nations. One had been put forward by Canada and the other by a group of Afro-Asian States prompted by India.

The Canadian resolution asked the Secretary-General to work out a plan within forty-eight hours for the creation of a United Nations force which would secure and supervise the ending of hostilities in the area of the canal. This was welcome to us. Reports reaching us from the United Nations, however, indicated that the purpose and composition of the force might not conform to our ideas. Sir Pierson Dixon was instructed to speak in favour of the Canadian resolution, while making our reservations clear and abstaining on the vote if they were not met.

The Afro-Asian resolution called upon the Secretary-General to arrange a cease-fire within the next twelve hours. A reply had to be sent to Mr. Hammarskjöld before midnight. The Government had a choice of three courses. We could proceed with our action at Port Said, repeating our offer to hand over to the United Nations as soon as an effective force reached the canal. Alternatively, we could postpone the parachute landings for twenty-four hours. This would give Egypt and Israel an opportunity to accept a United Nations force and allow time for the General Assembly to consider whether the Anglo-French forces might be accepted as its advance guard. Thirdly, we could defer all further military action on the grounds that we had in fact put an end to the Israeli-Egyptian conflict.

It was clear to me that a postponement could not be accepted. I was confident that the Commander-in-Chief, if consulted, would urge overwhelming arguments against it, which he properly and promptly did. The political objections were also obvious, once action was halted it could hardly be resumed. Postponement would, in fact, have meant calling off the operation. If we postponed now we should be doing so before we had gained our main physical objective, to insert an impartial force between Egypt and Israel along the canal. There was no United Nations force yet in being to fulfil our aims for us. Unless we persisted, it might never come into existence. The Cabinet was in favour of going forward and shouldering the political risks. It was determined by the news that reached us towards the end of our meeting. Though Israel had accepted a cease-fire in principle, she had not yet agreed to the United Nations force, wishing no doubt for information as to its location, duties and composition. All was still uncertain, there was every reason for proceeding with our action.

I gave an account of our opinion in a telegram to the President, in which I wrote:

> If we draw back now chaos will not be avoided. Everything will go up in flames in the Middle East. You will realize, with all your experience, that we cannot have a military vacuum while a United Nations force is being constituted and is being transported to the spot. That is why we feel we must go on to hold the position until we can hand over responsibility to the United Nations.

★   ★   ★   ★   ★

In the afternoon of November 5 the Minister of Defence announced the airborne assault on Port Said. The Egyptian air force had been destroyed by November 2, and the R.A.F. flew virtually without opposition. They took immense trouble to avoid civilian casualties. Egyptian military movements in the canal area were heavily intermingled with civilian traffic of all kinds. Many targets were not attacked by us for this reason. Our pilots reported that Egyptian military crews generally abandoned their vehicles on the appearance of our aircraft, while civilian traffic went on unperturbed. Such was the effect of our broadcast intentions to attack from the air military targets only.

At 8 A.M. on the 5th, some 600 British parachutists had begun their jump on Gamil Airfield to the west of the town, which itself lies on the west bank of the canal entrance. At the same time 500 French parachutists dropped to the south of Port Said near the waterworks, which they had seized, together with an important bridge over the interior basin. Gamil Airfield was quickly secured and the British parachute battalion advanced eastwards into the town itself. Continuous support was given by aircraft from the carrier force. At 1.45 P.M. a reinforcing drop of 100 men with vehicles and heavy equipment was made at Gamil Airfield. A further 460 French parachutists were dropped on the southern outskirts of Port Fuad, on the east bank of the canal, which they proceeded to occupy. Resistance was offered by the Egyptians during the morning, but at 3 P.M. the local Egyptian commander offered to discuss surrender terms on behalf of the Governor of Port Said. At 3.30 a cease-fire was ordered, while negotiations went forward. About an hour later I gave this news to the House, which was then noisily cross-examining the Foreign Secretary. I am not sure that I was wise to do so. The effect in the House was instantaneous, the Government's supporters rising to their feet to cheer and wave their order papers and the Opposition being temporarily subdued. By this announcement I told the world of the cease-fire, thus alerting those who would not welcome it and giving them an opportunity of working against it.

At seven o'clock in the evening a further signal arrived stating that the Egyptians had agreed to our terms. Their forces in Port Said had begun to lay down their arms, and their police were co-operating with us in the town. I was immensely relieved. It seemed that our operations had succeeded instantly and at remarkably small cost. An hour and a half later came a very different message. The Governor of Port Said reported that he could not now agree to the terms and that fighting must resume.

Who had caused him to reverse his decision? It is hard to believe that the Governor would have negotiated a cease-fire and then have proceeded to actual surrender without the knowledge of his Government. Nasser must have known during those five hours what was going on in Port Said. I am convinced that this reversal of action was prompted from further afield. We may never be able to prove it, but what is certain and significant is that loud-speaker vans toured Port Said announcing that Russian help was on the way, that London and Paris had been bombed and that the third world war had started. At this moment a menacing letter from Bulganin had been despatched to me, the first word I had received from him since our decision to intervene. Encouraged by the attitude of the United States and the United Nations, the Russians had taken their decision. The Soviet Consul became suddenly active in Port Said, stimulating resistance and promising help. The Russian hat was now in the ring.

When fighting was resumed it took the form of sniping and guerilla tactics in built-up areas. It was during this later period that the town was damaged. The parachute force had done its job swiftly and brilliantly, but it was too small in numbers to complete the capture of the town, now that the truce was off. The assault forces from Malta did so next day, arriving exactly on time. The Royal Marine commandos went ashore at Port Said in the early hours of the morning of November 6. French commandos and supporting troops landed at Port Fuad. The street fighting which followed was complicated by the fact that most of the Egyptian regular troops had discarded their uniforms and were indistinguishable from civilians, many of whom were also armed. Some centres of resistance held out until the afternoon, but by dusk organized fighting had ceased. Our forces had started upon an advance to the south and by 5 P.M. had reached El Cap, twenty-three miles down the causeway.

General Keightley had estimated that he could occupy Ismailia by November 8 and Suez by November 12. As he put it later in his despatch, "that would have completed the whole operation in twelve days from the start of air operations." Fighting between Israel and Egypt ceased on November 6 and our plans were therefore never completed. No other Arab state had joined in and the United Nations were scratching together a force to take up positions in the areas of fighting. Our intervention had compelled both these decisions. At 5 P.M. on November 6 the Allied Commander-in-Chief was given orders to cease fire at midnight.

It will be seen from an account of events in London how this fateful decision to cease fire was taken. Throughout the day of November 5 we were being continually pressed to accept a United Nations command in the Suez area, as meeting all our conditions for a cease-fire. This it did not do. A commander without forces could not fill the vacuum. During the night Marshal Bulganin's letter arrived. He had made it public before it reached me and its tone caused scare headlines in some sections of the press. The Soviet Premier declared that the war in Egypt could grow into a third world war. He threatened that Russia would resort to force and asked:

> In what position would Britain have found herself if she herself had been attacked by more powerful states possessing every kind of modern destructive weapon? And there are countries now which need not have sent a navy or air force to the coasts of Britain, but could have used other means, such as a rocket technique. We are filled with determination to use force to crush the aggressors and to restore peace in the East. We hope you will show the necessary prudence and will draw from this the appropriate conclusions.

We drew different conclusions. During the first four days the Soviets, both at the United Nations and in their wireless statements, remained extremely quiet and restrained. Their first intervention at the Security Council was more moderate than that of the United States and did not condemn Anglo-French action as Mr. Henry Cabot Lodge's resolution had done. Their propaganda was stepped up only some days after it became clear that the

United States was in the lead against us at the United Nations. Oblivious of Hungary, the Russians felt they could snarl with the pack.

This period of Soviet reserve was due to a number of causes. The Russians were determined not to risk putting themselves in an exposed position from which they might have to retreat, as over the Berlin blockade. They also recalled the warning I had given to Khrushchev and Bulganin when they came to London, that if need be we would defend our interests in the Middle East by force. Probably they were suspicious that official United States indignation against its allies could not really be as violent as it appeared. From the Soviet angle, it was rather too good to be true. To them it seemed unthinkable that the United States should not be as mindful of the interests of its allies as Soviet Russia was prepared to be of hers. There might be a catch in it somewhere and it would be wise to move prudently. Reassured on this point, and encouraged by the failure for several days even to discuss Hungary at the Security Council, the Russians thought they could take on something else. They made a leap for the lead.

We considered that the threats in Marshal Bulganin's note need not be taken literally. I returned him an appropriate reply:

> I have received with deep regret your message of yesterday. The language which you used in it made me think at first that I could only instruct Her Majesty's Ambassador to return it as entirely unacceptable. But the moment is so grave that I feel I must try to answer you with those counsels of reason with which you and I have in the past been able to discuss issues vital for the whole world.

I told Marshal Bulganin that we had virtually achieved our aim of separating the combatants in Egypt and that we welcomed the proposed United Nations force which would take over from us. I then went on:

> If your Government will support proposals for an inter- national force whose functions will be to prevent the

resumption of hostilities between Israel and Egypt, to secure
the withdrawal of the Israeli forces, to take the necessary
measures to remove obstructions and restore traffic through
the Suez Canal, and to promote a settlement of the problems
of the area, you will be making a contribution to peace
which we would welcome.

Our aim is to find a peaceful solution, not to engage in
argument with you. But I cannot leave unanswered the
baseless accusations in your message. You accuse us of waging
war against the national independence of the countries of the
Near and Middle East. We have already proved the absurdity
of this charge by declaring our willingness that the United
Nations should take over the physical task of maintaining
peace in the area. . . .

The world knows that in the past three days Soviet forces in
Hungary have been ruthlessly crushing the heroic resistance
of a truly national movement for independence, a movement
which by declaring its neutrality, proved that it offered no
threat to the security of the Soviet Union.

At such a time it ill becomes the Soviet Government to
speak of the actions of Her Majesty's Government as
"barbaric." The United Nations have called on your Government to desist from all armed attack on the peoples of Hungary, to withdraw your forces from Hungarian territory, and
to accept United Nations observers in Hungary. The world
will judge from your reply the sincerity of the words which
you have thought fit to use about Her Majesty's Government.

A more formidable threat than Marshal Bulganin's confronted
us. A run on the pound, at a speed which threatened disaster to
our whole economic position, had developed in the world's financial markets. Two months earlier the Cabinet had considered the
financial consequences of taking action at Suez. The cost of the
military precautions had been some £12 million. Holding our
proposed operation in readiness from mid-September onwards had been costing us about £2 million a month. The
operation itself was estimated to cost about £100 million, equivalent to one-sixteenth of the annual cost of the defence programme.

The Treasury had felt satisfied that these outlays could be borne without undue stress, though if the canal were blocked and the pipelines were cut indefinitely, our balance of payments would be endangered.

The position was made immediately critical by speculation against sterling, largely in the American market or on American account. Chinese balances were also withdrawn, no doubt for political reasons, and Indian balances reduced. The Chancellor of the Exchequer, Mr. Macmillan, later gave the House the figures. During the first half of the year, the gold and dollar reserves of the United Kingdom had been rising. Some pressure against sterling had been expected in the autumn and allowance had been made for it. This pressure was greatly intensified at the beginning of November. Our reserves fell by $57 million in September, $84 million in October, and $279 million in November; $279 million represented about 15 per cent of our total dollar reserves. This was gloomy foreboding and could have been decisive within the next few days.

There were reports at this time of a dissident minority in the Conservative Party in the House of Commons. I was told that if a cease-fire were not announced that day, some of them would not vote with us. I was not influenced by these reports, or by the knowledge that there had been some contacts between one or two members of our party and the Opposition leaders. The overwhelming majority was firmly loyal. There are always weak sisters in any crisis and sometimes they will be found among those who were toughest at the outset of the journey.

Popularly my problem was very different. The country had made up its mind that we were right to start; they would not be so easy to convince that we were right to stop. If I had been playing politics, nothing would have suited me better than a defeat in the House of Commons at this juncture. I had no doubt that failure to assert international authority would result in a sharp deterioration in the Middle East within the next year or two, until intervention became inevitable once again. That would be the moment for me and those who shared my views. But I was not playing politics and I expected to stay in office until that moment came.

None of these considerations determined our decision when we met at 9.45 A.M. on November 6, although all were in our minds in varying degree. The Chancellor of the Exchequer had rightly been to see the Foreign Secretary about our financial position earlier that day and I knew that it was grim. Another factor weighed even more in my mind, and I am sure in that of my colleagues. We had intervened to divide and, above all, to contain the conflict. The occasion for our intervention was over, the fire was out. Once the fighting had ceased, justification for further intervention ceased with it. I have no doubt that it was on this account more than any other that no suggestion was made by any of my colleagues, either then or in the hours which elapsed before my announcement in the House that evening, that we and the French should continue our intervention.

Our allies accepted this conclusion with understanding loyalty, though they would have liked to see what even a slightly longer period of action might have brought forth.

We knew, of course, that the heaviest pressure had been put upon Israel during the last forty-eight hours to accept the Assembly's resolution. The United States Government in particular had used every resource at their command, and they were many. There were promises also. President Eisenhower sent a personal appeal to Mr. Ben-Gurion in which he declared that once Israel had withdrawn from Egyptian territory new and energetic steps would be taken to solve the basic problems which had given rise to the present difficulty. It took eighteen months and Egyptian subversion in Lebanon and Jordan to compel any steps at all; the basic problems still remain untouched.

I doubt whether service was rendered to peace by applying this pressure. Nasser's position in Egypt was by this time threatened. Our patrols reported growing panic on the roads back from the Sinai peninsula to Cairo, but the fighting had stopped and we had no justification for going on.

★   ★   ★   ★   ★

We would have taken a second, and maybe a third, look at the problem had we understood what was to come. We were ashore with a sufficient force to hold Port Said. We held a gage. Nasser had received a humiliating defeat in the field and most of his Russian equipment had been captured or destroyed by the Israelis or ourselves. His position was badly shaken. Out of this situation intelligent international statesmanship should, we thought, be able to shape a lasting settlement for the Arab-Israeli conflict and for the future of the canal. We had not understood that, so far from doing this, the United Nations, and in particular the United States, would insist that all the advantages gained must be thrown away before serious negotiation began. This was the most calamitous of all errors. Had we expected it to be perpetrated, our course might have been otherwise, but we could not know. As it seems to me, the major mistakes were made, not before the cease-fire or in that decision, but after it. I did not foresee them.

Happily, by a combination of brilliant courage and firmness, Mr. Ben-Gurion was able to secure for his country one capital advantage, free passage of the Gulf of Aqaba to the port of Eilat, which could transform the economy of Israel and make everything that small country had endured worth while.

Optimists maintain that another forty-eight hours would have seen the occupation of the whole canal and the end of the fighting. That was not our military advice, which reckoned on five days more, and it is likely that the longer period would have been required. Even if fighting by organized units had not lasted long, the practice of the Egyptian army in Port Said of throwing away uniforms and using guerilla tactics in civilian clothes would in all probability have been repeated. It must have taken a little time to deal with, encouraged as it now was by Russian, and therefore by local Communist, support.

In the months after these events I repeatedly read and heard the comment, especially from the United States, even from those in high authority, "If only you had gone on." The implication being that, the canal once occupied and the main military operation over, the United States Government would have changed their attitude. I have never seen sufficient reason to accept this comfortable conviction and I do not believe that, if events had reached that point, they would in fact have done so. The United States Government had engaged their authority in the lead against us and would not have been appeased had Anglo-French forces occupied more of the canal or even the whole of it. In all probability they would only have been more indignant.

The factor which must now always remain unknown is the effect of a rapid advance down the canal, and its clearance, upon Nasser's position in Cairo. Militant dictators have more enemies at home than the foreigner ever dreams. It may be that even the Soviet entry into the lists would not have sufficed to save the regime in Cairo, humiliated by defeat and lacking the Voice of the Arabs to call disaster victory.

I had seen the chain of failure in the nineteen-thirties from Manchuria to Danzig and had tried in vain to break it. This time we had the opportunity and the responsibility. What we did was only partially effective, but it moved the United Nations to action. It led to later Anglo-American intervention in the Lebanon and Jordan, after the opposition of the United States to our Suez action had been seen to have brought disaster in Iraq. The consequences there may even have taught a little prudence in Cairo. Some of these checks to totalitarian plans may be judged late and feeble; even so they had their impact and their warning message, in revealing contrast to the fatal drift of the nineteen-thirties.

Much of the subsequent controversy over the Suez decision has been about the trees and not about the wood. The main question is whether inertia would have brought better results for the peace of the world than action. I think not. I thought and think that failure to act would have brought the worst of consequences, just as I think the world would have suffered less if Hitler had been resisted on the Rhine, in Austria or in Czechoslovakia, rather than in Poland. This will be for history to determine.

10

MYOPIA
November 7, 1956–January 18, 1957

The fighting is over – Casualties – President Eisenhower agrees to see M. Mollet and myself in Washington – He postpones the meeting – Clearance of the canal – Nasser is complacent – Egypt has to modify some demands – We agree to token withdrawal – My illness – Proceedings in the General Assembly – M. Spaak's amendment is defeated – His realistic views – Negotiations for withdrawal – British nationals and property in Egypt – Anglo-French harmony – My telegram to General Keightley – A summing up – A visit from Mr. Nehru – Christmas at Chequers – Illness and Resignation – M. Spaak calls on me – We sail for New Zealand

ON THE MORNING of November 7 the Anglo-French forces were firmly in command of Port Said and fighting had stopped, except for isolated clashes. We had cleared the causeway and advanced as far as El Cap. The total number of men landed in our operation was 22,000, of whom 13,500 were British. Our casualties were 16 killed and 96 wounded and the French 10 killed and 33 wounded.

The Egyptians circulated wildly exaggerated stories about their casualties. The President of the Law Society, Sir Edwin Herbert, later carried out a thorough investigation into the facts at the request of the Minister of Defence. His findings upon his mission to Port Said, published on December 22, were that the Egyptians had lost 650 dead and had had 900 wounded and detained in hospital. He also reported that not one bomb had been dropped on Port Said or its environs, and that the short naval bombardment had been entirely confined to the beaches.

He added:

Every possible warning was given by radio to the civil population. Indeed to one like myself, with a long experience of security in war-time, it came as a shock to find that the two overriding considerations in the minds of all concerned were firstly to inform the enemy of our plans and secondly to do him as little damage as possible in the execution of those plans, which I think is a fair summary of the steps taken.

In the afternoon of November 6 President Eisenhower telephoned to me when I was in my room in the House of Commons. He was vigorous and in good spirits. He was delighted by our order to cease fire and commented that we had got what we had set out to do; the fighting was over and had not spread. Mr. Eisenhower was naturally elated by the Presidential election results which had by then come in. I congratulated him and he told me he had increased his majority. This was our first conversation on the new undersea cable. The President commented on its remarkable clarity and encouraged me to keep in touch by this means and telephone to him at any time.

There seemed no doubt at that moment that friendship between our two countries could be quickly reanimated. I sent a telegram to M. Mollet in which I spoke of my confidence that friendship between the three of us was restored and even strengthened. I added that "as a result of all our efforts we have laid bare the reality of Soviet plans in the Middle East and are physically holding a position which can be decisive for the future." I was over-optimistic.

The President followed his telephone call with a telegram. It was cordial in tone, but contained some indications of the direction of American thinking which I was perhaps slow to recognize. I did not foresee then that the United States Government would harden against us on almost every point and become harsher after the cease-fire than before. Mr. Eisenhower urged that the United Nations plan for an international force should be immediately carried into effect in order to prevent what he considered to be developments of the greatest gravity in Egypt. By this I took him to mean the possibility of Soviet intervention in some form. I considered that the best guarantee against this was the presence of Anglo-French troops, until the United Nations force had built up sufficient strength on the spot to take over our police duties. In the days ahead we found growing divergence on this issue between the United States and ourselves. On November 6 and 7 this still lay in the future. To avoid giving Russia any excuse for a move, the President strongly recommended that we should consent to the exclusion of contingents from the great powers in the United Nations force. He also affirmed that any attack upon this force would meet with an immediate reaction from all the United Nations. I was glad of this and I thought that there was something to be said for the exclusion of all great powers from the force. I told the President so, but I had to consult my colleagues before decisions were taken.

The Government considered the position. Our object remained, as it had always been, to use this opportunity to secure a solution of Middle Eastern problems. We did not believe in Russian military intervention, but we realized how disastrous it would be if the United States became more intent on making us withdraw our forces than on seeking a comprehensive settlement. In spite of the friendly tone of the President's exchanges with me, we were not sure that his Administration understood the true situation in the area. At lower levels our warnings had been ignored. Our immediate purpose must be to resume close relations with the United States and induce them to recognize the real dangers of Soviet penetration. My colleagues agreed that I should consider the best means of making a further approach.

I thought that there should be an immediate consultation with Mr. Eisenhower and M. Mollet. During luncheon on the 7th I followed the President's suggestion and telephoned to him. The President was receptive. I told him I thought it important that we should meet and have a full discussion on the situation. He agreed and asked me what date I had in mind. I said the sooner the better and suggested that M. Mollet and I might fly over that evening. After a little discussion as to how to make the arrangements, the President authorized me to invite M. Mollet, since communication between us was quicker, and to tell him that a confirmatory invitation from the President would follow. I did this and M. Mollet, like the good colleague he was, at once accepted, although at no little inconvenience to his own plans.

About an hour later the President telephoned to me and said he wanted to be clear that I was not making the journey just to argue about the United Nations resolutions. I said certainly not, and that I did not even know what those resolutions might be at the present time. The purpose of our visit would be for much wider discussion on the whole Middle Eastern scene, and on what action we could take together about it. The President said he was glad of that, because it would be awkward if we were to argue about United Nations resolutions and then not agree. I assured him that was not my purpose.

Later he telephoned again and said that he would be much taken up in the days ahead in consultations with the leaders of Congress. He had come to the conclusion, therefore, that M. Mollet and I should defer our visit, though he did not rule it out for a later date. The conversation took place only a few minutes before I was going down to the House of Commons to announce the visit in the agreed terms.

Subsequently that evening I sent the President a telegram in which I said:

> I do hope that it will be possible for us to meet in the very near future. I should feel much more confident about the decisions and actions which we shall have to take in the short term if we had first reached some common under-standing about the attitude which we each intended to take towards a long-term settlement of the outstanding issues in the Middle East. I have for a long time felt that some at least of our troubles there have derived from the lack of a clear understanding between our two countries, ever since the end of the war, on policy in the Middle East. And I doubt whether we shall ever be able to secure stability there unless we are working towards common objectives.

After a reference to Soviet intentions and to the Swiss President's invitation to another Geneva meeting, I concluded:

On matters such as this it is difficult to come to considered conclusions by correspondence. I would feel much happier if we had been able to meet and talk them over soon. It was with these grave issues in mind that I suggested this morning that I might come out to Washington at once. I still hope that it may be possible for us to meet within the next few days, as soon as your immediate preoccupations are over.

The President replied agreeing to a meeting at an early date, but he held that the United Nations resolutions must first be carried out. This meant that the Anglo-French forces should be withdrawn from Egypt without delay. Mr. Eisenhower now considered that the ground would be favourable for a meeting only when this had been done. Thus we and the French were squarely asked to give up the gage we had won, before concerting with the United States any common policy for the Middle East.

★   ★   ★   ★   ★

In our discussions in London we had to determine our attitude to two resolutions which lay before the Assembly. One, sponsored by Afro-Asian powers, called for the immediate withdrawal of the Anglo-French forces. We could not agree to this. The other resolution was put forward by the Argentine. This accepted the Secretary-General's plan for the United Nations force and dealt with the separation of combatants and the withdrawal of Israeli units. It also allowed us to remain at Port Said while the United Nations force was built up. We decided to vote for this resolution, though it did not express concern for the future of the canal or for a final Arab-Israeli settlement.

Both resolutions were passed by the General Assembly. The Afro-Asian one had been amended to require us to withdraw in accordance with the earlier resolutions of the United Nations on the subject. However, we determined to keep our troops on the spot until the international force was there in strength. Our Commander-in-Chief was meanwhile authorized to open staff conversations with General Burns, the United Nations commander-designate, and to agree with him a plan for the orderly and effective transfer of responsibility.

We were now committed to the withdrawal of our forces from the canal, but not by any particular date. We had to avoid a vacuum between our departure and the arrival of a sufficient United Nations force. A phased withdrawal was the way to do this, timed to coincide with the building up of international contingents along the canal.

There were many complications and dangers. There was the possibility that the cease-fire might be broken, our troops and patrols were being frequently sniped at. Only their admirable steadiness prevented ugly incidents. Cairo radio, back on the air again, was inciting the population of Port Said to make trouble, thereby increasing the likelihood of demonstrations and rioting. We knew that the Russian Consul visited the Egyptian Governor of the town, who at once assumed a stiffer attitude to the allied commanders. The Consul was busy spreading inflammatory publicity against us; in these conditions we could not agree to dribble out our forces.

A further problem was the urgent need to clear the canal. The Egyptians had sunk twenty-one blockships in the harbour of Port Said. We got to work at once with our salvage equipment, which we had assembled in advance for just this purpose, and began removing these obstructions and also those in the short stretch of the canal under our control. In the rest of the waterway the Egyptians were busy sinking ships. By far the greater part of this obstruction to the canal was done after the fighting was over, when politically and physically it was safe to do so. By the time the Egyptians had finished, they had sunk thirty-two ships in the canal, while their propaganda was busy blaming allied bombing for their own act of sabotage.

The French and ourselves at once sought authority from the United Nations to clear the whole of the canal with the equipment which we, and we only, had at our disposal. Both countries were willing to place their salvage teams under United Nations control. Technically, France and Britain had the means to carry out this task far more quickly than anyone else. We wanted to get on with it at once. All the more so because the United States showed no signs of readiness to assist France and Britain with oil supplies from the Western hemisphere.

The Egyptian Government took instant advantage of this situation, and from a position of weakness were once again allowed to seize a position of strength. They declared that they would not contemplate the clearance of the canal until after the Anglo-French forces had gone. Nor would they even then agree to the use of Anglo-French salvage teams by the United Nations. There was no guarantee that they might not carry their opposition further and refuse clearance until after the United Nations force also had come and gone. Under this Egyptian pressure the United Nations gave way. Even before Mr. Hammarskjöld paid his visit to Cairo on November 16 he had largely accepted the Egyptian point of view. He informed us that no arrangements could be made about either the clearance or the future administration of the canal until we had withdrawn.

At this juncture the Foreign Secretary flew to New York, where he remained for ten days, struggling to inject some sense of values. His efforts were largely in vain. The President a few days earlier had granted a friendly interview to our new Ambassador, Sir Harold Caccia, when he presented his credentials. Mr. Eisenhower said he had differed sharply with us on tactics, but he shared my views on Colonel Nasser. He agreed that the urgent task ahead was to work out a settlement of both the Suez and the Arab-Israeli problems. These were promising words, but the President's attitude was not reflected in the actions of his Administration. Mr. Dulles at this time was ill and the authorities in charge of the State Department during his absence were aggressively negative when the Foreign Secretary urged our views upon them. In the possession of Port Said and the Israeli occupation of Sinai, we held strong bargaining counters. Before we agreed to relinquish them, we must ensure that the canal was promptly cleared and that a general settlement of the problems of the area was under negotiation. Soviet designs for penetrating the Middle East had gone much further than the United States believed. Russia regarded Cairo as a future Soviet outpost, and Communist sympathizers were busy throughout the area, notably in Syria and Iraq. As Nuri es-Said was to say in 1958, a few days before he was murdered: "All this shows that unless Nasser is checked, events in the Middle East will continue on a large scale in favour of Russia."

When the Foreign Secretary used these arguments, he was met

with expressions of moral disapproval of our action in Egypt and
with the reply that we must first withdraw before anything could be
attempted. The United States officials refused to co-operate at any
level of policy-making. They declared that Britain, France and the
United States must not appear to be conspiring together behind
the back of the United Nations. Their only reaction to reports
of Russian infiltration in the Middle East was to press us to remove
our forces more quickly.

We could not help contrasting the American attitude now with
our own attitude at the time of the Guatemala campaign. In that
country the United States had encouraged the overthrow of a Com-
munist-influenced government, which it considered a menace to
the peace of Central America. We had understood her action
there and done what we could not to hamper her in the Security
Council. The United States was now behaving in a precisely contrary manner towards us. When this point was put to the United
States officials, they had no answer.

It might have been thought that, however much angered, the
United States Government would wish to get the best possible results
out of the situation for the future of Western Europe, whose economic security was at stake. This was not so. The attitude was
rather that the President had been slighted because the allies had
acted without permission. The allies must pay for it, and pay they
did. The many warnings, both public and private, which had been
given by the allies over the waiting months did not help to assuage
official American opinion. On the contrary, they irritated it. If an
individual has been warned by his friend that the friend will take
some action, and has not heeded the warning, and his friend then
takes action, the individual is likely to feel sore. His own error of
judgment only increases his exasperation. So it can be with countries.

In London, the Government considered practical steps. They
were determined that arrangements for clearing the canal should be
made before ordering more than a token withdrawal of the Allied
Forces. They also wished to ensure that negotiations about the
future administration of the canal should begin before the withdrawal was complete. They were prepared to recall allied troops
unit by unit as the United Nations moved in, but a definite time-

table for the clearance of the canal had to be worked out at the same time. A guarantee that this time-table would be put in operation effectively was necessary before any withdrawal was made. The Government were confident that they enjoyed the support of public opinion in laying down these conditions. The Foreign Secretary was asked to make these minimum conditions clear to Mr. Hammarskjöld, who was about to set off for Cairo.

At the United Nations the outlook was darkening. The Egyptian Government were seeking to become the arbiters of the composition and functions of the international force. Having themselves sabotaged the canal, they were now saying that our salvage corps should take no part in the work of clearing it. Nasser was attempting to dictate terms as if he were a victor, while the Soviets were replacing the war material he had lost in the field.

The President had indefinitely postponed consultation with M. Mollet and myself. He did not receive the Foreign Secretary in Washington, nor the Australian Foreign Minister, Mr. Casey, who was the bearer of a message from the Australian Prime Minister. The United States Administration seemed to be dominated at this time by one thought only, to harry their allies. Mr. Dulles, who was still recovering from an operation, deplored to the Foreign Secretary that we had not managed to bring Nasser down and declared that he must be prevented from getting away with it. The actions of the United States Government had exactly the opposite result.

Hammarskjöld, on his visit to Cairo, found Nasser extremely complacent, as well he might be. The Egyptians were putting out much propaganda about the likelihood of riots in Port Said if the Anglo-French forces remained there for many more days. It was propaganda which found willing listeners among the delegates at the General Assembly in New York. The Egyptian Government next threatened to expel all British subjects from Egypt. The purpose of this move was also to bring further pressure to bear upon us.

Hammarskjöld returned from Cairo on November 19 to report the results of his discussions with the Egyptian Government. Some active political exchanges ensued in New York, in which the Foreign Secretary and his French colleague tried to secure results which were prudent and effective. They avoided a number of dangers. Egypt attempted to get a veto on the composition of an international force. This was refused, as was also the power which she demanded to determine where that force should be stationed. Egypt had wished to confine it to the Arab-Israeli armistice lines of 1949. The Egyptians also claimed that the United Nations force would have no further function once the Anglo-French and Israeli troops had left their soil. This was not accepted; it was decided that the force should not be withdrawn until the General Assembly resolved that its functions had been fulfilled.

The General Assembly was now due to meet in full session on November 23. The British and French Governments had to take a decision upon the question of withdrawal. We had already agreed to admit into Port Said an advance party of 100 Danes and Norwegians. We had promised landing and transit facilities to the Yugoslav contingent, which was on its way by sea. We were prepared to supply the United Nations with such vehicles and stores as they might need and they had undertaken to build up a force of 4000 by December 1.

On these terms the Cabinet decided to make a token withdrawal of one battalion of the Royal West Kent Regiment. They were not prepared to do more than this, until the debate in the General Assembly showed whether the United Nations would in fact carry out the responsibilities which it had assumed.

★ ★ ★ ★ ★

One Friday afternoon early in October, I had set out to drive down to Chequers with a private secretary and called on my way to see my wife, who was in University College Hospital. I had only been in the room a few moments when I suddenly felt chilled to the bone. My wife assured me that the room was the normal temperature. In a few minutes a severe ague fell upon me and I was put to bed, somewhat ignominiously, in a neighbouring room. I did not know much more after that for a while, but I was told later that my temperature had risen to 106 degrees. I spent the week-end at the hospital and I left on the Monday much refreshed by my rest. This refreshment was probably deceptive, for it is a common feature of these fevers and is apt to be followed by recurrent bouts of weakness. So it proved for me. But at the time I recovered well enough to carry on with my work.

In early November Lord Evans, who was taking care of me medically, began to be anxious at my state of health. Although the fever had not come back, there was no doubt that the bout had weakened me and he became concerned that it might be an indication of a return of my previous bile-duct trouble. As against this, the pressure under which I had been working, day and night, for so long a time, might have been held to account for the exhaustion from which I was certainly suffering. I had not had even a weekend off for many months. In this uncertainty, Lord Evans felt that I must somehow obtain a respite from my work, even for a short time, as a result of which we would be better able to tell whether my present state of health was only a passing phase, or indicated something more serious. Accordingly, and after consultation with my principal colleagues, I acquiesced in a decision to go for a few weeks to Jamaica. I flew there on November 23. Kind friends, Mr. and Mrs. Ian Fleming, lent us a peaceful retreat at Golden Eye. I arranged to be kept in touch with urgent decisions by cable and, though I was not present at the Cabinet whose conclusions I have just recorded, I approved them myself before I left for Jamaica. While I was away the Lord Privy Seal, Mr. Butler, presided at Cabinet meetings. He and his colleagues kept me informed and we exchanged opinions on the decisions they took.

★　★　★　★　★

Before the meeting of the General Assembly, President Eisenhower once more proclaimed in public that he wished to strengthen the Anglo-American alliance. Armed with this authority, the Foreign Secretary and our Ambassador in Washington both renewed their exchanges with high American officials. We were allies in N.A.T.O. and in S.E.A.T.O.; the present Soviet threat was directed at the Middle East, which lay between the spheres of these two pacts. We could hardly be allies in two parts of the world and not in a third. These efforts got us nowhere. One senior American authority frankly declared that it was not possible at this stage for the Administration to talk to Her Majesty's Government. We were accused of "stalling" on the resolutions of the United Nations and we were taxed with having created the "black-out" between our countries.

When the General Assembly met it approved the steps taken by the Secretary-General towards clearing the canal and it agreed to his definition of the functions of the United Nations force. The Soviet bloc alone voted against this resolution, which passed by 65 to 9. The next resolution before the Assembly was one of the Afro-Asian kind which regretted that Anglo-French forces were still in Port Said and told us to withdraw forthwith. Mr. Shepilov made a speech in which he accused us of having no intention of withdrawing. Choosing to forget his own country's actions in Hungary, he lauched a cynical attack upon Anglo-French "aggression."

Mr. Lester Pearson, who spoke next, drily described the Soviet Foreign Minister's remarks as "verbal aggression upon truth." Canada, Mr. Pearson said, believed that as Britain and France were already complying with the wishes of the United Nations, the present resolution was unnecessary. He urged the Assembly to apply itself to practical matters.

M. Spaak, as an experienced diplomatist, saw the opportunity which this situation created and seized it. He moved a friendly amendment to this resolution which omitted the call for immediate withdrawal, took note of the action which we and the French were already taking, and underlined the role of the United Nations forces. Had this amendment been carried, the negotiating position of the United Nations would have been immeasurably strengthened. There would have been a real opportunity to initiate negotiation on the wider issues of the Arab-Israeli dispute while some of the cards were still in the hands of the West. Equally, it would have been possible to treat the future of the canal as it should have been treated, a great international issue affecting the lives of many nations as closely as that of Egypt. At one time it seemed that this amendment might be carried. Had the United States put its full weight behind it, it certainly would have been. Even so, the amendment secured 23 votes, there were 37 against it and 18 abstentions, including the United States.

The countries which supported M. Spaak's amendment were Australia, Belgium, Brazil, Canada, China, Cuba, Denmark, the Dominican Republic, France, Iceland, Israel, Italy, Luxembourg, the Netherlands, New Zealand, Norway, Peru, Portugal, Sweden, Thailand, Turkey, South Africa and the United Kingdom.

Thus the Assembly rejected the advice of M. Spaak and Mr. Pearson. Delegates knew that the United States proposed once more to vote against us, which it did. The Afro-Asian resolution was passed by 63 votes to 5, with no less than 10 abstentions. The defence offered by the United States Government for their vote was that they were the prisoners of their own policy and had no choice. This vote caused much resentment in Britain, for it was cast when we were complying with United Nations resolutions.

M. Spaak soon afterwards gave his views upon the United Nations to the public. I print them here because I agree with them. In an article for the magazine *Foreign Affairs** called "The West in Disarray," he wrote:

> In the present United Nations set-up, which is not what its founders wished and hoped it would be, everything short of war is allowed. Treaties may be violated, promises can be broken, a nation is licensed to menace its neighbour or to perpetrate any sort of trick on it, just as long as there is no actual war. The attitude of Egypt during the last few months is a case in point. While Egypt denied transit through the Suez Canal to Israeli ships, sent death commandos onto Israeli soil, violated the Treaty of Constantinople, sent arms to be used against the French in Algeria and made preparations to attack its neighbour, the United Nations was powerless to intervene. Such intervention would not come within the scope of the Charter as at present interpreted. But let Israel in desperation send troops into the Sinai peninsula and let Anglo-French forces land at Port Said, and they are sure to be condemned. Meanwhile, those who were looking on impassively at the brutal repression of the revolt in Hungary could not find words harsh enough to damn them. . . .
>
> The spectacle which Soviet Russia and the satellite countries have presented in the course of debate in the present Assembly is indeed profoundly shocking. They become passionate defenders of the General Assembly's recommendations every time that Egypt is in question, but they treat all resolutions concerning Hungary like dead letters. This attitude is

* January 1957 issue.

so immoral that the very authority of the Assembly becomes deeply affected by it. Under such conditions it is impossible to believe that peace can be maintained and international justice assured.

In the days which followed the vote in the Assembly, no opening showed itself for negotiation on the important issues, of which this dispute was the expression. They remained to trouble the future and did so very soon. The United States Administration continued obstinately silent, so the Foreign Secretary and his French colleague returned home. The Arab-Israeli problem remained unsolved. The canal was handed back to the control of one man, who was picked up, dusted down and put in full authority again. At the time of this writing* Israeli merchant cargoes, on voyage in the ships of other nations, are being refused passage through the canal. The United Nations takes no action at this violation of the rights of nations in an international waterway. Western Europe would be naïve indeed to expect free passage of the canal at any time of emergency, unless it has the power to compel it, which it is not likely to have again.

The careless view has been taken that the events of Suez constituted a success for the United Nations. Unhappily this was not so. There is still no known instance of effective action by the United Nations when the two great powers of the world have been in opposition. The United States and Soviet Russia joined together in the General Assembly to issue their instructions on Suez. They were obeyed, but the fact that the United States and Russia were together did not mean that they were right. They could hardly both be so. The Russians are still in Hungary as the Egyptians are in sole command of the canal.

Distance may dim perspective, it should not distort it. The United States could not have taken up so legalistic an attitude if the security of its own continent had been at stake.

★   ★   ★   ★   ★

The British and French Governments were under heavy pressure at the United Nations to name at once a date for the with-

* August 1959.

drawal of their forces. In this the United States Government took a leading part. The Secretary of the Treasury, Mr. Humphrey, telephoned to Mr. Butler and made it clear that the United States would not extend help or support to Britain until after a definite statement on withdrawal had been made. In a further message he conveyed that the American Administration meant by this the announcement of an early date for such withdrawal.

This was unacceptable to us. Neither the French Government nor ourselves were willing to fix a definite date and announce it in public until certain conditions had been fulfilled. The immediate necessity was to secure precise assurances from the Secretary-General of the United Nations, before we handed over our responsibilities in Port Said to the United Nations contingents.

By persistent argument, we made some headway. It was accepted that the United Nations force should be built up to a competent size, though it did not in the end contain the Canadian contingent for which we hoped and which was made ready. The United Nations accepted responsibility for clearing the canal as quickly as possible. Surveying and diving operations were to begin before the allied withdrawal. On the other hand, no use was ever made of our offer to place Anglo-French salvage resources at the disposal of the United Nations. Our salvage fleet was working with high efficiency and success in Port Said harbour and clearing the entrance to the canal. If full use had been made of it, the canal could have been opened many weeks sooner. The delay was due to fear of offending Nasser.

We insisted that there must be no discrimination by the Egyptian authorities against British and French shipping when the canal reopened, and this we secured. It was agreed that negotiation upon the future of the canal should be resumed on the basis of the six principles unanimously approved by the Security Council. This was cold comfort for the canal users. I urged that we should stand upon the eighteen-power proposals. The United States had played a large part in formulating them and the fact that they had been vetoed by the Communist powers did not seem sufficient reason to drop them. The French Government shared my opinion and our Government's statement on December 3 reiterated this. It was not welcome to Mr. Hammarskjöld, who was now committed by his conversations with the Egyptians to regarding the eighteen-power proposals as superseded. We held that only something equivalent would provide acceptable guarantees for freedom of passage through the canal. This should have been the basis for further negotiation.

Though they had only received partial satisfaction on some points, the British and French Governments reluctantly agreed to resume the withdrawal of their troops. These negotiations had committed the United Nations force more seriously and on a larger scale in the area of the canal. They had also alerted United States opinion, if not yet the Government, to the combined dangers presented by growing Soviet penetration and intensified Arab nationalism. We refused, however, to name in public a specific date for final withdrawal. This would have given the signal for further demonstrations and disturbances in Port Said. On our insistence, the phasing was arranged between the Allied Commander-in-Chief and the United Nations Commander, in the light of transport problems and the needs for preserving public order on the spot. After discussion with the French Government, we fixed December 22 as the final day for embarkation.

During the closing weeks of the Anglo-French occupation, the Egyptians did all they could to stir up incidents and present them to the world as the result of allied provocation. In spite of the cease-fire agreements, they attempted ambushes, allied patrols were fired upon and grenades thrown at military vehicles. Arms were smuggled into Port Said and a virulent propaganda campaign was directed at its inhabitants inciting them against allied authorities. These Egyptian activities were of a pattern with the *fedayeen* raids against Israel and they caused further casualties on both sides. During this tense period, allied officers and men conducted themselves with remarkable coolness and forbearance. Their Commander in Port Said, General Stockwell, protested several times to the United Nations Commander against Egyptian actions, but with little effect.

I returned from Jamaica on December 14. During my absence I had a courteous exchange of messages with the President, an exchange which brought us no nearer a meeting of Heads of Government, urgent as this was. I was feeling much stronger and had no suspicion of the advice the doctors were to have to give me in January.

At London Airport, where many of my colleagues met me, I made a statement summing up the position and prospects at the moment:

> There is now, I am sure from my own post-bag as well as other evidence, a growing understanding in Canada, and also in the United States, about the action which Britain and France were compelled to take in the Middle East. I am sure that this will go on increasing.
>
> The formation of a United Nations force could be the turning point in the history of the United Nations. Does anyone suppose that there would have been a United Nations force but for British and French action? Of course not.
>
> It is true that it would have been perfectly possible to allow events to drift, to let hostilities spread and develop, to allow the Moscow-Cairo axis to perfect its plans. All this would have given us much less immediate anxiety than we have had to bear. It would have been easy to do nothing. It always is for any Government and it would have been popular in some quarters. It would have been easy, but it would have been fatal, just as it was fatal in the years between the wars.
>
> Everybody knows now what the Soviets were planning and preparing to do in the Middle East. Russia supplied arms in such quantities, as has now been revealed, because she knew the Egyptian dictator's ambitions suited her own book.
>
> The aim was just this — more satellites, but this time in the Middle East. I am convinced, more convinced than I have been about anything in all my public life, that we were right, my colleagues and I, in the judgments and decisions we took, and that history will prove it so.

Of the next steps I said:

> It seems to us two things are essential. The canal must be cleared by all available means, and without further delay. Its future must be settled, and permanently. Every country concerned must take a fresh look, and make a new effort to solve the problems that have beset the Middle East for far too long.

Soon after my return, my wife and I lunched alone with Sir Winston and Lady Churchill. We had a full discussion and at the end of it, Sir Winston summed up his judgment on the situation: "What a magnificent position to fight back from."

We now found the United States Government more helpful on two matters, the support of sterling and the supply of oil. Other problems arose, however, in connection with the canal area which complicated our plan of withdrawal, and on these they maintained a rigid attitude. The Foreign Secretary explained these difficulties to Mr. Dulles at a meeting in Paris on December 14. We wished to find solutions for them before our troops finally left. Dulles reacted as if we were seeking an indefinite suspension of our withdrawal, which was not so. He stated that he could not release us from our obligation to withdraw, since to do so would be " in some sense a breach of faith on the part of the Administration with Congress and United States public opinion." He maintained that our action had caused revulsion throughout the United States. This was strong language and at variance with the reports of our own representatives, who considered that the sharp feelings displayed at the time in Washington had not really represented American opinion.

The Foreign Secretary explained that we were concerned with the future of British nationals and their property in Egypt. About 10,000 were involved, many of them Cypriots and Maltese. By the middle of December 2500 had already been driven out by direct or indirect means. About 3500 French nationals had suffered likewise. Much British and French property had also been seized by the Government. The threat of general expulsion was now hanging over all the remaining British and French subjects in Egypt. By contrast, Egyptian nationals in Britain had not been molested.

We brought strong diplomatic pressure to bear at the United Nations and a general expulsion did not take place. We were also trying to settle upon some system of arbitration, either through the United Nations or directly with the Egyptians, to consider the claims and counter-claims for compensation, which would shortly arise. These included the value of the seized British and French property in Egypt, the cost of clearing the canal and a just assessment of the damage done during the fighting. When we withdrew, the argument was still going on.

Another controversy had a happier outcome. The Egyptians interned some 450 British civilian employees of the contractors in charge of the Suez Canal base. They had been engaged to work there under the 1954 agreement with Egypt and we were determined not to leave them interned. On our side we held some 250 Egyptians, mostly prisoners of war. An exchange was arranged and took place on the day before final embarkation.

Throughout the seven weeks of these operations, brief, inconclusive and exasperating as they were, Anglo-French co-operation at every level worked with unbroken harmony. A sense of mutual respect grew between the forces serving together. The gallantry of the paratroopers of both nations, the swift and careful execution of the air operation, the smooth timing of the naval landings and the operations which followed, each of these showed work together of a pattern rarely seen between two nations. There was no recrimination, political or military, either then or later. Our French allies showed wonderful generosity. They accepted our command in all the military fields. It would have been only human, when the task was completed, to blame us for not having found some swifter way. There was nothing of the kind. To the sincere respect which British soldiers, sailors and airmen brought back from their joint enterprise, should be added the gratitude of the British people for this understanding by their loyal neighbour.

As our forces were on the way home just before Christmas, I sent a signal to General Keightley:

> It is hard to imagine a more thankless task than has been yours and that of those who have served under you in these recent weeks. I have greatly admired the patience and discipline which all ranks of all three Services have shown throughout this period, and now that the main task is completed I should like to send congratulations and gratitude. I am confident that as history unrolls your efforts will have been shown not to have been in vain.

★   ★   ★   ★   ★

Suez was a short-term emergency operation which succeeded, and an attempt to halt a long-term deterioration whose outcome is still uncertain. A clash between Israel and Egypt was inevitable, given Nasser's declared intentions. Whenever this took place, it could bring grave danger to the general peace. It was far better that it should not happen at a moment of Egypt's choosing, and the explosion could not have occurred in circumstances less damaging, given the speedy action of Britain and France. On balance the world stood to gain by the fact that the conflict took place then and not some months later, when the consequences in relation to world events might have been infinitely graver.

We were not successful in our wider objective: we did not bring about Arab-Israeli peace or restore international control over the canal. It is true that some successes were gained. The military weakness of the Egyptian forces was exposed and duly noted, in particular by neighbours. This had important consequences. From the day of Egyptian defeat in the Sinai desert the chances of a Nasser empire were scotched, not killed. Even so, the Sudan did not hesitate to resist the grasping demands which Nasser later made upon her northern boundary. It is unlikely that Nasser or any other Arab leader will readily undertake a war of extermination against Israel in the immediate future, without support from outside. As against this, Nasser remains ruler of Egypt, his ambition still dangerous. The canal is under his control, Syria has become a part of his empire. Our intervention at least closed the chapter of complacency about the situation in the Middle East. It led to the Eisenhower Doctrine and from that to Anglo-American intervention in the following summer in Jordan and the Lebanon. It helped to show that the West was not prepared to leave the area wide open for infiltration and subversion by others. But these were only partial gains. The uneasy equipoise still continues.

A year and a half after these events, an army mutiny in Iraq murdered the King and former Regent, Nuri es-Said and their families and many more. Though instigated by Nasser's resourceful and unscrupulous propaganda, this event has not benefited him. The Governments of the Lebanon and Jordan, knowing themselves threatened by Nasser's subversive tactics in their own countries, asked for help from the West. The United Nations observers on the spot denied that there was subversive activity by Nasser in either country. The Secretary-General, Mr. Hammarskjöld, supported his observers. Ignoring this myopic testimony, the United States landed forces in the Lebanon and the United Kingdom flew troops into

Jordan, without prior reference to the United Nations. This action was necessary if the right to live of these two small countries was to be preserved; it was unquestionably against the terms of the Charter as interpreted at the time of our intervention at Port Said. Since the United Nations observers were already on the spot and proclaiming that the motives for Anglo-American intervention did not exist, it was rather more heinous.

The intervention succeeded in its limited purpose, the immediate rescue of the Lebanon and Jordan, though probably the more effective deterrent was the conviction that Israel would fight if the United Arab Republic took over Jordan. Egypt now knew beyond argument what Israeli fighting meant.

No attempt was made to redeem Iraq or to halt the deterioration in the Middle East. With Communist influence and authority in Iraq, the Russian dream of access to the Persian Gulf draws nearer. These developments will not be checked by support for Nasser in the role of an anti-Communist dictator. To attempt this would be as useless as it was to seek to use Mussolini against Hitler and would result in the final annihilation of the friends of the West. The position has a certain analogy with that which existed in Iran in 1951, when I returned to the Foreign Office. I was under strong pressure then from the United States to make terms with Musaddiq, communism being regarded as the only alternative. I did not believe that and refused to accept such a policy, preferring to bide our time and await an opportunity to do business with a more responsible authority. I felt sure that this would come. It will come also in the Arab lands, if patience is shown and opportunity and encouragement is given to those, and they are many, who believe that the future of this world must not be placed either in the hands of a militant dictator or of a Communist tyranny.

Whatever the transient phenomena of the visits and meetings of statesmen the danger of world conflict does not recede; it draws nearer. The period when the deterrent of nuclear power held the world in awe is fading. The wider manufacture and ownership of nuclear weapons spreads familiarity and with it an instinctive drift and carelessness. Nor are we entitled to remonstrate with others for making the weapons we have made. The numbers within the circle will grow and it has as yet no rules.

The United Nations has not been able to meet the need, because the charter has not been fulfilled. The abuse of the veto has nullified the effectiveness of the Security Council, while the failure to create an international force has deprived the United Nations of any backing for its authority. More serious is the attitude shown by that organization to international engagements in recent years. There has been an increasing tendency to condone breaches of international agreement. In order to obtain a temporary easement, it lays up further trouble later on. Up to February 1959, Israeli cargoes had freedom of passage through the Suez Canal. Since that date the Egyptian Government have blocked the passage of ships carrying Israeli goods and, when the captain of a Danish ship declined to yield, his ship was held and its cargo impounded. There was no attempt, even by the Egyptian press, to pretend that these cargoes were strategic. They complained that it was Israel's purpose "to increase trade with the Afro-Asian countries and develop its economy." No purpose could be more legitimate. Attempts by the Egyptian Government to halt it are contrary to every engagement given both under the Convention of 1888 and the Charter of the United Nations, to say nothing of the many assurances by Egypt and the United States in the last two years. On February 20, 1957, President Eisenhower said to the American people: "We should not assume that, if Israel withdraws, Egypt will prevent Israeli shipping from using the Suez Canal or the Gulf of Aqaba. If, unhappily, Egypt does hereafter violate the armistice agreement or other international obligations, then this should be dealt with firmly by the society of nations."

In the event there has been no more than a whimper from the United Nations. This attitude on the part of a world organization which should be the custodian of international agreement creates difficulties for Israel, but its consequences will be infinitely graver for all of us, for on this precedent the verdict of history cannot be challenged. To take the easy way, to put off decisions, to fail even to record a protest when international undertakings are broken on which the ink is scarcely dry, can only lead one way. It is all so much more difficult to do later on, and so we come full circle. The insidious appeal of appeasement leads to a deadly reckoning.

There is much that is unreal and unco-ordinated in the present Western position. The rivalry in Arabia has now serious consequences. The United States supplies weapons of war to Saudi Arabia, which gives encouragement and power to rebel pretenders against the Sultan of Muscat. We, as in treaty bound, help the ruler defend his territories. Nasser backs the rebels by any means to hand. All this is costing British and Arabian life in the fighting, and diplomatic damage in Western disarray. Few things are more important now than Western policy towards Africa. But the Western leaders do not even meet together on this subject, nor has there been effective discussion of it through the diplomatic channel. There is too little understanding of how closely France's position concerns the security of the Western nations. General de Gaulle's new plans for Algeria are characteristically courageous and far-reaching. They should receive steadfast support.

A strong argument can be made for a Marshall plan for Africa with all free Western countries contributing to it as much as they can and will. Russia could be invited to join and expert administration would be needed, and technical advice. Both could be provided and help given to projects and not to countries. Such a plan could influence Africa. The present multiplication of individual efforts does not.

A danger to the free world lies in the incompleteness of its alliances. In Europe N.A.T.O. and in South-East Asia S.E.A.T.O. are both fulfilling after a fashion the purpose for which they were originally created. At least there is no vacuum there. But in the vital intervening continents of central and western Asia and Africa, there is no common policy, plan or propaganda. Alliances cannot be limited geographically in a cold war which is global. The West has a common faith and a common philosophy; it must express both, in thought and action everywhere and always. The interests of allies cannot be regarded as vital in one area and expendable in another, without danger to the whole structure of the alliance. There must be the same unity of purpose and action in a cold war as in a hot. Failure to observe this obligation has resulted in great gains to the Communist powers in these post-war years.

There are remedies for this state of affairs, but they are difficult to accept and apply. They involve understanding among the European powers with overseas responsibilities about the aims and limitations of their policies. They involve an examination in the

United States of the realities of present-day colonialism and a determined effort by both groups to align their policies. If this is not done, the Western alliance will continue to weaken until it parts at the seams.

★   ★   ★   ★   ★

I have been blessed with a tough constitution which has served me well through more than thirty years of politics, nearly twenty in office and ten as Foreign Secretary.

At nineteen I was adjutant of my battalion, and a brigade-major at twenty. When my brigadier drew up a report after more than a year of service with him, I can recall one phrase: "He is possessed of staying power which his appearance does not suggest." I did not think the phrase particularly complimentary at the time, but it was true enough.

Even so, the three operations I underwent in 1953 had taken their toll and there was always some uncertainty as to whether or not the condition so brilliantly dealt with by the American surgeon, Dr. Cattell, would return. There had been one or two warnings over the past year, but slight enough, I felt, to be ignored. More serious was the high fever which had struck me down when visiting my wife in hospital.

We spent a quiet Christmas at Chequers with the family. On Christmas Eve, Mr. Nehru broke his journey in England on his return from a visit to the United States. He motored down to Chequers to see me, accompanied by his sister, Mrs. Pandit, who has made so many friends in this country as India's High Commissioner. Inevitably we were each a little constrained, but I have always felt a sincere liking for Mr. Nehru personally, which differences on policy could not affect. I like to think that he had the same feelings towards me, and our friendship was certainly unimpaired.

Lord Cherwell came over from Oxford to spend Christmas Day with us, firm in supporting our action and deploring the American attitude. It was the last time we were to see this generous and loyal friend; he died a few months later. I had found refreshment in his penetrating if sometimes acid analysis of events. Often critical, he was always true.

After Christmas, while we were still at Chequers, there was some recurrence of fever. This troubled us enough to seek Lord Evans' advice. After an examination, he advised me to come up to London as soon as possible when I could see him with one or other of the specialists who were familiar with this complaint. He did not disguise from me that the bouts of fever might be on their way back. This was grim news for me and it requires some little explanation.

If a man is told that he is suffering from heart trouble or from cancer and is doing some vital work, he may well decide that he can and will go on with it as long as his powers do not fail. Mine was a more difficult decision, for the truth was that these fever attacks, if they began to return at all frequently, were in themselves so weakening that nobody could suffer from them and at the same time do a good day's work, let alone a night's work. A Prime Minister's job in this country, if it is conscientiously discharged, can begin at eight-thirty in the morning and may end at one or two the next morning. There is no possibility of carrying through with work of this responsibility under any recurring disability. After talking over the situation unhappily with my wife, I decided to go to London early in the New Year. I eased off in the work as much as I could, but there was no improvement and the fever lingered.

When Lord Evans saw me in London he repeated his opinion that the indications of a return of my old complaint were serious and that I must expect them to become more frequent. It was impossible to tell how rapidly they would do this, whether there would be several attacks of fever in the next month or two, compelling me to lay down my work then, or whether the intervals would be longer, or shorter, but what was certain in his judgment was that the attacks would continue and increase in intensity. It was only natural that I should feel, in those early days of January, that this was just the time when I wanted to go on. There were difficulties and differences in the Conservative Party, but I was sure that the aftermath of Suez would justify our policy and do so soon. The United States was showing signs of taking action to meet a Middle Eastern situation now threatening to their interests. I was more confident than in 1938 as to how, unhappily, the position would unfold. Further intervention would be inevitable in some part of the Middle East, certainly by ourselves and possibly by the Americans. I wanted to be there when that happened.

We agreed to have a second opinion, that of Sir Gordon Gordon-Taylor, most respected and experienced of surgeons, who forcefully confirmed Lord Evans' opinion. On the following day we asked for a third opinion, from Dr. Thomas Hunt. He took the same view. After this firm and cumulative advice, I knew that I had no choice. If I had to hand in my resignation, I wished to do so at once, so as to give my successor the best chance to appoint his colleagues and take up his responsibilities before meeting Parliament. I asked two of my closest friends, Lord Salisbury and Lord Scarbrough, to see me separately, one from within my political circle and the other from outside it. Both saw Lord Evans, heard the medical opinions and were convinced that the decision must be taken. I felt it unfair to present the Queen with the facts of this situation without any kind of previous warning. I decided to ask Her Majesty whether she would receive my wife and myself at Sandringham. There was nothing exceptional in this, for I had often in earlier years been to Sandringham at this season, most recently as Foreign Secretary a few weeks before the death of King George VI.

We travelled to Sandringham on January 8. In the evening, before dinner, I had an audience of Her Majesty, when I told her of the medical opinion and my conviction that this could not be ignored without detriment to her service. The Queen said that in the circumstances she would go to London later the next day, and it was agreed that I should tender my resignation at Buckingham Palace on the following evening.

The next morning, on my return to London, I summoned one or two of my principal colleagues, among them Mr. Butler and Mr. Macmillan, and I told them the facts. At 5 P.M. I held my last Cabinet. I told them of the medical opinion and of my decision, for which most were entirely unprepared. I think that we were all affected by the personal side of this event, which I tried to make as short as I could. Thus, after twenty-two years, my periods of Cabinet office were ended. With Lord Salisbury I had worked in politics for half a lifetime, with others for lesser periods. While I was changing my clothes to go to the Palace, Antony Head came to see me. He was sad at my decision. The moment seemed to him such a bad one for a change, just as the Americans appeared to be evolving towards a new policy. In fact, the Eisenhowever Doctrine for the Middle East was announced a few weeks later. I thanked Antony Head and told him that I agreed with him entirely and I should be only too glad to stay, but that it would not be fair upon my colleagues or the country. Unhappily there was nothing to be done about it.

I then sent for the principal Ministers outside the Cabinet. These partings were painful, but none so much as the final duty which awaited me. I felt respect and devotion for the Sovereign I served. I drove to Buckingham Palace and submitted my resignation to Her Majesty.

The next few days and nights we spent at Chequers. M. Spaak came to England to see the Foreign Secretary at this time, in accordance with plans previously made. He asked to come to see me at Chequers from London Airport, before seeing any of my colleagues. I was grateful for this action by an old friend, whose opinions I had so often found penetrating and courageous. We had been through so much together in the past, Hitler's occupation of the Rhineland, the developing menace of the dictators, my first resignation and the war, when M. Spaak joined us with the Belgian Government in exile, that we understood events and each other more easily than could those who had not shared this experience. He was the last European statesman I saw at Chequers.

Among the messages which reached me was one from Mr. Sidney Holland, the Prime Minister of New Zealand, inviting us to spend the winter in that lovely country. I had been to New Zealand twice before and had often wished to stay there longer. The invitation made a strong appeal to us both. There were doubts on medical grounds, but there was at least a chance that the fevers might not become more frequent and that an improvement in general health, which the voyage would give, would strengthen me to meet them if they did. The risk seemed worth taking and we accepted.

On January 18 we sailed from Tilbury. I gave my final message:

> The difference between the West and Egypt has not been colonialism — it is the difference between democracies and a dictatorship. The British people, with their instinctive good

sense, have understood that. I am sure they will always understand.

Friends came to see us off, at dockside, on board ship and at the locks. At one of the locks my wife and I were looking casually over the side when a tall figure came running through the fog. It was my kind friend Lord Bracken, who had missed us at our sailing and headed us off this way to say good-bye.

We dropped down the river on a cold, misty winter's afternoon. Ships called to us and wirelessed their greetings as we passed. They continued to do so all across the Atlantic and across the Pacific into Auckland harbour.

A message from the Captain told us that the cadets of the training ship *Worcester* had asked to be allowed to man ship and speed us on our way. We came up on deck to see them. Their cheers were the last sound I heard in England. We went below.

INDEX